The Urban Towers Handbook

Eric Firley and Julie Gimbal

The Urban Towers Handbook

Eric Firley and Julie Gimbal

A John Wiley and Sons, Ltd, Publication

FRONTISPIECE: Tour Montparnasse in Paris

PAGE 6: View of 42nd Street and the Chrysler Building in Manhattan

PAGE 8: The hills of San Francisco

This edition first published 2011
© 2011 John Wiley & Sons Ltd

Registered office
John Wiley & Sons Ltd, The Atrium, Southern Gate, Chichester, West Sussex, PO19 8SQ, United Kingdom

For details of our global editorial offices, for customer services and for information about how to apply
for permission to reuse the copyright material in this book please see our website at www.wiley.com.

Executive Commissioning Editor: Helen Castle
Project Editor: Miriam Swift
Assistant Editor: Calver Lezama

ISBN 978-0-470-68474-0

Cover design and page design by Kate Ward
Layouts by Maggi Smith
Printed in Italy by Printer Trento Srl

For Pauline
Eric Firley

For my family and friends
Julie Gimbal

Acknowledgements

We would like to thank our sponsors who have made possible the realisation of this book not only through their financial contribution, but also through their continuous and personal interest in the subject:

Yves Aknin of Groupe Batima (as sponsor and initiator of the project)

Dominique Boré of EPADESA, La Défense – Seine Arche

Tatiana Delgado and Virginie Tenain of SemPariSeine, Front de Seine

Sébastien Bourgeois of The Carlyle Group

Our aim to produce a reference tool relies primarily on its graphical quality. We are therefore grateful to Dean See Swan and David Zink who produced the majority of the featured drawings.

During our long research and travel period we have been in touch with hundreds of people. Without their help the following material could not have been gathered. We can only mention some of them (in alphabetical order): Qurashi Elsheikh Abdulghani (Dubai Municipality), Kelvin Ang, Ronald Ansbach (Hines), Gilles Antier, Irene Avino (Studio Belgiojoso), André Balazs, Stefan Beck (Baumschlager Eberle), Ricciarda Belgiojoso, Peng Beng (ArcStudio), Neil Bennett (Farrells), Luiz Laurent Bloch (City of São Paulo), Prof Richard Burdett, Stefania Canta (Renzo Piano Building Workshop), Luiza Dedini Cardia, Cristina Carlson (Ennead Architects), Pierre Charbonnier, John Chu (Kohn Pedersen Fox Associates), Ray Clark (Perkins+Will), Emma Cobb (Pei Cobb Freed & Partners), Dr Joseph Colaco, Richard Coleman, David Crossley (Houston Tomorrow), Sarah Crouch (Ellerbe Becket – AECOM), Ellen Denk, David Dumigan (Henderson Land Development), Andrea Firley, Kathryn Firth, Stephen Fox, Dominic Grace, Gérard Grandval, Gerald Green, Craig Hartman (Skidmore, Owings & Merrill), Richard Hassell (WOHA Designs), Camille Henry (Atelier Christian de Portzamparc), Belinda Ho, Lonnie Hogeboom, Martin Hunscher, Yumiko Ichikawa (Tange Associates), Prof Jochem Jourdan, Frédéric Kappler (Principality of Monaco), Tetsuo Kawabe, Bridget Kennerley (WSP), Serena Khor (WOHA Designs), George Lancaster (Hines), Alexis Lee (Arup), Dr Ho Yin Lee, Didier Lourdin (EPADESA), Francesco Luminari, Richard Marshall (Buro Happold), Yutaka Matsumoto, Dr Cristina Mehrtens, Kamran Moazami (WSP Cantor Seinuk), Carlos Navarrete (Arquitectonica), David Nelson (Foster + Partners), Mieke van Nieuwenhoven (broekbakema), Markus Olechowski, Chad Oppenheim, David Peyceré, Camila Pineda (Sabbagh Arquitectos), Mélanie Pinjon (EPADESA), Prof Elizabeth Plater-Zyberk, Lee Polisano, Christian de Portzamparc, Alexandre Ragois, Cristobal Roig, Kristina Rosen, Hugo Samuelsson (AB Centrumfastigheter), Toshiyuki Sanada (Mori Building), Monica Schaffer (Gensler), Peter Cachola Schmal, Takis Sgouros (City of Berlin), Dr Li Shiqiao, Nam Hoi Sitt (Sun Hung Kai Properties), Manuel Tardits (Mikan), Dina Elisabete Uliana (USP), Klaus Vatter (City of Vienna), Ingrid Weger (Behnisch Architekten), Dr Johannes Widodo, Jorge Wilheim, Lena Wranne (Arkitekturmuseet Stockholm), Roger Wu, Norio Yamato (Mori Building), Thomas Yeung.

Special thanks also to Helen Franzen who performed a complete language check of the first and second part of the book before the handover to the publisher.

Last but not least, we would like to express our gratitude towards Helen Castle, Calver Lezama and Miriam Swift from John Wiley & Sons. They have shown a lot of dedication and patience for a project that has been particularly complex to wrap up and produce. We hope and believe that it was worth the substantial effort.

Contents

Preface

This project has been conceived as the continuation of a typological study that was based on residential low- and mid-rise construction, *The Urban Housing Handbook*. Initiated by the French developer Yves Aknin of Groupe Batima, the aim of this new book is to analyse whether and why the impact of high-rise buildings on their surroundings is different from that of lower constructions, and – most importantly – to determine how to control and adapt them in order to achieve the best results.

As much as possible, but hopefully not with complete success, we tried to divert our attention away from the glamorous top of New York's Chrysler Building, the colourful reflections of Barcelona's Torre Agbar and the breathtaking height of Dubai's Burj Khalifa, and rather focused on the base of these towers, and their insertion strategy in an existing or new urban context. The mainly famous examples in this book, products of so-called 'signature architecture', are eventually seen as placeholders for thousands of anonymous towers, that may leave little more impression on the local population than the direct impact on their lives through wind, shadow, entrances and walls.

Though susceptible like most people to the sheer attraction of size, a phenomenon that we do not seek to scrutinise in this work, we are not fanatics of high-rise construction. We do, however, believe that it is an interesting option: one that not only has its role to play in the future of denser and more sustainable cities, but also one that expresses creativity and our freedom to choose how to live and work. Mirrors of the constant power struggle of an essentially capitalist social order, high-rise buildings are arguably more appropriate and realistic case studies for our contemporary society than building types that grew in a fixed envelope with very limited liberties, most prominently exemplified by the late-19th-century urbanism of Paris, Barcelona or Berlin.

We hope that this book will contribute to this complex and exciting discussion, for which a definitive conclusion can hardly be expected.

Introduction

This book is conceived as a manual. It comprises three major parts: the first section provides a visual reference tool for high-rise construction; the second section outlines high-rise building regulations; and the third section investigates the notion of sustainability, with a special focus on the urban implications of towers.

    The general idea of our approach is to 'wedge' this highly complex topic into a fairly analytical form, and to accept the omission of certain information on one part of the spectrum in favour of coherence and clarity. We had the impression that there is a – constantly updated – supply of publications that deal with the newest contemporary examples and their record-breaking features, but relatively little choice of books that provide a comprehensive analysis of these structures as elements of the city's fabric. Therefore our choice of major topics, the classification logic and the type of featured analytic criteria is consistently urban – and not architectural – for all three parts of the book. However, due to their imposing size, their iconic importance and their role in a city's skyline, it would be pointless and impossible to try to convincingly separate these urban interests from the buildings' architectural features, and in the text we thus treat both at the same time.

    This volume is intended to contribute to the discussion about the future of our cities and the role that high-rise constructions can play in them. From our European perspective, the recent consultation about the future of the Parisian agglomeration ('Le grand pari de l'agglomération parisienne', 2009 – widely referred to as simply 'Le Grand Paris'), and the potential construction of towers as part of these plans, has been a revealing experience – both positively and negatively – of how quickly the topic of high-rise polarises opinions. One reason for the often confused discussion style seems to be directly linked to the major topic of this book and its motive to prevent the misleading understanding of high-rise as a single 'typology'. As long as this simplification persists, and all towers are perceived as belonging to a single group, it will remain impossible for an objective debate to emerge, and distinctions between public housing slabs with office point-towers, or podium developments with vertical garden cities, will be confused. We preferred to step back and, through the case-study structure and widespread examples, to analyse and understand, rather than to pass judgement on a hypothetical generalised use of high-rise construction as such.

BELOW: Four towers, and four completely different ways to relate to the surroundings.

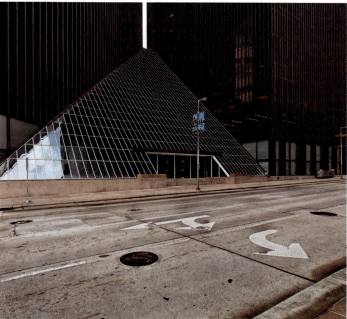

Despite some particularities that we will touch upon, there is no reason to believe that such a generalised judgement would make more sense in the case of high-rise than in that of low- or middle-rise. The wide spread of the featured examples, and the necessity to present some kind of appraisal for each of them, constantly pushed us in the role of a slightly schizophrenic devil's advocate, trying to understand and cast light from various angles on the emergence of what is still a fairly new urban phenomenon.

Before giving a brief overview of the book's three main parts, we would like to explain in further detail some fundamental issues which occasionally appear through the book, but which might not be sufficiently clarified without explicit mention.

IS HIGH-RISE A BUILDING TYPE ?

'Type' – or 'typology' – is the key word of this book. But without clear explanation of the tower's fairly specific case, it is – compared with lower and clearly repetitive building structures – at the same time an element of potential contradiction. First of all, as mentioned above, we strongly believe that height as such cannot be considered to be a sufficiently comprehensive parameter in order to define a whole typological group, just as the lack of height cannot either. Height is, rather, a selection criterion and a condition for our undertaking; but the process of classification, as an inherent component of the notion of type, needs additional information.

Compared with lower building types, the interesting feature of the tower is its extroverted character and forceful impact on neighbouring structures. While low- and mid-rise party-wall typologies of the 19th century such as the English terraced house, or Berlin, Paris or Barcelona apartment buildings, have been built within a very simple set of rules over hundreds or thousands of hectares – with one architect erecting a building right up against the next one as an extrusion of the available plot surface – this repetitive dynamic reaches its limit where taller buildings are concerned. In one extreme case it leads to a considerable loss of natural light and air levels and to questionable formal restrictions. In the other extreme case of spatial separation, it causes an explosion of the public realm and obstruction of social interchange through increasing distances

between the buildings. The 1920s and 1930s discussion of the New York setback and 1916 zoning rules clearly documents the first case (see page 88 in the second section of the book), while the latter case has been comprehensively theorised by the Modern Movement and can arguably not be considered as a true urban type. On the following pages we hope to convincingly present alternatives to these two extreme cases, but the urban problem provoked through the above-mentioned extroverted character remains valid.

The height of a tall building has not only the obvious and direct consequence of casting shadow on neighbouring structures, but it also has a strong impact on the organisation of spaces within the building. Many of the early Chicago skyscrapers like the Rookery (1888) or the Santa Fe Building (1904) still had internal courtyards, but growing building heights and the increasing impracticability of such courtyards led to the loss of any inward-looking element and a quasi-total extroversion of the building's interior, reinforcing the aforementioned impact on its surroundings. It is not by chance that the vast majority of towers – office or residential – simply group surfaces around a central service core. This layout is architecturally quite restrictive, and excludes the notion of open communal spaces, the central feature of analysis for the classification of the low- and mid-rise housing types (see *The Urban Housing Handbook*).

A distinction has therefore to be made between the upper part of the high-rise construction, the more or less slender 'needle' with a fairly restricted diversity of plan layouts, and the formally more versatile base which serves as a link between the often recessed tower, the ground and neighbouring structures. This distinction between the lower and the upper part of a tower does not necessarily depend on major urban or cultural differences, and can be exemplified with the rather local comparison of two of history's most famous skyscrapers: the Lever House (1952) and the almost contemporaneous Seagram Building (1958) (see page 39) on New York's Park Avenue. While both of them deal with the stepback laws in an arguably similar way, recessing from the street in order to build a straight and monolithic volume, the strategy for the base is completely different, and opposes an empty plaza to a carved-out podium. Cruder extremes can be highlighted through the confrontation of Vancouver's recent tower-on-podium revival (see page 193) and the 'green' point-towers of Higienópolis in São Paulo (see page 154).

Our aim was therefore the classification of towers according to their base and respective urban insertion strategy, and not according to their architecture. This insertion strategy will rarely be completely repetitive, as in the case of the above-mentioned low- and mid-rise types, but it will follow a similar logic. In the end it is probably fair to say that we classify single projects and suggest typologies, rather than presenting established and recognised ones.

THE ALLEGED UNIQUENESS OF THE ICONIC TOWER
AND ITS EXTRAORDINARY BRANDING CAPACITY

In this book we explore further the notion of type and repetition, clarifying from a non-formal perspective why this classification is so elusive to establish and promote. We also address the tendency to discuss high-rise almost consistently on the basis of the most extreme examples, a fact that is understandable but obstructive to identifying the relevant stakes in terms of urban planning.

Economically, the enormous investment and risk attached to projects of such pharaonic dimensions tend to reinforce the particularity of their spatial insertion artificially, emphasising the alleged exceptional character as the base of all marketing activities. This aggressive branding is an economic necessity, due to the fact that the rising construction costs associated with increasing heights only make sense if they are covered by increased rental income for the upper levels. The natural and self-evident advantages of better views and clarified corporate hierarchies

OPPOSITE: Due to the obvious structural constraints imposed by the height of tower buildings, there is limited scope for variation in the plan layouts of their upper floors. The Commerzbank building in Frankfurt (1994–7), by Foster + Partners, is one of the few examples in which an internal courtyard provides additional spatial complexity. From an urban point of view, it is thus the design of the bases of towers that tends to offer the greatest differentiation between them.

CLOCKWISE FROM TOP LEFT: Mies van der Rohe's Lake Shore Drive, Chicago (1951) and Skidmore, Owings & Merrill's Lever House, New York (1952) belong to the group of the high-rise superstars. The real question – and typological challenge – is, however, raised by millions of anonymous towers, exemplified by an aerial view of São Paulo.

might not be sufficient and self-communicative enough to assure this premium, and 'uniqueness' in terms of design and status is often the chosen sales strategy. Underlining 'uniqueness' as a selling point is not reproachable, but neither is it conducive to establishing a rather technical classification in which the tower in all its appearances is seen as one typological option next to others. The powerful emphasis on notions like the 'icon', the 'superlative', 'signature architecture' and (the often over-suggested and fake) 'novelty' and 'technical revolution' tend to overshadow the fact that the basic demands on the creation of a successful urban environment have not substantially changed over the last 100 years. It is rather the prevalence and speed of development which have increased considerably in some areas of the world. In view of this spectacular urbanisation process, and the urgent sustainability questions that it raises, high-rise can, and already does, play an important role. From this point of view, and in the case of China, it is not the example of Shanghai's Lujiazui Business District (see page 170) or Hong Kong's Kowloon Station (see page 190) that are thus most relevant, but the endless repetition of similar and simpler high-rise developments in less prominent areas.

Crucially, we are on the cusp of witnessing an unprecedented scale of development in which the tower will by definition lose its exceptional status. We now have an opportunity to establish a typological understanding of high-rise as a planning tool, similar to those established a long time ago for low- and mid-rise constructions. It is indeed one of the simple, but important outcomes of our study to realise that the modern office and residential tower is still a comparatively young building type, and that it leaves great scope for future improvements. Not all buildings can be a new Eiffel Tower, and the non-iconic tower has its role to play. But this is not to say that the iconic tower is redundant of function. Several of the examples featured in this book have kick-started a successful regeneration process for entire urban districts, a recognised trait which for many local communities has increased the appeal and the motivation for high-rise developments.

HOW TALL IS A TOWER ?
THE POINT-TOWER AND THE SLAB – MODERN PLANNING PRINCIPLES
In writing this book we have opted out of participating in the definition of a minimal height limit for a tower to be called a tower, as such a detail may make sense in relation to an existing local context, but is far less meaningful for our inherently international comparison. Our typological perspective even suggests that low-, mid- and high-rise structures should be analysed in a similar way, without clear distinction. We are, however, acutely aware that planning authorities have to apply distinctions in terms of height, particularly concerning issues of safety. As a rule of thumb – and in the European context – a height of over 10 storeys might be considered as the minimum in order for a construction to be defined as a tower. But this ordinal definition has to be considered in conjunction with the elongated relationship between building height and building footprint. This leads automatically to the rather more relevant distinction between the point-tower and the slab, and opens wide avenues of discussion concerning the theoretical origins of modern high-rise architecture and urbanism. Several of the featured examples in the first part of the book will make reference to the relationship between these two types of high-rise, particularly in the case of the European context influenced by the rather Taylorist vision of the *Zeilenbau* (linear block) as one of the starting points of the Modern Movement.

Our own selection largely concentrates on point-towers, and does so due to their greater ability to integrate in an environment of smaller cadastral subdivisions. Unlike the slab with its massive footprint, the point-tower is not necessarily linked to an urbanism of the tabula rasa and the erasure of a historically grown plot structure. Projects like La Défense in the outskirts of Paris (1958 onwards) or the Hansaviertel in Berlin (1956–60) are good examples in which the large-scale and

ABOVE: The cliché of the self-sufficient Modernist residential slab: the 1959 Alton West Estate in Roehampton, Surrey, designed by the London County Council Architects Department.

LEFT: Oscar Niemeyer's Copan Building in São Paulo (1966) is one of the few slab constructions whose massing adjusts in a very dense context to the constraints of an existing plot structure.

public planning approach did not require such a formal distinction, and the first drafts of both schemes did almost exclusively rely on the slab type, before eventually experiencing a shift towards the point-tower typology. From the 1920s, the prevailing design method prescribed the artistic, cost-efficient and hygienic distribution of architectural objects on an empty (and expropriated) canvas of land, and in this context the aforementioned typological and practical differences between slabs and point-towers were understandably not of major consequence. Space was not an issue, and density a mere theoretical notion that was not measured on the scale of the whole agglomeration. But assessing, even in these simplified terms, the comparison of contemporary and modern planning paradigms is not the objective of this book. The difficulty of such a potential study has also to do with crucial differences in regional planning attitudes: it was not only in communist countries that the inner city was neglected in favour of peripheral developments, and projects like the French *grands ensembles*, situated on former farmland somewhere around the major cities, cannot seriously and fairly be compared with Singapore's new Pinnacle@Duxton (see page 127) as an explicitly inner-city housing redevelopment. Lastly, recent projects which evolved in similar conditions without cadastral constraints – in Dubai (see page 104) or China (see Lujiazui, page 170), for example – and their sometimes similar urban results compared to Modernist developments, do also highlight that the planning paradigms depend on the projects' brief, size and site, and that the relationship between architectural type and production of space works in both directions. Simply put, Modernist urbanism would not have produced the same results if it had not received state support for the disruption of the historically grown plot structure (and this admittedly often for the satisfaction of urgent social needs). The history of high-rise and of the point-tower has thus emerged out of this complex dialectic, and needs to be considered in this context.

The development of high-rise in the United States is slightly different, and the history of New York's Rockefeller Center (see page 88) is a good example demonstrating that some American cities had already roughly 40 years of high-rise experience behind them before the Modern Movement took root in Europe. Furthermore, the emergence of the American tower, unlike that of its European counterparts, was primarily related to commercial rather than residential uses, and it grew out of the same grid logic as the developments of the former generations. But this is not to say that the typological and social issues were completely different; and projects like Stuyvesant Town in Manhattan (see page 103) bear a surprisingly strong resemblance to contemporaneous European developments. For a short period of time, however, in the early post-war phase and before the construction of the European business districts, it would be fair to say that the typical metropolitan American white-collar worker commuted from his family home to a high-rise office, while his European colleague left his tower apartment in the morning to spend the working day in a low-rise *fin-de-siècle* building.

WHERE TO BEGIN AND HOW TO ANALYSE: HIGH-RISE AND HISTORY

The organisation of this book – and especially the first part – according to a strictly formal classification of distinct types emphasises that it is not our intention to write a chronological history of the tower. It is also not our aim to situate each example against its theoretical historical background, but rather to highlight some points in its development history that appeared specifically relevant from our contemporary view as designers. The featured examples, however, cover approximately one century of high-rise experience, and the question was where to begin? To comment on the eternal quest of man to scale new heights seems arbitrary, as does the suggestion that our skyline has lost its role as the expression of a holy hierarchy, with religious buildings as formerly dominant elements.

The towers of Sanaa in Yemen and San Gimignano in Italy are just two of a wide range of historic examples which have grown under very different circumstances, but still remain appropriate references.

It seems therefore appropriate to separate physical artefacts from social, cultural or psychological motivations, and to recognise that the nature of these physical artefacts has considerably changed, and this at a fairly specific moment in time, while socio-cultural or psychological motivations have gradually adjusted according to the rules of our contemporary society. Following the line of most other works in this field, we consequently started our research and selection process with the beginning of the modern 'skyscraper' in 1880s Chicago, where the commonly cited milestone is the Home Insurance Building (1885) designed by William Le Baron Jenney. This metal-frame building, considered to have been the first of a new kind, combined the structural use of metal with a height of at least 10 storeys and the installation of an elevator. More significantly, it marks – in conjunction with its immediate successors of the Chicago School – the beginning of a new generation of office buildings. The combination of three essential elements – the apparent need for large office space; technical progress in terms of building materials and structural solutions; and the invention of the secure elevator – eventually led to the emergence of a vertical building type that cannot simply be seen as a derivative of medieval castle towers, pyramids or cathedrals. This does not, however, mean that the earlier references are without virtue of comparison, and this especially from a typological perspective. Due to a more comparable set of development motivations, secular rather than religious structures are for us of particular interest, and include examples like the tower houses of Yemen, ancient in origin, or the medieval family towers as seen in San Gimignano, Italy.

With a maximum of about eight floors, the Yemenite tower houses might not meet our height constraints, but they do deliver highly interesting insights into the type of urban fabric that is created by tall elements with small footprints in a specific cultural and environmental context. Intriguingly, they do so in a very repetitive way, and thus represent early examples of non-iconic towers. San Gimignano's interest is situated on a rather macro-urban level, and represents the very successful creation of a skyline through a network of occasional tall elements. Incidentally, they also support the claim that height has long been associated with an expression of private wealth, as these slender towers were commissioned by the city's foremost trade families and not by the church.

THE BOOK'S THREE SECTIONS
Section A: A visual dictionary of high-rise buildings
As a consequence of the precepts explained above, we spent many months on an urban review and analysis of hundreds of historic and contemporary examples, finally identifying three major groups and 21 classes of high-rise buildings in total. To make our typological approach clearer, each class – except for the vertical cities – features one main example and two secondary ones. The subdivision into three groups – solitaires, clusters, and vertical cities – is admittedly artificial, because the latter two notions obviously depend on an accumulation of the former one, the solitaire. Their existence is, however, helpful in order to grasp the notion of scale and to identify questions that could otherwise be lost in an endless accumulation of the solitaire's sub-types. It also acknowledges the fact that our urban environment does not only consist of (orthogonal or non-orthogonal) grid systems and adjacent single plots. Large parts of Dubai, Hong Kong's impressive megastructures and the La Défense business district have been developed according to a very different logic, and it did not seem appropriate to analyse all high-rise phenomena with exactly the same small-scale tool. The solitaire group therefore focuses on the integration of a tower in a block structure, the cluster group on the creation of large-scale developments, and the last group on the vertical city in the sense of a regional high-rise identity.

Section B: High-rise building regulations in seven cities worldwide
In the first section of the book we analyse and classify urban situations in a very formal way. The project descriptions try to elucidate the reasons for a specific architectural and urban response, but they have not been conceived to document the relationship between built structures and planning policies or with a focus on current legislation. The second section therefore explains how cities try to actively influence the development of building heights, and on what kind of vision the resulting regulations are based. It elucidates how the vertical element is used for the implementation of a specific planning strategy, and as a result it rapidly becomes clear that these strategies gravely diverge and that the motivations for the interference in the 'natural development' of the city are manifold. A simple example is the notion of 'view corridors', and the fact that they are legally relevant only for a small selection of cities. Some planning authorities regard high-rise as a primarily aesthetic feature, while others focus almost exclusively on density and transport issues. We chose seven cases from around the world, aiming to cover the widest possible range of planning strategies. European examples are London, Paris, Vienna and Frankfurt, the American example New York, and the Asian situation is highlighted through Singapore and Hong Kong. Our primary aim is to explain the current legislation for each chosen city, but a succinct historic outline helps to understand the origins of each specific case.

The regulative frameworks of all seven cities have been analysed according to seven themes: 1. Background / context; 2. Originators of urban regulations and responsibilities; 3. Zoning / urban planning; 4. Urban skyline / cityscape; 5. Tower design; 6. Building codes / fire safety; 7. Ecology. The examples are written to stand alone, but cross-references help to identify major differences between planning policies and sometimes refer to specific built examples of the first section.

Section C: High-rise and sustainability

A sustainable city is a 'good and successful' city, and a place that contributes to the respect, development and improvement of each society's values. High-rise is therefore – just like all other building forms – an expression of diversity and freedom of choice. As such, it is an option that has been adopted in most parts of the world, and this at least quantitatively with increasing success. Yet there remains the issue of individual rights and the question of how to prevent one person's freedom from restricting the freedom and well-being of another. With growing experience in high-rise development, these questions are generally subject to the aforementioned building regulations. The unfortunate fact that tower projects are often – and especially in developing countries – the reason for the inappropriate destruction of historically grown urban environments, is not directly linked to the issue of high-rise, and does evenly occur in favour of lower structures.

Over the last few years the discussion about the future of ever-growing cities and their impact on our ecosystem has led to an important change of paradigm, and high-rise has been rediscovered as a potential tool for the prevention of further urban sprawl or even retrofit. The argument as such is not new, but the analysis of most built examples reveals that this vision was rarely the motivation for any major tower project. This situation may soon change, and the third and last section of the book therefore constructs a rationale based on the tower as a potentially sustainable element of the urban fabric. It gives an overview of the major issues, and combines strictly ecological features of new building techniques and materials with crucial density and transport considerations. In contrast to most similar essays, it focuses in large part on the comparison with low- and mid-rise developments as the obvious building alternative, and tries therefore to set the tower in context with a technically more familiar environment. Too often, energy-saving building features are solely assessed in relation to alternative high-rise projects, and their urban conclusiveness is therefore of limited value. It is crucial to understand that the sustainability and density issue directly relates back to the first two parts of the book, as the notion of density makes no sense without formal ideas of how to implement it in a successful and lasting way.

OPPOSITE: There can only be one – the 'useless' Eiffel Tower as ultimate icon.

A visual dictionary of high-rise buildings

Kingdom Centre

SOLITAIRES: MONUMENT
LOCATION: RIYADH, SAUDI ARABIA
DATE: 1999–2002
ARCHITECT: ELLERBE BECKET
CLIENT: KINGDOM HOLDING

The tower as an exceptional construction is inherently linked to the two notions of the icon and the monument. The Kingdom Centre in Riyadh is one of the purest contemporary examples of this type, and lives up to these expectations from an architectural as much as an urban point of view.

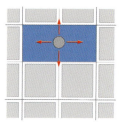

Typological group:
Solitaires – monument
Building height: **302 metres**
Site coverage: **48%**
Plot ratio: **3.19**

HISTORY / DEVELOPMENT PROCESS

Originally the project in Riyadh did not set out with the vision of creating a super-tall building. HRH Prince Alwaleed Bin Talal Bin Abdulaziz Al Saud – nephew of King Fahd, owner of the Kingdom Holding and one of the world's most influential businessmen – initiated a masterplan competition for a vast site that he had bought in the northern periphery of Saudi Arabia's capital. Twelve teams were invited to participate in the competition and the first prize was awarded to the Minneapolis-based design company Ellerbe Becket. The concept of potentially incorporating the entire building programme into a single tower, rather than several low-rise buildings, only emerged during the competition process. Two separate proposals were therefore included in the final presentation, submitted in collaboration with the runners-up, WZMH Architects. Prince Alwaleed was quick to grasp the huge potential of a grand project, and discarded the masterplan option in favour of a single iconic tower. As the tower only covered 40 per cent of his estate in the form of a large urban block, the remainder of the property was subsequently sold to third parties. A smaller architectural competition followed, and the team from Ellerbe Becket had to prove itself against internationally acclaimed specialists in high-rise building including Kohn Pedersen Fox (KPF), Skidmore, Owings & Merrill (SOM) and Cesar Pelli (who, though approached, declined due to his workload).

URBAN CONFIGURATION

The reason for choosing the Kingdom Centre as the main example for the typological class of the 'high-rise monument' is based on the interesting combination of two main features: firstly, the impressive contrast of height compared with the majority of its surroundings, and secondly, a very clear urban situation in which the tower covers a whole block in Riyadh's orthogonal street grid. Compared with many, if not the majority of towers, which assert an iconic claim solely on the grounds of height and originality of design, the Kingdom Centre extends its iconic role also on the ground and within the wider urban context. A potential first impression of heavy set, accentuated not only in the way in which the site was planned but also in the building's perfect symmetry, is therefore deceptive and reveals itself, at a second glance, as well-conceived simplicity. The impact of this symmetry is particularly worth noting, as it was not incorporated in Ellerbe Becket's initial proposal, and emerged only after a study of the local architectural culture.

The Kingdom Centre's prominence against the city skyline is facilitated by the striking lack of tall structures in Riyadh and the location of the building plot on the city's major north–south-oriented arterial road, defined by Al Olaya and King Fahad Streets. In a car-oriented city with over 4 million inhabitants which has quickly outgrown its small historic core, the projection of this axis in the third dimension is of major importance, and takes place in conjunction with the city's second skyscraper, Foster & Partners' Al Faisaliyah Center, which was completed in 2000 just 2.5 kilometres south of the Kingdom Centre complex. Urbanistically, the linear relation between the two skyscrapers appears as an inversion of Dubai's Sheikh Zayed Road (see page 104), where the axis is defined through a wall of towers rather than two reference points.

ARCHITECTURE

The inspiration for the tower's prominent top emerged through extensive analysis and review of international built structures demonstrating iconic qualities. The curved shape of an arch, reminiscent of an inverted St Louis Gateway Arch, presented itself as an option which conformed to the client's vision of beauty and elegance. The most decisive factor influencing the eventual size of the decorative top was the fact that the local building regulations limited the scale of any new construction on this site to only 30 occupied floors, but no height limits for the building were defined. In the absence of height

Side view of the tower and its base with driveway.

restrictions, Prince Alwaleed and his design team were left a wide margin of scale to work with, and they decided upon a height of around 300 metres – similar to that of the Eiffel Tower – in their creation of a new major iconic construction. The fact that size matters is thus clearly illustrated, and the Kingdom Centre can therefore justly be seen as an oversized sculpture, with approximately one third of the building holding no interior spaces except for the elevators leading to the spectacular skywalk at the very top. An additional perhaps irreverent reason for the tower's height may

have been stimulated by the proximity of the above-mentioned Al Faisaliyah Tower, which stands at 267 metres in height.

The design of the large structures at the foot of the Kingdom Centre has been principally defined by three elements: firstly, the significant number of surfaces and functions that could not be accommodated in the tower itself; secondly, the desire to ensure there was an interaction between the building and its immediate surroundings; and thirdly, the client's insistence on separate, representative and centrally located entrances. The last point with respect to the entrances is probably the most original one, and represents an atypical approach to the architectural treatment of hybrid structures. Also, the architect's idea of integrating pedestrian landscaped areas into the concept is unusual for new constructions in one of the world's hottest climates. The wing-like design of the base of the building, with the street-fronting shopping mall and convention centre, allows direct access through these green areas to the tower on the northern and southern sides of the block. Even though the mixed-use tower houses numerous facilities, including the Kingdom Holding's headquarters, luxury condominiums, the skywalk, a hotel and a bank, due to the separate entrances visitors can avoid walking through the shopping mall or any other intermediate space to reach the central core – a feature that distinguishes the project from a podium development.

SUMMARY

The Kingdom Centre thus effectively illustrates the notions of the icon, the landmark and, most ambitiously and ambiguously, the monument. In a society characterised by a mass-media visual culture and where semiotic communication is intrinsic to the urban condition, these notions are often interlinked with a well-calculated process of branding: either the branding of a building to an icon, or the use of an icon for the branding of a company. Or both. It is part of the intention of this book not to dwell on these intriguing notions – which have already been deservedly studied by others in their own right – but, rather, to concentrate on the analysis of the building's physical position in the urban fabric. Obviously things are not that simple, and most of the book's featured examples have been chosen due to a particular iconic quality, the analysis admittedly following an intuitive and partly taste-driven selection process on the part of the authors.

One of the Kingdom Centre's qualities and particularities is therefore the fact that, due to its almost archaic simplicity, it urges us to reconsider the relationship between the symbolic and physical realm – the sign itself and the communication that it provokes – and to question the specificity of the tall building for these notions in contrast to lower structures. What we mean is that there are not many cities in the world in which a tower still manages to achieve a monumental effect, and this through its simple existence. As an urban icon, it is often said that skyscrapers, a product of the modern era, have

1:2500 section showing that about a third of the building height is not used.

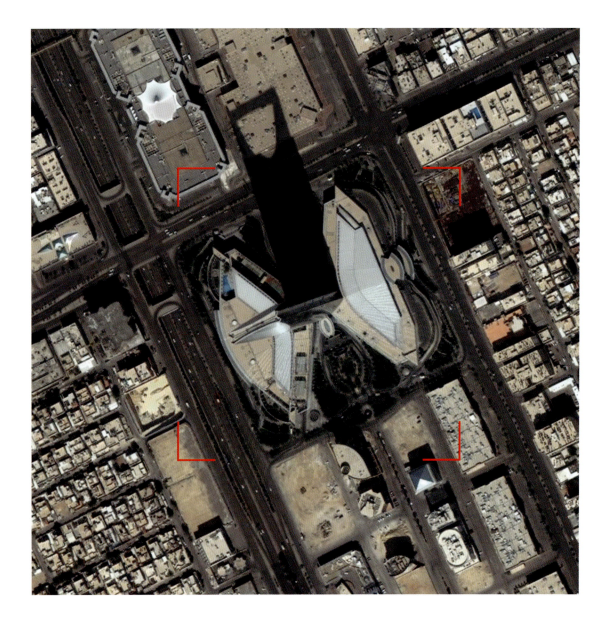

replaced the traditional role of the church, or mosque. But in contrast to a centralised religious institution, the liberal nature of the modern economy is reflected in the difficulty of maintaining a specific hierarchy and prominence of vertical objects. The skylines of cities like Tokyo, Chicago, London and São Paulo are well-known proof of the fact that now thousands of developers and multinational companies have the means to erect monuments to their own memory, channelled rather than controlled by the authorities. At the same time, these skylines and their innumerable towers are also testimony to the fact that height as such does not assure glory or even long-lasting attention. This seems to be an inevitable consequence of our individualistic, secular and highly competitive society. As part of the global urban narrative, the Kingdom Centre represents

an explicit symbol of Saudi Arabia's modernisation and increasing openness. It therefore plays a very special, if not contradictory role, and its success as an urban artefact is arguably due to the fact that, for whatever reasons, Riyadh's skyline does not yet reflect the reality of such development. The stunning and almost medieval relationship to its low-rise surroundings, comparable to that exerted by a religious building, will potentially be lost in the case of further modernisation and economic diversification, and give way to a restless process of overtrumping and reconstruction, in which the expression and extent of the individual's ambition will, by definition, never endure.

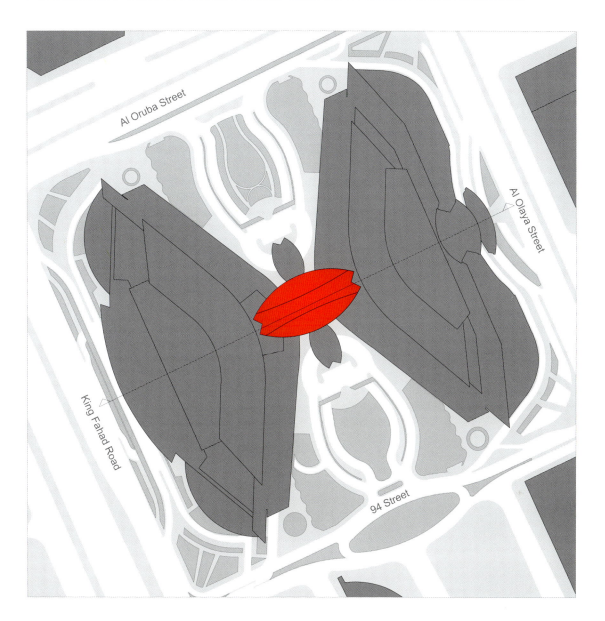

Urban plan 1:2500

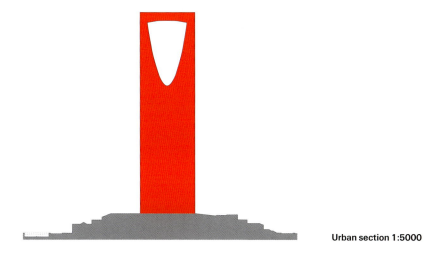

Urban section 1:5000

MOSCOW STATE UNIVERSITY (LOMONOSOV)

LOCATION: MOSCOW, RUSSIA
DATE: 1949–53
ARCHITECT: LEV RUDNEV

The tallest of Stalin's so-called 'Seven Sisters' (see also Hotel Ukraina, page 47) is situated in a green area close to the Sparrow Hills, the city's highest viewpoint. Like a dotted line around the nucleus of the Soviet capital, the seven tall buildings were meant to trace the contours of the 'Great General's' and 'Supreme Architect's' realised utopia. In a figurative sense, this spatially quite successful system extended much further, and Warsaw's Palace of Culture can be considered to be part of the same group of highly symbolic and political constructions that were meant to express the unity of the Communist regime. In addition, on a more local level, the strictly symmetrical and freestanding university building marks the end of a triumphant perpective that reaches from the Kremlin to the southwest of Moscow.

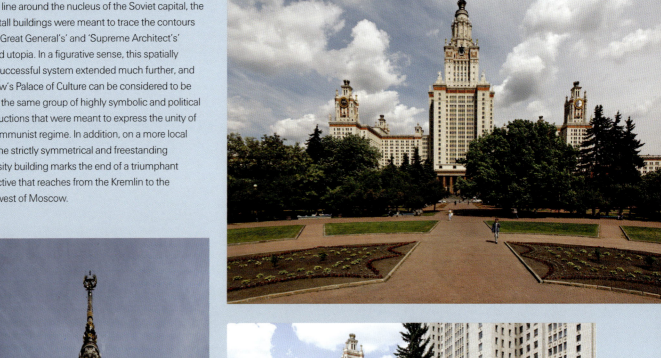

BURJ KHALIFA

LOCATION: DUBAI, UNITED ARAB EMIRATES
DATE: 2004–10
ARCHITECT: SOM (SKIDMORE, OWINGS & MERRILL)

From an urban point of view, the most remarkable feature of the world's tallest building is the fact that it has been planned as the centrepiece of a completely new district, called Downtown Dubai. It is therefore the most extreme representation of a new way to develop cities, in which commercial structures take the place of public buildings, and architectural superlatives feature as major marketing tools. Real estate value is maximised through the view from surrounding buildings of the tower, as much as it is in a more conventional way through the breathtaking views from the tower to the outside. The landscaped surroundings of the tower's base have been carefully designed and are situated on an artificial peninsula, dramatically increasing the project's obvious monumental claim.

30 St Mary Axe

SOLITAIRES: MONUMENT IN BLOCK
LOCATION: CITY OF LONDON, UK
DATE: 2000–2004
ARCHITECT: FOSTER + PARTNERS
CLIENT: SWISS RE

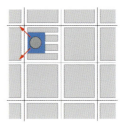

Typological group:
Solitaires – monument
in block
Building height: 180 metres
Site coverage: 37%
Plot ratio: 8.37

Situated in one of the world's oldest banking and business districts, the so-called 'Gherkin' shows that a high-density urban fabric does not necessarily preclude the existence of freestanding structures. The monumental effect of the perfectly monolithic point-tower on its environment has been intensified through the minimalist treatment of the surrounding plaza.

HISTORY / DEVELOPMENT PROCESS

The first tower to be granted a building permit by the City of London Corporation since 1978, it has been interpreted to symbolise the City's ability to defend its status as one of the world's major financial hubs. From a real estate point of view, the challenge was rather local: situated just five miles to the east, the development of Canary Wharf in the Docklands had been promoted since the late 1980s and was increasingly attracting some of the City's top names due to more liberal planning constraints, good traffic connections and an extensive land reserve. The same exodus threatened to happen with the insurance company Swiss Re, scattered after several acquisitions over five separate City offices. Not finding appropriate spaces available for rent, a move to Canary Wharf had been contemplated, but finally the company decided to stay and to lead the construction of a new building as an owner-occupier. The rare opportunity to take control of a site of appropriate dimensions ironically arrived through an incident whose

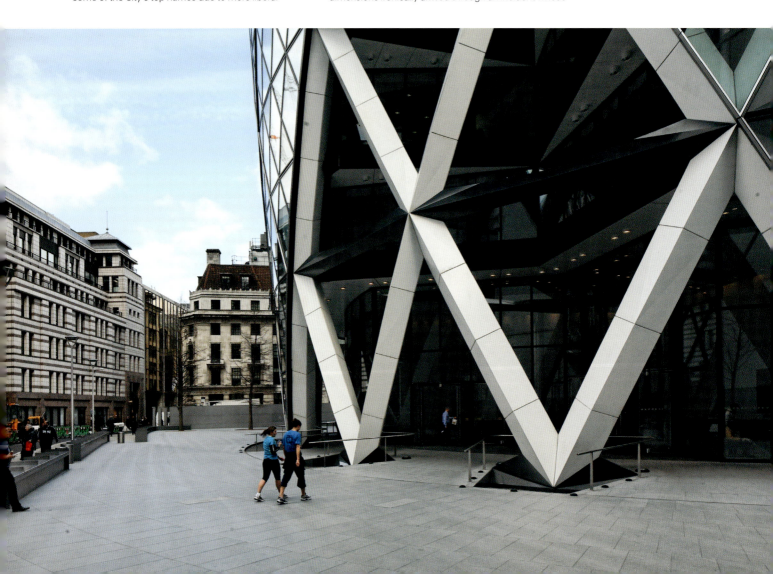

consequences could not be fully insured: the detonation of an IRA bomb in front of the Baltic Exchange, leaving the 19th-century listed building in a pitiful state. Not appropriate for contemporary and efficient office use, but partly of historic relevance, discussions and negotiations over the future of the building remains and the site went on over years, seeing ownership in the meantime move from the Baltic Exchange, via Trafalgar House and Kværner, to Skanska. After eight years a building permit was finally granted, English Heritage and the City of London Planning Authority loosening their formerly rigid position in favour of a project that was considered to be of exceptional quality, and therefore superior to an earlier, slightly bizarre scheme that was meant to incorporate the main hall with the stained-glass windows of its dome and elements of the historic facade. The long planning history should not,

however, disguise the fact that the position of the plot is rather advantageous in the planning context of the City: it is – unlike the majority of the City's estate – neither part of a conservation area nor affected by one of the protected viewing corridors towards St Paul's Cathedral. This is also one of the reasons why Norman Foster had initially imagined a scheme of far taller dimensions, the Millennium Tower, strongly inspired by his earlier studies for a vertical city in the Tokyo Bay.

The acquisition of the building permit was a condition in Swiss Re's purchase contract with Skanska, and the Swedish contractor secured in exchange their appointment for the execution of building works. These were finalised in only 33 months, between early 2001 and late 2003 when Swiss Re's staff moved in – almost exactly 100 years after the opening of the former Baltic Exchange building.

ABOVE LEFT: View along Lime Street in-between Richard Rogers' Lloyd's Building (left) and Foster + Partners' recent Willis Building (right).

ABOVE: View from the south across Leadenhall Street.

FAR LEFT: The plaza offers new pedestrian connections through a formerly impermeable site.

LEFT: For fire safety reasons, the spiralling atria are organised in stacks of six.

BELOW: The new tower as an imposing addition to the skyline of the City of London, seen from the south side of the River Thames.

URBAN CONFIGURATION

High-rise is neither new nor exceptional in the City of London. Famous examples include Richard Seifert's NatWest Tower (1980) – now Tower 42 – and Richard Rogers' radical, but more modestly sized scheme for the Lloyd's Headquarters (1986). Due to the city's long history, and gradual and continuous redevelopment above a predominantly medieval block structure, a genuinely freestanding point-tower is, however, a rather rare incident. The few existing towers tend to be wedged into the pre-existing fabric, at least one side being attached or quasi-attached to neighbouring structures. Foster's proposal is different and obviously denies any front or back orientation, seen from the direct vicinity as much as in the skyline of London. Compared with the prevailing situation, he actually inverted the figure-ground logic: from the impermeable perimeter development of the Baltic Exchange with a centrally lit hall, he switched to a centrally positioned tower with a surrounding empty plaza. Ironically, the new dome could be seen as a clone of the one that had previously crowned the Baltic Exchange's hall, lifted 180 metres up into the sky in order to offer brighter working conditions to its approximately 3,500 occupiers.

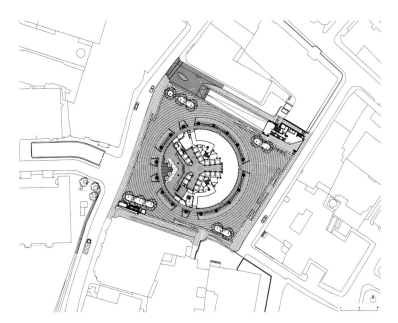

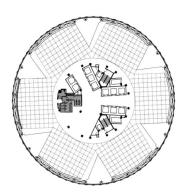

1:1250 typical floor plan with peripheral courtyards.

1:2000 ground-floor plan and surroundings.

The public plaza, one of the important elements for convincing the authorities of the project's merits, not only allows new pedestrian cross-connections, but directly benefits from the unusual architectural form of the tower. It does this first of all through the smaller diameter of the tower at its foot, leaving a maximum of space for public outdoor use, and secondly, through the advantageous wind conditions at ground level which are likewise linked to the building's curved shape. The plaza's character as such is rather awkward. Monumental, but small (essentially a leftover); anonymous, but animated through commercial ground-floor uses – it feels unconditionally dedicated to the building itself.

ARCHITECTURE

In order to understand the architectural principles of the building, it is worth highlighting Foster + Partners' main themes and the practice's architectural development during the 1990s: its insistence on a qualitative improvement of work spaces, its research in the development of vertical cities, and its increasing fondness for a curved geometry. Sustainability for high-rise structures has been one of the firm's primary concerns since the 1997 construction of the Commerzbank tower in Frankfurt (see page 40), and was also one of the central demands of the client for 30 St Mary Axe. The built scheme complies with these demands through technical engineering, including an energy-saving climate buffer in-between the facade's two adjustable glass skins, and some rather conceptual design

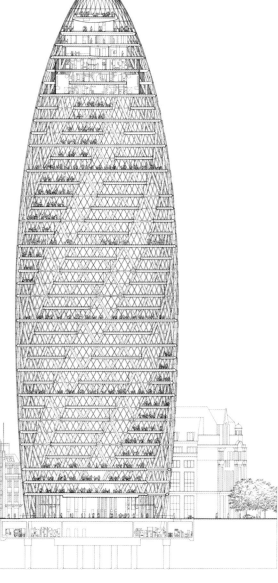

Section 1:1250

principles, such as high natural lighting and ventilation levels through shallow floor plates and extensive internal atria. An interesting architectural feature of these spiralling atria is the mediation of the tower's scale and verticality towards the interior and the users of the offices. They appear as a contemporary answer to the light wells of the early Chicago towers (for example Burnham's Santa Fe and Rookery Buildings), adjusting to growing heights and therefore increasingly difficult light conditions by turning the spatiality of the light wells inside out, from the centre to the building perimeter. On the ground floor, as an answer to the practical requirements of the main entrance, these internal atria are spatially matched by the recess of the doorway area behind the structural elements of the facade, offering a very different kind of intermediate space.

All these elements combined – the round and perfectly symmetric shape of the tower, the recess of the entrance behind the structure, and the leftover character of the plaza – somehow, though on a different scale, make allusion to Bramante's Tempietto in Rome (1502), exposing the weighty 'Gherkin' as a very Londonian compromise of classical beauty, ingenious engineering and contemporary pragmatism.

SUMMARY

The long planning history behind this tower, and its 'happy ending', underline the fact that extraordinary buildings are almost invariably the result of very specific circumstances, and can hardly just be commissioned as an architect's stroke of genius. Always political, regardless of whether they involve the demolition of

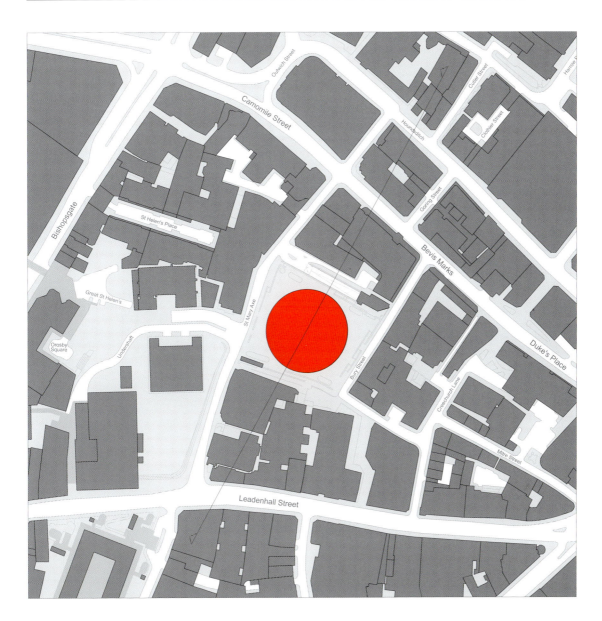

Urban plan 1:2500

an existing listed structure, they are not only symbols of the client's and the city's ambitions, but also exhaust valves for the public and the media's wish to participate, in one of the most spectacular ways possible, in the (hopefully) democratic process of weighing up so many different public and private interests. Economically, this is expressed through great risks and highly divergent estimations of land values according to the expected results of such negotiations. It is intriguing to realise that the Baltic Exchange sold their site for only 12.5 million pounds to Trafalgar House, expecting the authorities to insist on at least partial retention of the historic building, while any developer would have paid a multiple of this sum for a cleared site, as was eventually the case.

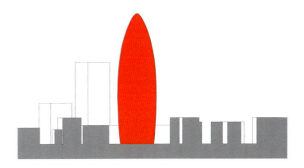

Urban section 1:5000

TORRE AGBAR

LOCATION: BARCELONA, SPAIN
DATE: 2005
ARCHITECT: JEAN NOUVEL AND B720 ARQUITECTOS

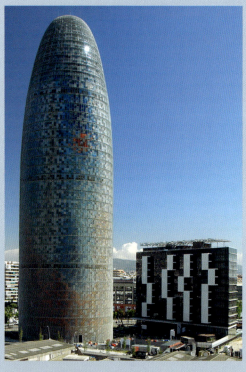

The tower project is the consequence of a masterplan study undertaken by b720 Arquitectos on a plot of formerly industrial land. Situated in the southeastern limit of Ildefons Cerdà's famous 19th-century extension plan for Barcelona, the run-down area was in urgent need of change. The resulting high-rise, designed by Jean Nouvel, became on its opening a new icon of the Catalan capital, and the signpost of a wider urban renewal zone called 22@Barcelona. In contrast to the St Mary Axe tower in London, it has been positioned along the boundary of the site and is intended to better define Avenida Diagonal and the oversized roundabout in front of it. The square, with its exterior seats, is therefore positioned behind the tower and between neighbouring structures. It can be assumed that the impact of this extraordinary piece of architecture on its direct surroundings will be further strengthened through the densification of the developments around it.

SEAGRAM BUILDING

LOCATION: NEW YORK CITY, USA
DATE: 1958
ARCHITECT: MIES VAN DER ROHE AND PHILIP JOHNSON

Strongly influenced by Louis Sullivan and the Chicago School, Mies van der Rohe was interested in the uncompromising vertical expression of the tower ('a proud and soaring thing'), and did therefore not appreciate the common stepbacks provoked by the New York zoning laws from 1916. For this milestone of modern architecture, he therefore decided to concentrate all the development potential on the 25 per cent of the plot without height limitation and to position it off Park Avenue. The remainder became one of the very few squares in the Manhattan grid, and had a strong impact on the following modification of the planning laws. In the future, the deliberate provision of publicly accessible space would come along with development incentives granted by the authorities. The tower itself became through its monumental simplicity the archetype of the glass box and the International Style, but it has rarely been equalled in terms of elegance and ingenuity.

Commerzbank Tower

SOLITAIRES: TOWER AS BLOCK
LOCATION: FRANKFURT, GERMANY
DATE: 1994–7
ARCHITECT: FOSTER + PARTNERS
CLIENT: COMMERZBANK AG

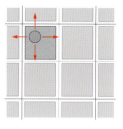

Like an oversized machine, the Commerzbank tower sits heavily on the Frankfurt skyline. Famous for its revolutionary interior organisation, it also excels with an urban insertion strategy that respects Frankfurt's historic urban fabric.

Typological group:
Solitaires – tower as block
Building height: 259 metres
Site coverage: 87%
Plot ratio: 10.99

Frankfurt has gained a global reputation as one of Europe's few high-rise capitals. But a cursory glance at an aerial view also reveals a predominantly intact and repetitive urban structure of perimeter blocks with a well-preserved heritage of *fin-de-siècle* buildings. Early on, the city's planning officials were aware of the potentially negative impact of oversized building masses on the existing urban fabric, and from 1953 established a series of *Hochhausrahmenpläne* (high-rise planning frameworks). These frameworks were designed to define a clear strategy that would control as much as support future growth of the city.

The proposed solutions for vertical development have, however, not always been consistent over time, and a radial vision had been superseded by a finger-plan, which then gave way to the current definition of specific high-rise clusters. The reasons for these modifications are not only linked to changes of planning paradigms, but are also a consequence of the fact that the realisation of such exceptional structures cannot, even in one of the world's financial capitals where demand is high, be precisely forecast. Frankfurt's experience of constant planning modifications shows that the development pressure can be successfully organised and channelled, but not precisely controlled over a longer period of time. Several towers from the 1998 plan have not been built, while others managed to receive a building permit outside of the designated cluster zones. A major change and revision is currently under way due to the failure of the Frankfurt 21 project (1996–2002), which prescribed the construction of several towers above and next to the tracks of a new underground railway station. This revision will also include the site of the new European Central Bank, a tower designed by Coop Himmelb(l)au and scheduled for completion in late 2013.

URBAN CONFIGURATION

One of the qualities of the Commerzbank scheme is its ability to integrate high-rise architecture within the spatial logic of a perimeter block. Stimulus for a new project came at the end of the 1980s when the Commerzbank, which had undergone significant expansion, had outgrown its existing location. With the workforce scattered in over 30 buildings, the subsequent and acute loss of efficiency gave rise to growing pressure for change. The Commerzbank was finally able to purchase the site right next to its 29-storey headquarter tower that dated from the 1960s, but was forced to wait for the establishment of a new high-rise framework in order to legally secure the permit for a building that would finally become Europe's tallest skyscraper.

From an urban point of view, the result can be described as a mixture of a tower-on-podium and a tower-in-block configuration. Inspired by the surviving 19th-century buildings on the south side of the block perimeter, the architect decided to rebuild the perimeter above the torn-down structures. He filled these new low-rise building masses with functions which did not need to be accommodated in the actual tower, and presented the main entrance as one element of a row of new and old perimeter developments. On entering the building, the visitor is drawn to the elevated interior of the block, with its public and skylighted restaurant

ABOVE: The base of the tower mimics the closure of the historic perimeter block.

LEFT: Behind the southern entrance, stairs lead up to the canteen and the lobby. The whole ground floor is publicly accessible and can be used as a short cut.

and a generously sized lobby. On the northern side – less restricted by existing structures – the architect's scheme is bolder, and allows the creation of a far more modern space, a monumental flight of stairs leading up to the unwrapped and freestanding base of the tower.

ARCHITECTURE

The Commerzbank tower is perhaps no masterpiece of beauty and elegance, but it was never planned to be. The overriding feeling is of some Japanese Metabolist projects, and this assumption gains credibility in view of Foster's almost contemporaneous proposal for the world's tallest tower in Tokyo.

The tower's antagonistic relation between shape and building regulations is intriguing, because the enormous total width of the construction is directly linked to the fact that German light regulations for work spaces do not permit the design of large floor plans. Foster's ingenious solution therefore prescribes a pluralithic tower, in which built and unbuilt areas alternate vertically much as horizontally in a spiralling way (see for comparison his tower for Swiss Re at 30 St Mary Axe, London (page 32)). This technique reveals it as one of

the only built examples of a modular system that could be the base of a genuine vertical city, with several, at least aesthetically separated and autonomous elements. The constructivist nature of this approach was even more developed in earlier stages of the project, when the vertical circulation was excluded from the triangular building plan as the so-called 'fish-tail' in order to be potentially linked to an envisaged redevelopment of the adjacent second Commerzbank tower.

SUMMARY

The first proposals for the Commerzbank tower were considerably over budget, and important savings had to be accommodated to make it viable. Finally, financial viability of the project was only assured through the extension of the calculation period, making full use of the tower's numerous energy-saving features and its comparably low maintenance costs. In connection with this is a striking realisation of how many of history's most famous, most advanced, but also most expensive high-rise buildings have been commissioned by clients who were owner-occupiers, and had therefore a slightly different interest in the building than a professional developer for whom the optimised cost–rental income relation should be paramount. Examples include New York's Woolworth Building (Cass Gilbert, 1913), Seagram Building and Lever House, as well as London's

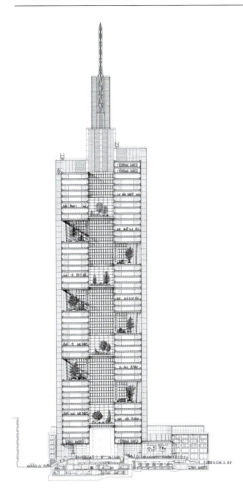

Section 1:2500 showing the spiralling skygardens.

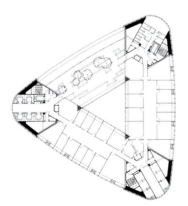

1:1250 floor plan: through its spiralling configuration, one side of the triangular building is always open to the exterior.

30 St Mary Axe and the Frankfurt Commerzbank Tower presented here. For the 'Formula One' of the technically most advanced high-rises, this marketing logic might be accurate. However, at a second glance, a clear-cut distinction of 'expensive brand names' versus 'cost-efficient rental machines' seems not that easy to uphold. If a multinational company does not build its own headquarters, it might still want to rent into a first-class address. In numerous cases a developer-built tower can hold the name of the sole or major tenant, leading to a similar identification as if the client had been the direct occupier. Also, the image of the rationally calculating real estate professional might not always be true, and many developers (and non-occupiers) have gone bankrupt through their own enthusiasm and obsessive will to leave an extraordinary heritage to future generations.

The economically rather more relevant point is therefore the tower's superlative nature as such, and the premium payment that it inflicts as an item of extraordinary branding capacity. Only very few cities could actually explain the construction of high-rise buildings solely on the basis of a lack of space and therefore exorbitantly high land prices. And even in these cities, the super-tall building will not be able to pay for its surplus costs without imposing higher rental charges for the upper floors. The rational evaluation of

The tower and its dominant position in the skyline of Frankfurt, seen from the south side of the Main river.

this premium's precise value is, however, very difficult, and for a short time after the attacks of 11 September 2001 it even seemed as if it could adopt a negative value. But height alone is not sufficient to generate maximal rental income, and as a second important economical point the location of the future building becomes an equally relevant argument. The analysis of these two simple points – height and location – is of major importance for the differentiation of solitaires, clusters and vertical cities in terms of development pressure, and for the evaluation of the impact of high-rise regulations on the gentrification of surrounding areas. The sheer suspicion of a potential cluster will have consequences on the land prices, and the sometimes animated if not violent disputes in Frankfurt's planning history – most famously at the

beginning of the 1970s in the residential Westend district – document this point as especially difficult to control in the case of solitaires in a historically grown area, when an unclear legal situation can lead to instant land speculation. The 1967 *Fingerplan* (a name derived from the plan's 'five-finger' form), a still-vague vision rather than a valid legal framework, had at the end of the 1960s led to the eviction of residents and to the deliberate neglect of the existing low-rise structures in view of a high-rise redevelopment. Eventually, the plan was not adopted, and the construction of towers was limited to the southern boundary of the district along the Mainzer Landstrasse, part of the so-called Bankenviertel.

Urban plan 1:2500

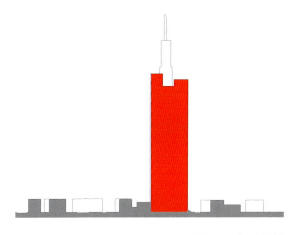

Urban section 1:5000

TRANSAMERICA PYRAMID

LOCATION: SAN FRANCISCO, CALIFORNIA, USA
DATE: 1969–72
ARCHITECT: WILLIAM L PEREIRA

Pereira's immaculately white office building plays an ambivalent role in the city's grid, and dramatises its urban position as focal point of the oblique Columbus Avenue through the symmetric recess from the plot boundaries. This non-alignment with neighbouring structures perfectly fits the tower's iconic and monolithic shape, and it eventually reads as a single block of monumental expression, even though the eastern cross-connection is in reality only a pedestrian link through an actually wider block. As explained in the case study of Houston (page 146), this alleged situation – the equation of a block and a tower – is surprisingly rare and challenges the notion of the American grid as a homologous juxtaposition of piecemeal-developed perimeter blocks. The tower's pyramidal shape is coherent with the programme and the client's iconic ambitions, because the drastic loss of surface in the upper floors attends with the site's limited plot ratio and the fixed maximum development area.

HOTEL UKRAINA

LOCATION: MOSCOW, RUSSIA
DATE: 1953–7
ARCHITECT: ARKADY MORDVINOV AND VYACHESLAV OLTARZHEVSKY

Just like Lev Rudnev's Moscow State University (see page 30), Hotel Ukraina is one of Stalin's 'Seven Sisters'. Situated in a more central location in the direct vicinity of the river, it shares with the other buildings some neoclassical architectural features, often dismissed as 'wedding cake' style. In contrast to the university building, it appears as an independent block and encloses a landscaped courtyard, creating an arguably more urban and complex environment with extroverted and introverted features. Unlike similar examples of megablocks in Manhattan's Upper West Side, for example The Apthorp or The Belnord, the courtyard of the Russian example is publicly accessible and appears as a green square rather than a building courtyard. The surprising tranquillity of this space is preserved through the fact that the entrance of the hotel, situated on the ground level of the tower, is mono-oriented towards the block exterior and the river.

Torre Velasca

SOLITAIRES: TOWER IN BLOCK
LOCATION: MILAN, ITALY
DATE: 1956–8
ARCHITECT: BBPR (GIAN LUIGI BANFI, LUDOVICO BARBIANO DI BELGIOJOSO, ENRICO PERESSUTTI, ERNESTO NATHAN ROGERS)
CLIENT: SOCIETÀ GENERALE IMMOBILIARE

Famous for the architectural debate that it inflamed at the last CIAM (Congrès International d'Architecture Moderne) congress in Otterlo, The Netherlands in 1959, the Torre Velasca also represents an ingenious solution in urban terms.

Typological group:
Solitaires – tower in block
Building height: 106 metres
Site coverage: 45%
Plot ratio: 5.64

Several Italian cities were heavily bombed during defeat in the Second World War. Milan, the country's economic capital, was not an exception, and the question of how appropriately to rebuild the destroyed structures in the historic cores remained a major, preoccupying theme for the post-war generation of Italian architects. The situation was aggravated through an enormous demographic growth, a continuing lack of residential space and the city centres' increasing loss of functional mixture in favour of office uses during the subsequent period of economic revival. The initial

lack of adequate legal tools did not facilitate the reconstruction according to the plans of the city officials. In the case of the Torre Velasca, a 9,000-square-metre surface had become available through the bomb destruction of several older residential structures, and a redevelopment scheme was sought.

The involvement of the local design studio BBPR (Banfi, Belgiojoso, Peressutti, Rogers) in the project holds, from today's point of view, a symbolic role for the history of Italy. The four architects knew each other from their studies in Milan and had founded an office

in 1932. Their early sympathies for the Fascists quickly evaporated, and the members of the group over time became opponents of the regime. Rogers, who was of British origin, had to leave the country and Gian Luigi Banfi eventually lost his life in a concentration camp. After the war, the three remaining partners reconvened and continued a successful career as university teachers and practitioners. Initially strongly influenced by Mies van der Rohe, Le Corbusier and the Italian Rationalists, their post-war work became deeply personal and contextual, and eventually clashed openly with the anti-historicism of their former CIAM colleagues. In particular Ernesto Nathan Rogers, as former publisher of *Domus* and editor of *Casabella* until 1964, made his mark as one of the intellectual leaders of his time, and had the capacity to challenge the increasingly dogmatic views of his formerly congenial comrades on an international level.

URBAN CONFIGURATION

Due to the aforementioned damage suffered through bombings from the war, the structure not only of the block on which the Torre Velasca now stands, but of the whole surrounding district has been considerably altered. Previously, Via Larga continued at its full width along the length of what is now Piazza Velasca, and found its end in a perpendicular T-junction with Corso di Porta Romana. During the post-war work on town planning and traffic rearrangements, Via Larga was shifted to the west towards Piazza Giuseppe Missori

through the creation of the large Via Alberico Albricci. The newly created block, historically further subdivided by a narrow lane, therefore acquired in terms of connectivity a rather more secretive character, which somehow stands in intriguing contrast to the ambitious size and programme of the tower that it holds at its heart.

This background information is important in order to understand the complexity of the urban redevelopment, which involved far more than just resurrecting a destroyed apartment block. Hence the architect's decision to subdivide the programme into three chapters, to rebuild – or rather invent – a formerly non-existent block, and to 'hide' a 106-metre-tall structure at its centre. In contrast to both other examples of this typological group presented in this book – the Kudamm-Karree in Berlin (see page 54) and the Norddeutsche Landesbank in Hanover (see page 55) – the central space is not only publicly accessible, but open and incorporated into the city's street network. This feature, together with the much-needed accommodation of residential spaces, was also the reason for the administration's support of the privately

CLOCKWISE FROM TOP LEFT: View down Corso di Porta Romana from Piazza Giuseppe Missori.

View of Piazza Velasca with the tower and its front and entrance building. Via Larga can be seen in the left-hand background. The residential corner blocks were part of the same development programme.

The ground floor of the front building is transparent and accommodates retail uses. The first floor of this low-rise structure is linked with the spaces within the tower's actual volume.

ABOVE: The tower demonstrating its exceptional capacity to melt into Milan's historic fabric.

RIGHT: Torre Velasca and one of the corner buildings seen from Via Larga.

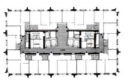

1:1250 typical office plan layout, situated in the lower and thinner part of the tower.

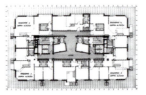

1:1250 lower level of the duplex apartments at the top of the tower.

financed project. Working within the margin set by existing building regulations, it would have been possible to build over 142,000 square metres of gross area in the shape of a stepped megablock; but the high-rise solution, though in conspicuous proximity to the Duomo, offered a civically far more interesting result.

Analogies with the fabric of the historic city could easily be over-interpreted. Nevertheless, similar to the building's intensely discussed architectural aesthetics, the almost playful, if not antagonistic strategy – in which a tower is positioned in the centre of an invented urban block – is certainly atypical for most other modern architects. This is especially true of those who were, like BBPR since 1935, members of the CIAM group. Giò Ponti's contemporaneous Pirelli Tower, lean as a sword, and situated next to the railway station just outside the historic core of Milan, is a good local counter-example which confronts the surrounding space in a far more provocative and open way. Some Parisian examples of the same period, such as Front de Seine (see page 136) and La Défense (see page 178), are even more radical, and position the tower on an artificial datum above the historic city, therefore avoiding the question of typological insertion.

ARCHITECTURE

The building's mix of uses as such was not really new: many of the early American high-rises, as well as the few existing in Europe, incorporated a greater number of functions than most post-war examples. What was, however, very unusual was the expression of this mixture on the exterior. Officially, the architects explained the recess of the lower storeys by the need to save space on the ground (compare to 30 St Mary Axe, page 32), combined with the assumption that the 6-metre width of the lower office floors would not have suited the needs of the upper storeys' residential areas. However, it can be guessed that these rather functional explanations masked a lyrical and contextual approach, in which references to medieval defence towers and the neighbouring Duomo have been stated and assumed. The treatment of the building envelope follows these ideas, and the exaggerated expression of the structure – in theory following modern design principles – can hardly be misunderstood as a fairly literal reference to Gothic architecture. The treatment of the facades with comparatively small windows, and the use of mixed-surface facade panels containing some of the same materials that had been used in the surrounding older structures, complement this picture. Initially the architects planned a steel construction, but switched for financial reasons to reinforced concrete. Among

many inspirations, the early experimental work of Auguste Perret in the use of this building material seems to have influenced the Italian architects strongly.

Also remarkable is the use of a duplex typology for the apartments of the two top floors. Probably meant to facilitate and justify the creation of a formalised building crown through a recess from the tower's perimeter line, they can be understood as a negation of the modern principles of equality, and might have provoked the critics' evocation of London's Big Ben as a pejorative reference for the tower. This point is also linked to the fact that – in contrast to the United States – high-rise

Giò Ponti's Pirelli Tower, situated in front of Milan's main railway station.

living was still a fairly rare phenomenon in Europe and became in the following two decades increasingly associated with social rather than private housing.

SUMMARY

At first glance, the building fits in well with its environment: so well in fact that it is difficult to determine its age. Depending on the reader's inclinations and taste, this characteristic can be perceived as a positive or negative attribute, but in any case it gives an idea of what high-rise can achieve, albeit rarely, in terms of character and atmosphere. If the tower is often understood as an element of disturbance, if not of destruction of the traditional urban grain, Torre Velasca in contrast establishes rather more subtle dialectics with its surroundings, and indirectly

provokes the question why form and materiality of the post-war tower have in general followed such a homogenous path. In the narrow limits of the rules of structural efficiency, the previously mentioned negation of the tower as a monolithic vertical extrusion – the notorious 'box' – can lead to challenging design solutions which have recently regained importance, not least because of an increasing size and functional diversity of the projects.

Unlike other milestones in the history of high-rise construction – such as the Chrysler or Seagram Buildings in New York, which quickly became precedents for numerous copies worldwide – the importance of Torre Velasca seems, however, to be based on its exceptional and critical character, rather than on its role as a model.

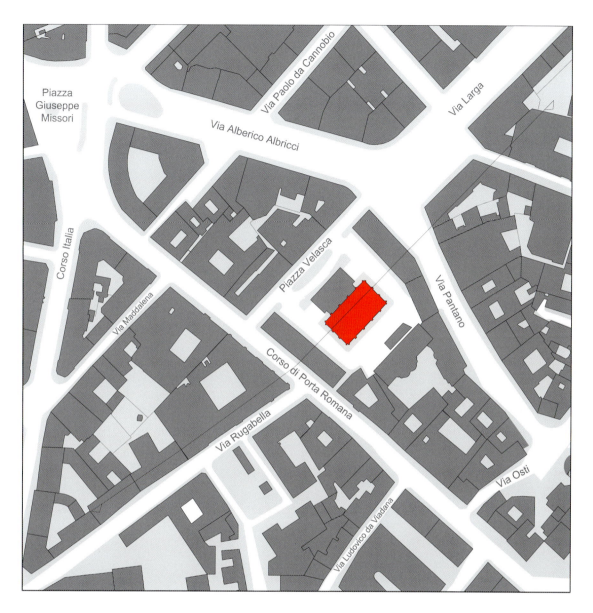

Urban plan 1:2500

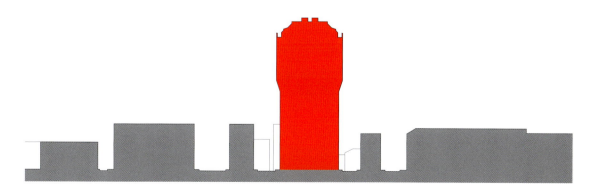

Urban section 1:2500

KUDAMM-KARREE

LOCATION: BERLIN, GERMANY
DATE: 1969–74
ARCHITECT: SIGRID KRESSMANN-ZSCHACH

Designed, developed and built by the flamboyant female architect and entrepreneur Sigrid Kressmann-Zschach, this 40,000-square-metre mixed-use scheme includes a 20-storey tower, a car park and a network of retail passages. The latter element provides the pedestrian connection from the centrally located tower to all four sides of the block perimeter which is essentially composed of typical *fin-de-siècle* apartment buildings. The Kudamm-Karree is predominantly known for its two historic theatres that have been incorporated in the prominently located 1970s redevelopment. Almost indistinguishable from the outside, the unusual high-rise proposal represents an 'anti-iconic' solution in which the height seems to be solely caused by the need for more space. The Irish developer Ballymore has bought the site and is currently exploring its renewal together with the British architect David Chipperfield.

NORDDEUTSCHE LANDESBANK

LOCATION: HANOVER, GERMANY
YEAR: 1996–2002
ARCHITECT: BEHNISCH ARCHITEKTEN

The 75,000-square-metre bank development covers a large urban block in the centre of Hanover, and combines a strictly orthogonal perimeter building with a 70-metre-tall tower of far more complex and playful geometry at its centre. The interior courtyard of the glazed block is accessible to the public through generous corner openings, and incorporates retail, restaurants and cafés. It is shielded from the noise of Friedrichswall, one of the city's busiest traffic arteries, and has been designed as an oasis as much as transitional zone that mediates between the diverse activities and scales of the city centre. The generous width of the main street also explains the strong visibility of the tower in the urban context, despite its protected central location.

Kungstornen

SOLITAIRES: TWIN TOWERS
LOCATION: NORRMALM, STOCKHOLM, SWEDEN
DATE: 1919–25
MASTERPLANNER: SVEN WALLANDER, BASED ON ALBERT LINDHAGEN'S PLAN OF 1866
ARCHITECT: SVEN WALLANDER (NORTH TOWER) AND IVAR CALLMANDER (SOUTH TOWER)
CLIENT: AB NORRA KUNGSTORNET (NORTH TOWER); AB L M ERICSSON (SOUTH TOWER)

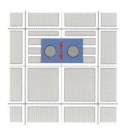

Typological group:
Solitaires – twin towers
Building height: 60 metres
Site coverage: 91%
Plot ratio: 6.84

Better known for its decidedly horizontal geography, Sweden is also home to Europe's first 'skyscrapers'. Planned before the beginning of the Modern Movement, Stockholm's neoclassical Kungstornen represents one of the rare cases where high-rise construction meets 19th-century urbanism in a harmonious manner.

HISTORY / DEVELOPMENT PROCESS

The origins of this ambitious project date back to the mid-19th century and the city's efforts to modernise the capital to the level of its continental European neighbours. In 1866 the lawyer Albert Lindhagen drew up a plan for the city's long-term extension to the north and south of the old town, situated on the small Stadsholmen Island. The nature of this urban development needs to be considered in the context of Sweden's delayed but swift industrialisation process and the subsequent growth of Stockholm's population from 100,000 inhabitants in 1856 to 200,000 in 1884 and rising to 300,000 in 1900. The complexity of the

enormous task, combined with the lack of technical, legal and financial means, caused delays and significant alterations to the plan, but it remained the city's most influential planning document until the mid-20th century. Lindhagen was not only the driving force behind this plan, but was also responsible for initiating the subsequent establishment of building statutes which among other points set out clear rules for the relationship between street width and building heights, in addition to maximum plot coverage for new developments. Limitations on plot coverage were designed to avoid the emergence of Berlin-style 'rental barracks', characterised by large apartment buildings

with overly small and dark interior courtyards.

The implementation of the northern half of the 1866 plan was made difficult by the existence of the Brunkebergsåsen, a north–south ridge which led to the de facto separation of the Norrmalm and Östermalm districts. Through already densely built-up areas, Lindhagen had designed a new street grid with Kungsgatan as the major east–west link and the north–south Sveavägen as the city's new main boulevard. The Sveavägen boulevard was never constructed according to the plan, and Kungsgatan – cutting right through the ridge – only opened to traffic in 1911. The sale of plots and the construction of buildings along the carved-out artery progressed very slowly, probably due to their lowered situation. For many years, it was only the area around Stureplan public square that demonstrated any momentum in becoming built up. The two viaducts at Regeringsgatan and Malmskillnadsgatan, the latter framed by the two towers featured here, are a result of Kungsgatan's cut through Brunkebergsåsen.

URBAN CONFIGURATION

The young architect Sven Wallander worked from 1915 to 1917 for the Stockholm City Planning Commission,

and in this role developed a masterplan for Kungsgatan that was based on Lindhagen's then almost 50-year-old vision. Along the viaduct that connects the northern with the southern part of Norrmalm, Wallander envisaged a neoclassical ensemble with two towers and six-storey buildings. The combination of the vertical elements with the horizontal impact of the strictly aligned lower structures was designed to produce a monumental effect and to symbolise Stockholm's aspirations as a modern and emerging metropolis. Except for some minor changes – for example the decision not to include the continuous colonnades along the ground floor of the lower structures – the scheme was realised between 1919 and 1925 when Wallander had already left the Planning Commission in order to set up his private practice.

The resulting construction is remarkable on many levels, and represents an inherently urban type of European high-rise construction that complements the often deliberately anti-urban picture of the post-war period and its radical interventions. In the case of the Kungstornen towers, the decision to build tall is neither limited to symbolic considerations nor to the quest for cost-efficient space supply, but the verticality in essence helps to aesthetically accomplish the formally

BELOW LEFT: View towards the north on Malmskillnadsgatan.

BELOW RIGHT: Stairs leading down to Kungsgatan.

LEFT: The three-storey base of the north tower and its connection to the viaduct.

BELOW LEFT: The radically modern slabs of Högtorgshusen as the high-rise counter-example to Kungstornen, which is visible in the background on the right-hand side of the image.

demanding insertion of a viaduct and an entrenched traffic artery in an existing urban fabric. Wallander's decision to build twins and not a single tower further supports this endeavour, and presents Kungstornen as both the major gate of Kungsgatan and the signpost of the perpendicular north–south link above it. Among the very few tall buildings which exist in Stockholm, the towers remain today prominent points on the urban landscape and stand out clearly on the approach to Stockholm by sea.

ARCHITECTURE

The two towers and the lower constructions along Kungsgatan are good examples of a building style that strongly influenced Scandinavian architecture from around 1910 to 1930, referred to as 'Nordic Classicism'. As a more vernacular version of neoclassicism, it evolved from National Romanticism, or *Jugendstil*, and ended with the beginning of Functionalism and Modernism, marked by the opening of the Stockholm Exhibition in 1930. Rediscovered by the Post-Modern

1:1250 plan of the 15th floor,
at the top of the building.

1:1250 ground-floor plan of the
south tower with access from
the viaduct.

movement in the late 1970s and 1980s, its most famous
exponents include the Swedes Gunnar Asplund, Sigurd
Lewerentz and the Dane Kay Fisker.

From a planning point of view, more relevant than
the architectural style is the large degree of involvement
by the city administration in prescribing the form of
the buildings. This strong public control in urban
development represented a new step in Stockholm's
planning policies, and an unequivocal will to ensure
design quality through fairly restrictive guidelines to
be respected by the contractors responsible for
construction of the buildings. In this specific case,
the twin towers had private clients, but were built on
land owned by the city.

Wallander himself implemented the construction of
the northern tower, but the second tower was attributed
to the architect Ivar Callmander and indeed features
some spatial and stylistic differences. Since the
masterplanning stage in 1915, several points had been
adjusted, and the towers eventually became taller than
previously intended – a fact that Wallander welcomed.
His tower was initially conceived for a single user, but
the interior distribution had to be adjusted when the
taker spontaneously decided to move the headquarters
abroad. Last-minute changes were also necessary
due to the decision to accommodate a three-storey
restaurant at the top of the building, which no longer

exists today. The fountains and generous planting
arrangements that Wallander designed for the
exterior staircases connecting Kungsgatan with
Malmskillnadsgatan on the upper level fell by the
wayside.

SUMMARY

Kungstornen is distinctive in European urban history,
for it is clearly not cut from the same cloth as the 19th-
century European city yet it is seamlessly woven into
the urban fabric of the Stockholm context and, unlike
its later counterparts, was not intended to represent a
deliberate break with the past.

**The Nordic Classicism of
the south tower, designed
by Ivar Callmander.**

The development of the tower typology was closely linked to the housing question and often built as a slab rather than a point-tower, if possible surrounded by green open spaces (see Unité d'Habitation, Marseilles, page 134). Another type, specifically dominant in France, combined high-rise with a large podium, as in Paris at Front de Seine (see page 136) or around the Montparnasse tower, or on the outskirts of the city at La Défense (see page 178). Högtorgshusen (see image page 58), a massive adjacent development with five juxtaposed slabs, is an excellent local example of a podium construction, and clearly demonstrates, despite its architectural value, the difficulties associated with introducing a structure which stands in such stark contrast to the more organic evolution of Stockholm's urban fabric. Kungstornen, in contrast, is more in line with the earlier American tradition in which high-rise grew out of the traditional city and led – unlike the Modernist version of the tower – to an almost proportional increase in density, with New York and Chicago as its best examples. Besides the otherness of the plot and grid structure, a crucial difference with these American predecessors in terms of cityscape is Sweden's horizontal landscape and building tradition. In light of this, Kungstornen appears in a double sense as an ingenious signpost for an exceptional urban situation, masterminded by the city administration and not private investors. Formal similarities can be found with the equally public Villeurbanne project (see page 94) near Lyons and the Frankfurter Tor towers in Berlin (see page 130), but none of these projects achieves such a degree of integration.

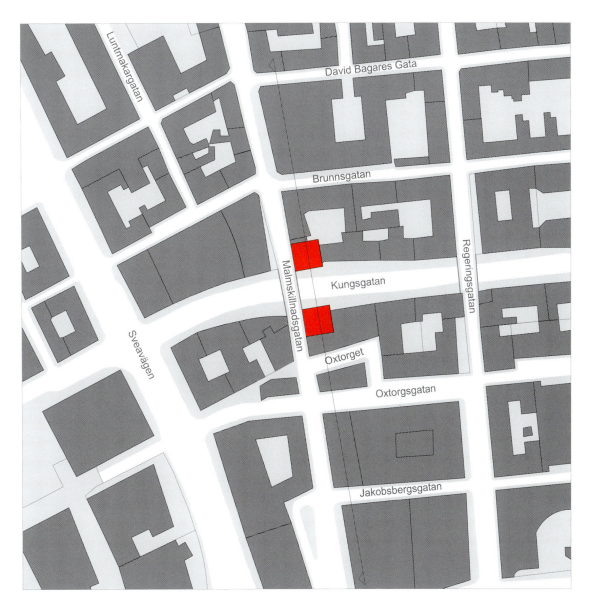

Urban plan 1:2500

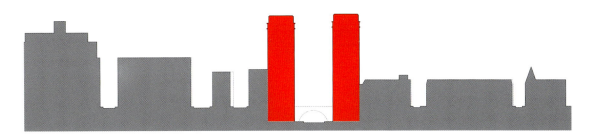

Urban section 1:2500

MARINA CITY TOWERS

LOCATION: CHICAGO, ILLINOIS, USA
DATE: 1959–64
ARCHITECT: BERTRAND GOLDBERG

Financed by building unions and built on a three-storey podium along the Chicago River, the famous development comprises not only the two residential towers with their generously sized balconies and the famous vertical parking decks, but also a mid-rise hotel building and a saddle-shaped concert and theatre hall. Due to the narrowness of the site, the ensemble of four large volumes does not achieve the same harmony on the ground floor that the two towers brilliantly provide as major players in the river front's skyline. Skilfully, the shift of the two corncobs against each other mimics the nearby turn of the river. The spectacular mixed-use development – marketed as a 'city in the city' – was an early attempt to revitalise the downtown area and to prevent the flight of the middle classes to the suburbs, which it did by offering retail, restaurants, offices, a television studio, a gym, an ice rink, a swimming pool and a marina. Unlike the other two examples of this group, Marina City does not form a gate situation, and is a particularly iconic example of the vast group of twin towers.

PUERTA DE EUROPA (KIO TOWERS)

LOCATION: MADRID, SPAIN
DATE: 1989–96
ARCHITECT: PHILIP JOHNSON / JOHN BURGEE

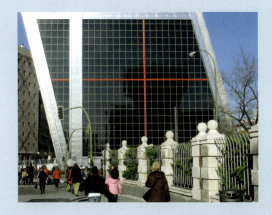

Situated at a distance of approximately 5 kilometres from the historic centre of Madrid, Puerta de Europa marks a strategic point along the city's major extension axis to the north, the Paseo de la Castellana. Through the inclination of the two twin towers, the new development area around the roundabout is experienced as Madrid's major northern gateway. The structural novelty of oblique towers, a tribute to Russian Constructivism, has been explained by the architects through the need to physically converge the two vertical masses as much as possible in order to imply the urban meaning of a gate, previously not envisaged by the city's masterplan. The existence of several underground tunnels and subways beneath the site perimeter imposed heavy technical restrictions, forcing the architects to allow an additional distance between the edges of the broad avenue and the bases of the towers.

Tokyo Metropolitan Government Building

SOLITAIRES: TOWER AS TEAM PLAYER
LOCATION: NISHI-SHINJUKU, TOKYO, JAPAN
DATE: 1988–91
ARCHITECT: KENZO TANGE
CLIENT: TOKYO METROPOLITAN GOVERNMENT

The TMG complex, with Tokyo's tallest tower as its central element, is charged with a multitude of symbolic meanings. Its urban form is clear but highly unusual, challenging the grid layout of the Nishi-Shinjuku business district.

Typological group:
Solitaires – tower as team player
Building height: 243 metres
Site coverage: 64%
Plot ratio: 8.86

HISTORY / DEVELOPMENT PROCESS

Together with Ikebukuro and Shibuya, Shinjuku was designated in the National Capital Region Development Plan of 1958 as one of Tokyo's new sub-centres that would assure the multi-nodal development of the capital's economic, political and cultural functions. Built around one of the world's busiest train stations, linking metro lines with the JR (Japan Rail) and several private train lines, Shinjuku has consequently become the largest of these sub-centres, and at the end of the millennium achieved Tokyo's highest figures in terms of retail turnover and office surface area. The train station and its tracks sharply divide the district into two major parts: the eastern historically older part renowned for entertainment and shopping activities, and the western (Nishi) proudly presenting Japan's high-rise answer to Manhattan. This separation between east and west, attenuated by the presence of some large retail stores on the western side of the station, has an almost caricatural quality: every evening an army of 'salary-men' wander out of the austerity of their open-plan floor plates towards the glittery, often nefarious and mainly Yakuza-controlled amusements of the Kabukicho red-light district on the other side of the tracks. This character, however, has historical roots: at the time of the Tokugawa Shogunate (1603–1868), Shinjuku was already a place where people sought easy entertainment before entering the walls of the city that was then known

The Tokyo Metropolitan Government complex seen from the Shinjuku Park Tower, also designed by Kenzo Tange.

as Edo. After the Second World War, it was the site of Tokyo's largest black market.

The move of the city hall from Marunouchi to Nishi-Shinjuku happened only in 1991, long after construction in 1971 of the Keio Plaza Hotel, the area's first high-rise. It was a pet project of Suzuki Shunichi, Tokyo's governor from 1979 to 1995.

URBAN CONFIGURATION

Nishi-Shinjuku was masterplanned to become a modern high-rise district, and is not the result of a historically grown redevelopment process. It is located on the site of former waterworks. A wide-meshed and regular network of broad avenues delimits large rectangular blocks, which usually coincide with a plot

of single ownership, accommodating a point-tower or a very large mid-rise building. More than 30 of these constructions are over 100 metres tall, many of them offering public access to viewing decks and restaurants on the top floors. If the chequerboard of juxtaposed megastructures bears similarities to the urbanism of Pudong-Lujiazui (see page 170), the main particularity of this office and hotel district is marked out by a level difference between the east–west and north–south avenues. Designed to facilitate car travel and deliveries through the minimisation of traffic lights, the result of this complicated arrangement for the public realm and pedestrian street life is ambivalent, and cannot conceal its 1960s origins. The system can indeed be seen as a more moderate alternative to European or American podium-urbanism (compare with Front de Seine (see page 136) in Paris or La Défense (see page 178) on the outskirts of the city), and produces some similar spaces and problems. Shinjuku Central Park to the west of the TMG complex is an inherent part of the masterplan, and a modest reminder of the fact that the city – inspired by Patrick Abercrombie's 1944 plan for London – initially intended to adopt a green-belt policy which, due to pressures for redevelopment, was finally abandoned.

ARCHITECTURE

Kenzo Tange was already the designer of the former city hall in the Marunouchi district. His career as Japan's most influential modern architect took off in 1949 with a victory in the competition for the Hiroshima Peace Memorial Museum.

Thirty-six years later, after countless successful built works and following the foundation – with other colleagues including Kisho Kurokawa – of the Metabolist movement, Tange's office also won the competition organised in 1985 for the pharaonic project of the new city hall, which was meant to accommodate 425,000 square metres on three blocks owned by the city administration. His proposal established a very clear hierarchy between the three building masses and their respective urban blocks: the main and tallest building with two iconic twin towers, a stepped lower building that adjusts to the average height of surrounding

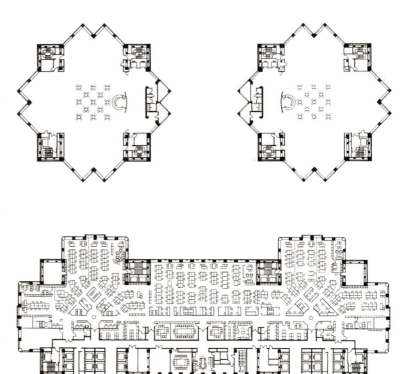

1:1250 typical and top-floor plans.

Close-up showing the level differences around the city hall complex. They even extend into the adjacent park.

structures, and a much lower building, the assembly hall, which circumscribes with colonnades a square in front of the main building. More explicitly than in most of his other works, Tange evokes historic references, and the outcome of the Tokyo Metropolitan Government complex is a decidedly Japanese mixture of Metabolist and Post-Modern influences. While the twin top can hardly be missed as a reference to a Gothic cathedral – most probably Notre-Dame in Paris – the treatment of the base with moats and blank walls has been interpreted by some as an allusion to the architecture of traditional Japanese castles. Most importantly, the great urban gesture of the assembly hall conveys the impression of a modern version of St Peter's Square in Rome.

SUMMARY

Tange's skilfully intellectual proposal is not limited to Post-Modern allusions, but represents, deliberately or not, a critique and analysis of urban forms and public space strategies. In this context, the square, as not only an architectural but also an urban-planning element of the traditional city, is confronted by the modern, car-oriented urbanism of the whole Nishi-Shinjuku district. The slightly awkward atmosphere of the sunken space and its complicated multi-level relationship to the main building underline the aforementioned pedestrian issues of the grid rather than solving them. By circumscribing an interiorised square rather than opening it towards the surrounding public realm, Tange effectively redefines this urban space as an architectural feature, an uncovered hall rather than a *plaza mayor*. In fact, the allusion to St Peter's Square and its colonnades is provocative, because the Roman reference is, unlike the city hall, part of a kilometre-long Baroque axis that leads to a building of monumental dimensions in a context of

CLOCKWISE FROM TOP LEFT: South approach to the space of the assembly hall. In the Shinjuku grid, the north–south avenues are elevated to optimise the traffic flow.

View from the park along one of Shinjuku's main avenues. At far left is the Mode Gakuen Cocoon Tower, a university tower built by Kenzo Tange's son (Tange Associates).

Situated one level beneath the city hall's main entrance, the square is defined by the rounded assembly-hall building and its colonnades.

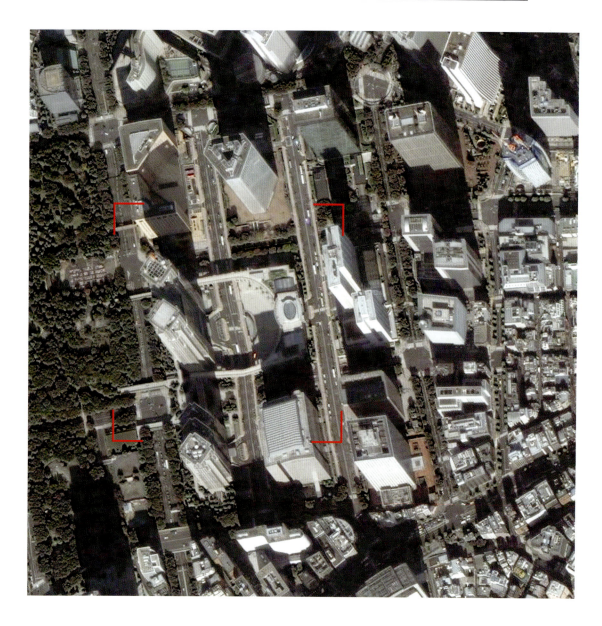

far smaller surrounding structures – St Peter's Basilica. Neither is the case in Shinjuku's grid, and the decision to turn public space in on itself can be understood as the multi-level grid's incapacity or the architect's refusal to create a European-style public space – a fact that is understandable in the context of a very different relationship of Japanese and Asian cities to the public realm. The fascination of this project is eventually based on the use of openly incoherent signs, mixing the classical American grid and a rather European, CIAM-inspired separation of circulation levels with Japanese, French and Italian architectural elements. A reminder of Metabolist influences can arguably be seen in the above-mentioned incorporation of public space into the building programme of a superstructure that hosts over 10,000 civil servants. It seems that the perfect operation

of this organism and its potential flexibility and growth have been given more importance in the long run than its connection to the ground and its relation to the surroundings.

It is therefore surprising to realise that the genuine urban quality of this high-rise district is more concerned with the creation of exterior spaces in the sky than on the ground. More than in any other major business district in the world, public access to the top of the towers has been established as an almost common rule, making accessible to the collective memory a view over the city that can usually only be gleaned from the virtual reality of television screens or books.

Urban plan 1:2500

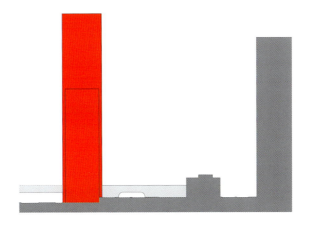

Urban section 1:5000

THYSSEN-HAUS

LOCATION: DÜSSELDORF, GERMANY
DATE: 1957–60
ARCHITECT: HPP (HENTRICH–PETSCHNIGG & PARTNER)

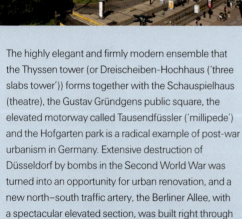

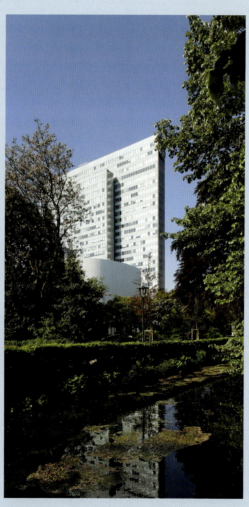

The highly elegant and firmly modern ensemble that the Thyssen tower (or Dreischeiben-Hochhaus ('three slabs tower')) forms together with the Schauspielhaus (theatre), the Gustav Gründgens public square, the elevated motorway called Tausendfüssler ('millipede') and the Hofgarten park is a radical example of post-war urbanism in Germany. Extensive destruction of Düsseldorf by bombs in the Second World War was turned into an opportunity for urban renovation, and a new north–south traffic artery, the Berliner Allee, with a spectacular elevated section, was built right through the remains of the pre-war urban fabric and the city's major park. The theatre opened only in 1970, with a curved form that was conceived as an explicit counterpoint to the tower's corporate coolness. An early attempt to think outside the usual Modernist box, the scheme as built was initially merely an alternative by the same architects to the one that had won them the commission. Not being in a position to suggest the construction of the earlier option, which was his own favourite, Helmut Hentrich took the opportunity of a study trip to the US to ask star architect Gordon Bunshaft of Skidmore, Owings & Merrill for his opinion, in the client's presence. On hearing Bunshaft's praise, the client was left with little choice but to accept the alternative proposal.

UNITED NATIONS HEADQUARTERS

PLACE: NEW YORK CITY, USA
YEAR: 1949–50
ARCHITECT: HARRISON & ABRAMOVITZ (CONCEPT BY INTERNATIONAL DESIGN TEAM)

Deterred by the poor outcome of the 1926 competition for the League of Nations building in Geneva, the organisers of the new 'workshop for peace' had decided to directly commission an international team of 12 architects for the elaboration of a radically modern design. With Le Corbusier and Oscar Niemeyer particularly instrumental in forming the final concept, the buildings themselves were, however, detailed by the lead consultants Harrison & Abramovitz (a firm founded in 1945 that had its origins in Corbett, Harrison & MacMurray – see also Rockefeller Center, page 88). The result is a fascinating hybrid between radical European Modernism and well-conceived American building culture. An interesting tension can be felt in terms of urban insertion, as the modest extent of the site forces the 'slab-in-park' configuration back into the logic of the Manhattan grid. Ultimately, the water of the Hudson river and the skyline of Midtown combine to embody Le Corbusier's definition of architecture, which is outlined in his seminal work of 1923, *Vers une Architecture*, as 'being the masterly, correct and magnificent play of masses brought together in light'.

The Standard Hotel

SOLITAIRES: TOWER ON INFRASTRUCTURE
LOCATION: NEW YORK CITY, USA
DATE: 2008–9
ARCHITECT: TODD SCHLIEMANN OF ENNEAD ARCHITECTS (FORMERLY POLSHEK PARTNERSHIP)
CLIENT: ANDRÉ BALAZS PROPERTIES

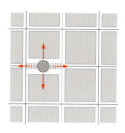

Typological group:
**Solitaires – tower
on infrastructure**
Building height: **71** metres
Site coverage: **80%**
Plot ratio: **5.30**

A signpost for, as much as a consequence of, the new High Line Park, the Standard Hotel in Manhattan's Meatpacking District takes advantage of a very atypical urban situation. Previously considered a scar in the city, this alleged handicap has turned out to perfectly support the Standard hotel chain's claim for exceptional solutions.

HISTORY / DEVELOPMENT PROCESS

When André Balazs bought the site, the rapid transformation of the historically industrial Meatpacking District, on the Lower West Side of Manhattan, from a run-down red-light district into one of New York's most fashionable shopping areas and nightlife hotspots, was already well under way. The plan to transform the elevated freight railway line, built in the 1930s but out of use since 1980, into a linear park, had been around for several years, though nothing had yet been made official. The site of today's Standard Hotel, like many others along these elevated tracks, was therefore considered to be an urban blight. Balazs, however,

realised its exceptional potential, being surrounded by much lower protected structures and having itself a fixed maximum FAR (floor area ratio) but no height limitation. A potential construction above the line had not seriously been considered by the owner – the CSX railway company – or by the city, and as a result there were no existing planning restrictions for this case. In addition, Balazs' offer did not have to compete with condominium builders, as this use was prohibited by the zoning laws for this area.

Only much later, in November 2005, was the construction of the High Line Park – initiated by a local interest group – decided, the legal preservation of the

RIGHT: The twisting form of the main volume dramatises the building's highly unusual setting.

BELOW: The hotel entrance with exterior seating area in front of it. It was part of the design intention to present the new-build ground floor as a reminder of the district's warehouse culture.

tracks concluded and the land given over from CSX to the city. The project was gaining momentum. The design, inspired by the 'Promenade Plantée' in the east of Paris, was undertaken by the landscape architect James Corner's practice Field Operations and the architects Diller Scofidio + Renfro. The implementation of the project under ownership of the city precludes future construction above it, providing the Standard Hotel with a genuinely unique status.

URBAN CONFIGURATION

The site has to be seen in relation to the Manhattan grid, and in this grid it holds, independent of the High Line, a specific role as the southwestern edge of the Commissioners' Plan of 1811. It therefore reflects the edgy shape of Manhattan as much as it marks the point of transition from the several grids of the southern older part of the island to the northwards extension following a spatially unified pattern.

Due to its situation at this turning point between two orthogonal geometries, the impact of the tracks on the site is especially pronounced. In contrast to most other plots along its route towards 30th Street, it does not cut them perpendicularly and therefore neatly, but in an oblique manner. This is essentially the reason for the specific shape of the plot which, in contrast to the typical Manhattan plot, is not small, narrow and deep, but large, long and parallel to the street.

Interestingly, this shape is very apt for the construction of a hotel, because it minimises the existence of backward-oriented and service areas that make little sense for the provision of space-efficient temporary accommodation. This does not necessarily apply in the same way to apartments or offices, where a larger proportion of the surface does not have to be in direct relation to the exterior. Due to the elevation of the tower and the low height of the surrounding structures, the guests of the Standard Hotel can benefit from a unique view which, for simple typological reasons, could not have been provided in Midtown's or the

CLOCKWISE FROM TOP LEFT: Approach from the south along the High Line Park.

The hotel terrace is situated between the base and the western part of the elevated volume.

The project combines modern architectural language with a decidedly non-minimalist conceptual approach.

Upper East Side's perimeter block developments, on orthogonal plots with courtyard-and-street orientation. The twist of the glazed slab underlines this fact and appears as a gesture of liberation.

It is worth mentioning that the exploitation of the site's atypical geometry in this way was not self-evident from the start, even though the solution as built may now seem to have been the obvious choice. Before purchase of the land by Balazs, another developer had elaborated a proposal which took advantage of the lack of height limitation and concentrated the totality of the development potential on a small part of the site,

adjacent to and not above the railway tracks. Though proposed by star architect Jean Nouvel, the scheme was abandoned at an early stage due to the criticism expressed by the local community.

ARCHITECTURE

It is hard to believe that the building was finished in 2009, and several articles have indeed (mis-)presented the new-build as a simple renovation. At first glance, the southern glazed facade and its concrete frame may evoke images of the United Nations Headquarters (see page 71), situated nearby on a similarly atypical

site. The strong formal design references to 1950s
and 1960s Modernism are no coincidence, but part
of the design brief and a consequence of the client's
architectural and urban inclinations which regard the
city as a harmonious yet simultaneously mutating
whole. Balazs would ideally have preferred to find an
old building and to convert and improve it. But this
was not an option, and the project therefore artificially
creates this impression, transforming in the playful,
undogmatic, but rational spirit of Morris Lapidus a fake
modern carcass into a contemporary hotel. In a skilful
game of references and allusions, the architects
addressed some issues that had been identified as
typical shortcomings of the 'average' Modernist
construction, including formal oversimplification,
mirroring glass, unattractive ceilings and incoherent
interior shading. The last point in particular – the choice
of simple white curtains behind a facade of clear,
whitish glass – reveals the strong urge to play and
improve architectural history, and to solve, as just one
example, the often aesthetically unsatisfying problem
of individualised curtains, typical for modern residential
buildings. In a similar spirit, but more directly related
to the history of the place, the ground floor and its
entrance area underneath the formally expressive
pilotis appears as a converted warehouse, strictly
avoiding the impression of a monolithic construction
and emphasising the vertical layering caused by the
elevated tracks of the High Line.

From an economic point of view, the efficient
combination of a narrow floor plan and a glazed facade
helped to achieve the project's crucial mission: to create
the highest possible profitability at an affordable price,
an unusual combination for Manhattan standards. The
solution to achieving this objective was to convert the
greatest amount of area into space that could be rented
out to generate the highest return. The mercenary
design which cuts the rooms short is exchanged for
excellent light conditions and breathtaking views over
the city.

SUMMARY

In contrast to the Shard in London (see page 78) and
similar to the Tour Dexia in Paris (see page 79), the
Standard Hotel's relationship to infrastructure is linked
to the scar that such an infrastructure can cause in the
urban fabric, rather than to the potentially advantageous
topics of transport capacity and passenger flux. As
mentioned above, this spatial exception can have
typological advantages for certain kinds of uses. In this
case, it is the hotel use and its fairly specific spatial
programme which seem to benefit from an alteration
of the typical Manhattan block. This is a historically

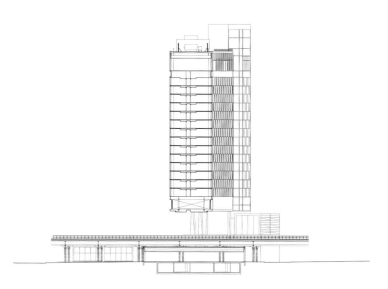

1:1250 section along the High Line Park.

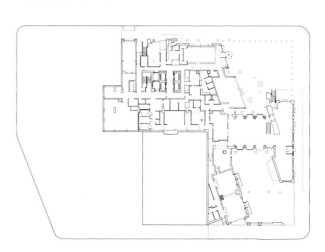

1:1250 ground-floor plan. The plan extends in both directions
underneath the High Line Park.

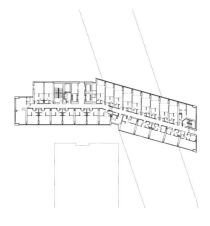

1:1250 upper level plan, along the High Line Park.

intriguing observation, because hotels hold a special position in the early development of residential high-rise in New York, though for legal rather than typological reasons. In the second half of the 19th century, building restrictions had been conceived only in view of housing for the poor, and the Tenement House Act of 1867, the nation's first, limited the height of any building with three or more rental dwellings, with independent living and cooking, and more than two per floor. This definition did theoretically also include luxury dwellings, and the developers of the ever-growing apartment blocks were therefore trying to find legal loopholes, usually declaring the apartments as 'apartment hotels'. This situation ultimately changed only with the Multiple Dwelling Act of 1929, which exercised a uniform control on all types of housing.

In the meantime, the importance of the apartment-hotel was, however, not only limited to these legal considerations, as the provision of hotel-like services helped to attract wealthy customers who were previously accustomed to living in brownstone family houses or in freestanding mansions.

Urban plan 1:2500

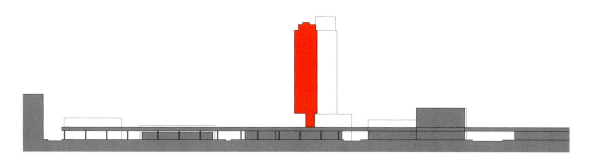

Urban section 1:2500

SHARD LONDON BRIDGE

LOCATION: LONDON, UK
DATE: 2009–12
ARCHITECT: RENZO PIANO BUILDING WORKSHOP

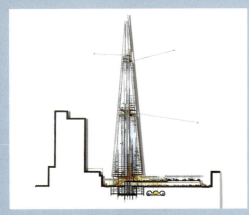

Currently one of Europe's most prominent construction sites for a single building, the Shard, previously known as London Bridge Tower, is scheduled for completion in 2012. Its design is inspired by a shard of glass, and at 305 metres it will not only be the tallest building in the European Union, but more importantly will redefine the skyline of London, being the first major tower on the southern side of the river Thames – all the city's most prominent towers are currently located on the northern side. It supersedes a tower from the 1960s and sits almost directly above the tracks of London Bridge Station with its two Tube lines and a multitude of rail services, serving over 50 million passengers a year. The construction of the tower goes along with a regeneration of the whole area, and another mid-rise building will eventually complete the masterplan. The tower will contain offices, a hotel, apartments, restaurants and a viewing platform. Through its base, it will be directly connected to the transport network.

TOUR DEXIA (FORMER TOUR CBX)

LOCATION: LA DÉFENSE, PARIS OUTSKIRTS, FRANCE
DATE: 2002–5
ARCHITECT: KOHN PEDERSEN FOX

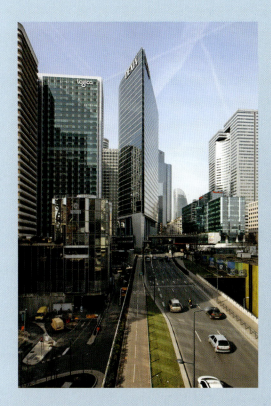

Situated on a 'non-site' above a traffic island of the busy Boulevard Circulaire, this spectacular project shows how tall buildings can create value in circumstances that would be completely inappropriate for lower constructions. The scenario here is especially complicated, because the entrance level is not at the base of the tower, but in line with the elevated level of La Défense's podium. The building therefore performs an additional function as the middle section of a public bridge that links the main pedestrian space with the northern extension area of the expanding business district. Due to the lack of any building approach or exterior spaces, one part of the tower's section has been elevated to accommodate an open plaza. This gesture, formalised through imposing columns, underlines the elegance and weightlessness of the tower.

Tour Ar Men

SOLITAIRES: TOWER AS MODULE
LOCATION: PARIS, FRANCE
DATE: 2008
MASTERPLANNER OF MASSÉNA NORD DISTRICT: CHRISTIAN DE PORTZAMPARC
ARCHITECT: PIERRE CHARBONNIER
CLIENT: ARC PROMOTION

Typological group:
Solitaires – tower as
module / business as usual
Building height: 36 metres
Site coverage: 80%
Plot ratio: 5.18

Following Christian de Portzamparc's ideas of the *'îlot ouvert'* ('open block'), this modestly sized tower in the Masséna Nord district of Paris cleverly balances the position on the block perimeter with the advantages of a freestanding object. And that is exactly the plan's concept.

HISTORY / DEVELOPMENT PROCESS

The Masséna Nord area is just one part of Paris's largest inner-city development zone (130 hectares), known as Paris Rive Gauche and situated along the river bank in the 13th arrondissement. Partly built above the tracks that lead to the Gare d'Austerlitz, the vast majority of the land was initially owned by the public railway company, SNCF. After the formation of a mixed development company, SEMAPA, the land was subdivided and masterplan competitions were organised for the gradual redevelopment of each zone.

In 1996 Portzamparc won the redevelopment competition for the northern part of the Masséna zone with a proposal that was based on his concept for the *îlot ouvert*. The simple idea was to combine the civic strength of perimeter block developments and their ability to clearly define the street spaces – typical for Paris – with the superior living quality of a freestanding object, interweaving traditional and modern design principles. Of particular significance for our high-rise study is the proposal made by the urban designer, for density and aesthetic reasons, occasionally to exceed

the height limit that had uniformly been set for the whole Paris Rive Gauche development zone. This height limit was defined by a gradient which grew from approximately 24 metres on the river front up to 34 metres along the new Avenue de France. But these proposed exceptions were hard to legally define, and in 1997 it was eventually decided that 10 per cent of the buildings would be allowed to surpass the ceiling by up to 10 metres, those fronting the Avenue de France being however excluded from the derogation. Charbonnier's Tour Ar Men was one of these exceptions, and its height was raised from a theoretical limit of 30 metres – according to the 24-to-34-metre rule – to 36 metres (ground plus 11 floors) in the final built state. In 2003 the height regulations were again modified to a maximum of 37 metres in the capital's peripheral zones, but this new rule, which superseded the former one, did not apply to buildings which had already received a building permit. Today, the city administration has become more open to 'real' high-rise buildings, and a legal process has been started in which several exceptions might be granted in the Plan Local d'Urbanisme (PLU), including the vast neighbouring site of Masséna-Brunéseau – another district of Paris Rive Gauche.

URBAN CONFIGURATION

This architectural project is of particular interest due to the fact that it is inseparable from its urban intentions, and this not only based on a simple set of rules in the form of written building regulations, as would be the case for most architectural projects, but more specifically in the form of predefined massing envelopes that are an outcome of a holistic, if not sculptural masterplanning approach. The office of Christian de Portzamparc defined a network of streets and relatively small blocks, and then carried out extensive tests as to how the future building volumes could best relate to each other, the principle of light and air being determining factors. In order to allow enough margin for the individual creativity of each plot's privately commissioned architect, the prescribed building envelope is larger than the permitted amount of buildable surface. Portzamparc tries here to solve a common problem in the relationship between architects and urban designers, similar to the situation that arose in the Front de Seine project (see page 136), when several architects refused to participate in competitions in which the building volume had already been precisely defined by the masterplanner. His concept therefore accommodates a certain formal individualism in the frame of an urban blueprint. He explicitly emphasises the importance of an iterative design process, and

remains during the whole planning and development period an important link between all intervening parties for the resolution of deliberately open questions. This mixture of control and loose supervision allows him to contrive a 'fake random spatiality' as an ad hoc situation that would usually only evolve over a longer period of time.

ARCHITECTURE

As already mentioned, the plot of the Tour Ar Men ('ar men' meaning lighthouse as well as granite in Breton) had been designated to accommodate a taller structure in order to improve the legibility of the new

TOP: The massing of the Tour Ar Men (right) and all the neighbouring buildings has been defined by the masterplan.

ABOVE: View of the tower from the back of the university building. The verticality of the structure has been visually enforced through the tapering of the white envelope.

district. Its situation on one of the greenest blocks with the lowest densities, right opposite the district's centrally located park, facilitated this undertaking, even though the total height was eventually lowered by one storey as a reaction to the neighbours' concerns. The plot, one of three in this block, extends all along Rue des Frigos, and hence includes the lower structure right next to it, eventually designed by the same architect. When it was acquired by Arc Promotion, ownership and development rights were granted together with the set of urban and architectural rules described above. Central to Portzamparc's urban concept is the fact that the base unit of these rules is the block, even if it contains several plots. In the specific case of plot 'M1F1' in block 'M1F', it was therefore necessary to position the tower in the corner of the block, and to erect two distinct volumes along the northeastern site boundary. The data sheet as an appendix of the sales agreement also defines the rights of view in relation to neighbouring structures.

The architect's concept for the exterior finishes is simple and efficient. Adopting the idea of the tower, he concentrates his efforts on visually narrowing the top of the building, and skilfully accentuates its verticality in a pyramidal way without loss of development space. With the exception of the penthouse apartment, the upper levels do not actually step back, but appear to

do so through the oblique treatment of the white envelope and the gradual growth of the balconies. The ground floor of the building accommodates retail and hence contributes to the functional mixture of the district, in which educational institutions take an important part next to apartments and offices. A direct outcome of the 'tower' typology is the space gained on the ground, which is used for private gardens and reads as an extension of the public park.

SUMMARY

The intriguing contrast between the apparent chaotic disposition of the building masses and the centralised and fairly tight control of the design and implementation process is key to this project. The masterplanner's influence on the approximate shape of the actual buildings is far from unusual, especially in the French system where the massing prescriptions often do not allow any formal deviation. In this case, however, the topic of design freedom appears underlined through the use of the point-tower typology which historically was – among other positives – also felt to be liberating from the architectural restrictions imposed by the Haussmann-style development principles, the perimeter block and its traditional cadastral logic. A minus point of this liberation was the usual inability to couple such architectural freedom with the creation of

ABOVE LEFT: A typical street view in the Masséna Nord district (Rue Françoise Dolto). Portzamparc's concept of the '*îlot ouvert*' supports a play of light that is different from the closed perimeter blocks of 19th-century Paris.

ABOVE: The massing clearly defines the block perimeter, and the building's ground floor accommodates retail and a restaurant.

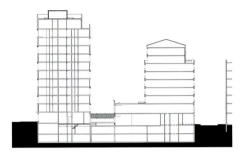

1:1250 section through the tower and adjacent building, designed by the same architect.

1:1250 typical floor plan with four apartments.

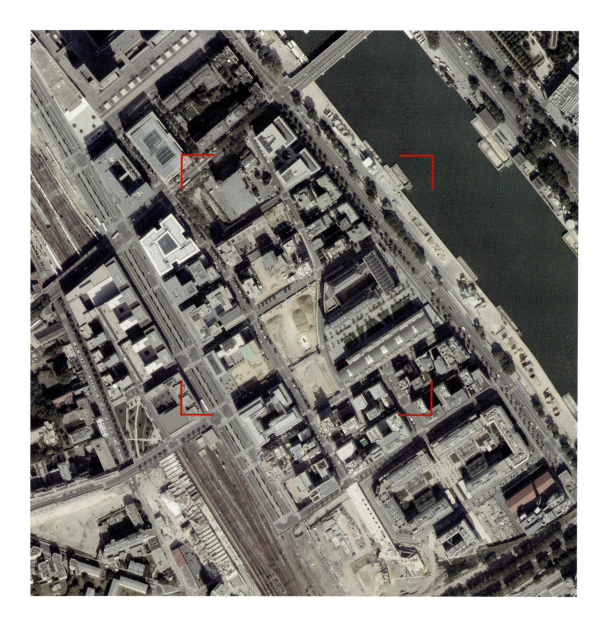

a meaningful public space through the loss of the street as a clearly defined negative of the built form. Portzamparc's approach tackles this problem through the respect of the block perimeter in conjunction with the use of a very pragmatic and flexible version of the point-tower. Typologically this is a highly interesting exercise, and it reveals the tower in a new dimension as an extroverted element in the urban fabric, with inherent advantages, but also the need to carefully plan the relation to public, communal and private green spaces. In this respect, Charbonnier's work delivers convincingly and calmly, proving in a non-iconic and structurally modest and efficient way that a tower can relate to the street, incorporate commercial uses and still offer the advantage of surrounding green spaces and views for all inhabitants. Critically, the Masséna Nord area shows

that such a development can be done in a repetitive way, though preventing the creation of the *'rue corridor'* as abhorred by Le Corbusier as the destruction of the street-space in the Modernist tradition. The question is to what height, density and mix of uses Masséna's modestly tall vision could grow without losing these qualities.

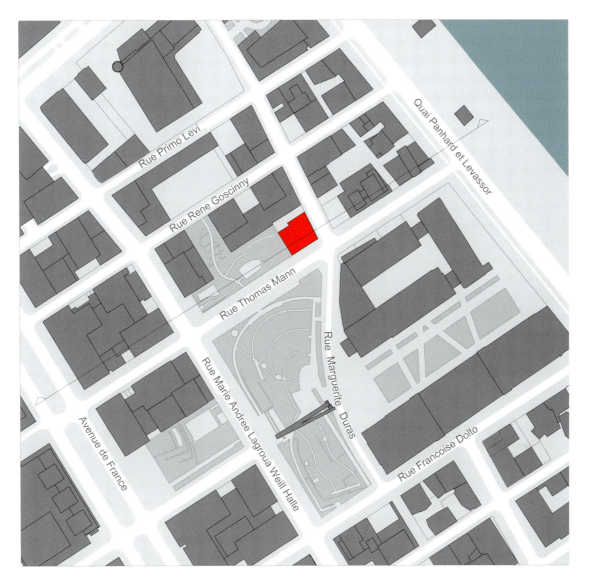

Urban plan 1:2500

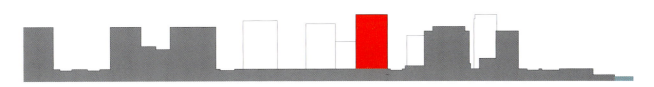

Urban section 1:2500

DUOC CORPORATE BUILDING

LOCATION: SANTIAGO DE CHILE, CHILE
DATE: 2005–7
ARCHITECT: SABBAGH ARQUITECTOS

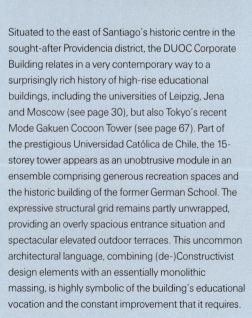

Situated to the east of Santiago's historic centre in the sought-after Providencia district, the DUOC Corporate Building relates in a very contemporary way to a surprisingly rich history of high-rise educational buildings, including the universities of Leipzig, Jena and Moscow (see page 30), but also Tokyo's recent Mode Gakuen Cocoon Tower (see page 67). Part of the prestigious Universidad Católica de Chile, the 15-storey tower appears as an unobtrusive module in an ensemble comprising generous recreation spaces and the historic building of the former German School. The expressive structural grid remains partly unwrapped, providing an overly spacious entrance situation and spectacular elevated outdoor terraces. This uncommon architectural language, combining (de-)Constructivist design elements with an essentially monolithic massing, is highly symbolic of the building's educational vocation and the constant improvement that it requires.

BANCO ATLÁNTICO (NOW BANCO SABADELL ATLÁNTICO)

LOCATION: BARCELONA, SPAIN
DATE: 1966–9
ARCHITECT: FRANCESC MITJANS MIRÓ

In terms of architectural form reminiscent of Giò Ponti's Pirelli Tower (see page 51) in Milan (1958), this urbanistically interesting solution has been included as an ironic if not caricatural example of a non-iconic tower. By this is meant the provocative combination of modern architecture and traditional urbanism, through the insertion of the high-rise element on the corner of a typical Barcelona block. As if the plan of Cerdà's traditional perimeter block did not come with a certain massing envelope and height limitation, the tower rises far above the roofs of its neighbours' even height. This overly bold urban gesture relates on the one hand to its situation on the corner with the prominent Avenida Diagonal, but follows on the other hand – in a typologically intriguing way – a rationality in which the spatial problematic of the Eixample district's corner plots becomes thematised. The traditional apartment buildings on these plots, in contrast to those on the middle plots, do not have access and views to the block-internal courtyard, and the high-rise option elegantly minimises the impact of this fact.

Rockefeller Center

CLUSTERS: INTEGRATED IN EXISTING CITY FABRIC
LOCATION: NEW YORK CITY, USA
DATE: 1930–9
ARCHITECT / MASTERPLANNER: REINHARD & HOFMEISTER; CORBETT,
HARRISON & MACMURRAY; HOOD, GODLEY & FOUILHOUX
CLIENT: JOHN D ROCKEFELLER JR

The Rockefeller Center is far more than just the most famous and still one of the largest high-rise clusters in the world. It has achieved the status of an urban ideal, the apparently perfect symbiosis, rather than compromise, of urban coherence and capitalist gain for profits. Inherently part of Manhattan's historic grid, the scheme introduces a distinct character, and does so by offering to the public one of the city's most successful plazas.

Typological group: Clusters
– integrated in existing city
fabric
Building height: 259 metres
Site coverage: 84%
Plot ratio: 11.46

HISTORY / DEVELOPMENT PROCESS

Early in his career John D Rockefeller Jr, the only male heir of the immense Standard Oil fortune, decided to quit leading positions in the family business in order to dedicate his life to philanthropic works. He donated large sums in activities ranging from archaeology and art to medical research, conservation and international relations. Even before the beginning of the Rockefeller Center episode, real estate and architecture were not new to him, and he had for example supported the renovation of the Chateau de Versailles and of Rheims Cathedral in France, and the reconstruction of colonial Williamsburg in his home country.

Interestingly, his arguably most famous project, the Rockefeller Center, was not part of these philanthropic activities, and had been started and led as a profitable investment rather than a gift to the public.

The kick-start for what was to become one of the largest American building activities of its time came through the Metropolitan Opera Company's wish to

relocate its premises. A vast and potentially attractive plot of land had been offered on Columbia University's Upper Estate in Midtown Manhattan, and the opera company immediately asked the architect Benjamin Wistar Morris to prepare a first scheme for the site. He soon realised that the construction of a new opera house had to be combined with a substantial commercial development in order to cover the inevitable running deficits of the Opera. A public square was meant to dignify the Beaux Arts-inspired setting, but also to maximise land values and customer flows, inevitably pushing the already ambitious project in ever-growing spatial dimensions.

URBAN CONFIGURATION

Among other reasons, it is the detail of the plaza that attracted Rockefeller's attention. He initially refused to meet the Opera's board of directors and to sponsor the acquisition of land for the plaza, on the grounds that it should be financed by the owners of the adjacent properties due to its value-raising function. Very soon afterwards, however, he contacted Columbia directly and offered to buy or lease large parts of the Upper Estate, one of Manhattan's largest privately owned pieces of land and a major source of income for the university. In September 1928 he signed the lease alone, but expected the Metropolitan Opera Company to subsequently sublease a central plot of substantial size. It had been agreed that the plaza itself would not be paid for by the Opera and would be dedicated to the Rockefellers as donors. Unfortunately, some open questions and the 29 October 1929 crash thwarted the realisation of these plans, and the Opera left the scene. Later on, another entertainment company, the Radio Corporation of America (RCA), took over as the project's main leaseholder, and eventually gave its name to the RCA Building as one of New York's tallest towers.

In view of the vast project team, the presence of such strong egos and talents, and the production of numerous design options, it is intriguing to realise that the 1928 plan remained the cluster's major inspiration until completion of the first part of the Center in the late 1930s. Nevertheless, fundamental changes have been the repositioning of the tallest towers from the outside to the inside, the densification of masses within the legal zoning envelope and an arguably fortunate loss of the project's original perfect symmetry in favour of a more open and airy constellation. Morris himself had left the project team after cancellation of the Opera scheme in 1929.

Only much later, with the 1960s and 1970s extension of the Center to the west, would its former spatial logic be superseded by a different kind of urbanism, linked also to changes in the city's zoning laws and the establishment of a new generation of tall buildings. Its public-realm strategy of wide (and predominantly empty) open spaces along 6th Avenue, based on a bonus system established by the city government in which the provision of open space is rewarded with a higher plot ratio for the developer, has had much less success than the more intimate and protected spaces of the original part of the cluster.

ARCHITECTURE

Probably better known than Morris's is the role of Raymond Hood in the creation of Rockefeller Center. He was part of a large team of architects supervised by the energetic and highly assertive developer John R Todd, including Reinhard & Hofmeister as lead architects, the office of Corbett, Harrison & MacMurray, and as a third entity the office of Hood, Godley & Fouilhoux. The renderings were done by Hugh Ferriss and John Wenrich. Truly a result of teamwork, important elements of the final scheme's architecture and today's landmark buildings – especially of the slab-shaped RCA Building as central focus – have been attributed to

Avenue of the Americas, with the landmark buildings from the 1930s to the right and the 1950s to 1970s extension of the Center to the left.

Hood, an international star since his victory in 1922 in the competition for the Chicago Tribune Tower. As an excellent communicator with great theatrical talent, Hood knew how to implement his own architectural visions in constantly referring to the financial interests of his clients, and declared the Center explicitly as an opportunity to prove that architects could build commercially viable products as partners of the capital. His deep interest must have been awakened through Morris's early scheme, not so much because of its architectural language, but because of its size and the above-mentioned will to explore alternative ways of

building on the Commissioners' Plan grid. In his 1927 book *City of Towers*, Hood had detailed his ideas about a change of the zoning laws and the construction of towers as isolated and freestanding elements rather than constituents of the ever-repeating perimeter blocks. The building density was meant to be a function of open space on the ground, producing ever thinner and taller needle-shaped towers. In several of his high-rise realisations, he had implemented parts of these ideas in setting the towers back from the plot boundaries, presenting them as individual detached objects rather than extruded building masses that had to share party walls with all their neighbours. In addition, he was fascinated by quasi-autarchic megastructures that would absorb external traffic congestion through internal transport systems – something that the Center does at least on a symbolic level, through pedestrian connections, its underground network and direct access to the metro system.

SUMMARY

From today's perspective, large-scale developments are rather seen as a potential threat to the city, endangering the architectural and social diversity compared with a more carefully grown and rather

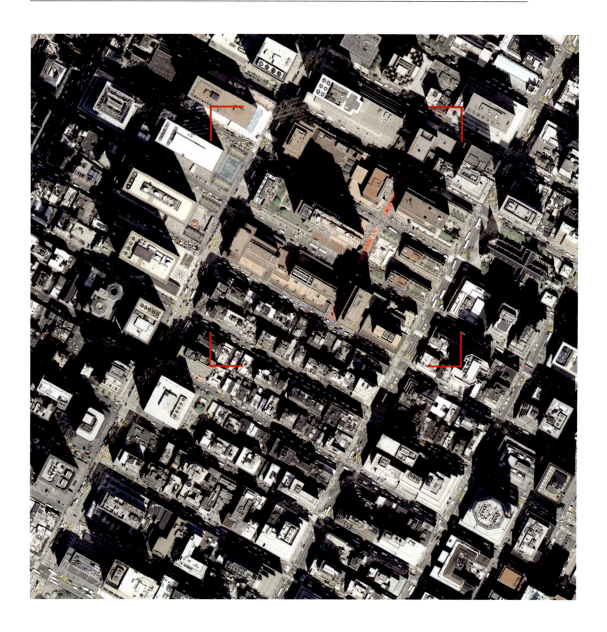

more robust piecemeal approach. The Rockefeller Center is an early counterpoint to this thesis, and the coverage of almost three complete Manhattan blocks has to be seen as a condition for the establishment of a new urban form. Even the largest perimeter block developments like the competing Chrysler (1930) and Empire State Buildings (1931) were in the end spatially anonymous elements of the grid's logic, extraordinary jewels in the skyline, but rather traditional on the ground level. New perspectives, pedestrian walks and the creation of a square which is at a safe distance from the street, required a scale that surpassed the already frequent merger of five, six or seven traditional plots. The Center inverted Manhattan's grid logic from closed

extroverted perimeter blocks with avenues and streets as only public realms, to a more complex megastructure which infuses life into the centre of the blocks.

From a European point of view, it is also remarkable that the economical background and programme of the project was by definition based on customer crowds and congestion on several levels. Whereas the famous European thinkers were mainly focusing on the separation of functions and on theories about nature, light and ventilation, the initiators and creators of the Rockefeller Center saw those elements rather as ideas for the space above the customers' heads, and realised a playful landscape of extensive roof gardens.

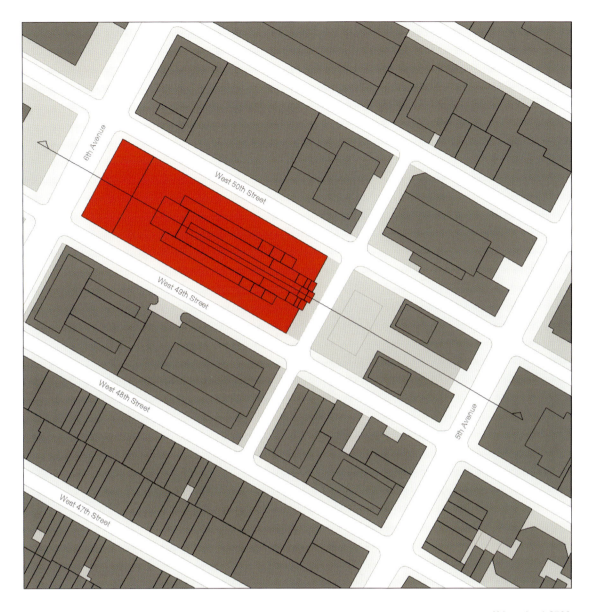

Urban plan 1:2500

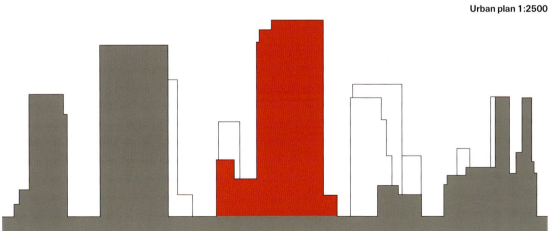

Urban section 1:5000

VILLEURBANNE TOWN HALL AND NEW CENTRE

LOCATION: VILLEURBANNE, LYONS OUTSKIRTS, FRANCE
DATE: 1934
URBAN DESIGN: MÔRICE LEROUX

This ambitious scheme was initiated in the 1920s by the mayor of Villeurbanne, at that time a fast-growing but neglected industrial suburb of Lyons. Though based on a real need for a new town hall, a theatre and social housing, its major purpose was spatial and symbolic: the impressive bulk was meant to define the new centre of a politically independent community which had remained since its creation in the shadow of its wealthy neighbour. From an urban point of view it is therefore rather to be understood as a kick-start than as a continuation, and succeeding developments were expected to follow the proud example in terms of urban form. This, however, did not happen, probably because of too abrupt and unrealistic an increase of scale compared with the modesty of the surrounding structures, and because of its rather closed, linear and introverted spatial character. The two 19-storey towers on the northern entrance of the scheme clearly evoke Hermann Henselmann's 1950s towers at the Frankfurter Tor in Berlin (see page 130).

RIVERSIDE CENTER

LOCATION: NEW YORK CITY, USA
DATE: SCHEDULED FOR 2018–20
ARCHITECT: CHRISTIAN DE PORTZAMPARC

The mainly residential Riverside South neighbourhood, initiated by Donald Trump in the mid-1970s, has been built over a former freight rail yard. The last piece to be redeveloped covers four urban blocks and is called Riverside Center. Portzamparc proposes to combine the two westerly blocks in order to create a central public park whose landscape concept respects the continuation of the grid towards the river. Architecturally, he conceives the towers as sculptures that follow a tripartite low–medium–high graduation: the lower part up to 25 metres with its mixed-use facilities referring to the pedestrian and vehicular scale, and the top one over 160 metres being part of the New York skyline. Due to its sheer size and the holistic planning approach over four blocks, it represents a rare opportunity to create an alternative urbanism to Manhattan Island's strictly plot-oriented development logic. Here lies a clear parallel to the Rockefeller Center, even though Riverside Center is destined to become a retail and entertainment hub on the local rather than city level. The project is a continuation of Portzamparc's built work in Manhattan, and follows on a larger scale similar ideas to the 400 Park Avenue Tower, currently undergoing development (see tower below right).

Quartier du Palais (Immeubles 'Choux')

CLUSTERS: TOWERS AS URBAN PATTERN
LOCATION: CRÉTEIL, PARIS OUTSKIRTS, FRANCE
DATE: 1968–74
ARCHITECT: GÉRARD GRANDVAL
CLIENT: OCIL

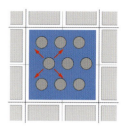

Typological group: Clusters
– towers as urban pattern
Building height: 38 metres
Site coverage: 18%
Plot ratio: 1.06

The so-called 'cabbage' towers are an eclectic by-product of France's post-war housing era. Completed in 1974, they combined the 1950s and 1960s categorical request for efficiency with a new search for identity and sense of place.

HISTORY / DEVELOPMENT PROCESS

In the aftermath of the Second World War, France faced a particularly bleak housing situation compared with several other industrialised European nations. The severe winter of 1954 left many out in the cold, and mounting public pressure led the state to commission a housing survey which identified a lack of at least four million modern dwellings. In France, the post-war era marked a new beginning in construction and spatial extension, inseparably fuelled by the country's post-war run to prosperity known as the 'Trente Glorieuses' ('the Glorious Thirty', 1945–75).

While strong economic growth and the immigration of foreign workers were not unique to France, local particularities included a bad housing situation (especially in the Parisian agglomeration, and this even before the war), a strong rise in the birth rate and the abrupt need for reintegration following a painful decolonisation period, primarily from Algeria. As a result, approximately six million housing units were built between 1954 and 1977, half of those as publicly commissioned social housing, the other half as a result of substantial subsidies channelled through the national mortgage bank, the Crédit Foncier de France.

RIGHT: The entrance area of the residential towers is fenced off in order to protect the intimacy of the neighbouring ground-floor apartments.

BELOW RIGHT: The towers are set back from the pedestrian walkways and part of a holistic landscape design with an artificial relief.

In a short space of time a highly efficient mechanism had been established, through which the state kept tight control not only of the planning and construction of modern apartment buildings – the single-family housing option having been abandoned – but also of the spatial relationship of these apartment buildings towards the rapidly growing network of infrastructures.

Housing provision and the construction of new infrastructures were not only the consequence of social endeavours. They were also a necessity for the sustention of an explosive production growth which necessitated the improvement and development of a formerly underperforming building industry. The future had to be engineered. The *grands ensembles*, housing operations characterised by a minimum size of 500 units, but often far larger, were the answer and remained so until 1973, when operations of over 500 dwellings were declared illegal. Effectively what was being created were dormitory towns and in many cases social hotspots. From an organisational point of view, the change in paradigm translated through a change of legal status, and the ZUP (*zone à urbaniser en priorité*) – created for the fastest possible implementation of large-scale housing programmes by the state – was after 1969 superseded by the still-existing ZAC (*zone d'aménagement concerté*). Projects with a legal status of ZUP or ZAC were both 'top-down' systems and excluded from local planning regulations, but the ZAC facilitated the mixture of uses and the inclusion of private funds.

URBAN CONFIGURATION

The Quartier du Palais, built on the site of a former wasteland on the outskirts of the city, covers only a small part of Nouveau Créteil (New Créteil), and its insular situation between intimidating new

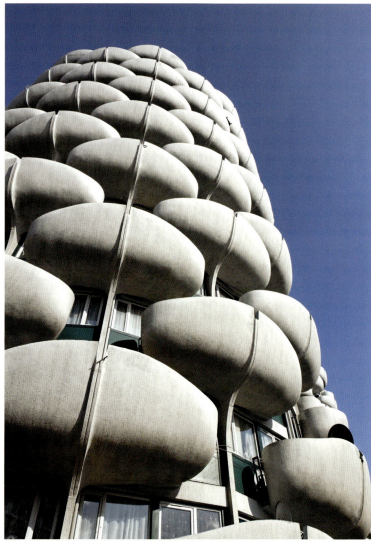

infrastructures had been identified as a problem by the architect Gérard Grandval, the fairly inexperienced Prix de Rome winner who had been commissioned by the director of the social housing company OCIL. Grandval's solution was simple: his idea was to artificially reinforce the insular character of the area and to attribute a sense of place and protection through spectacular architecture and skilful principles of landscaping. In the spirit of the *villes nouvelles* that were beginning to be developed at around the same time (Cergy-Pontoise, for example, initiated in 1969), the mayor of Créteil wanted to avoid the ennui of the infamous *grands ensembles*, perceived not only as increasingly unimaginative, but more importantly lacking a mix of uses, which in turn hindered the development of urban life. An amenity such as the small shopping centre was therefore an integral feature of the project, and during the design process and construction period of the new district, the decision

was made to move it from the centre out to the boundary of the site, so it would serve the inhabitants of the residential towers as well as the students of the neighbouring university. The symbolic eponym of a housing project with high ambitions, and perhaps the most important feature in this respect, was the construction of the courthouse in direct western vicinity of the towers. Three large and equally curvilinear residential slabs, designed by Louis-Gabriel de Hoym de Marien, frame the tower district to the north, south and west, and sustain the idea of a social mix through the provision of market housing. As the site was liable to flooding, the construction of underground parking would have been too expensive, and the architect skilfully incorporated sets of one-storey garages in his landscape concept. This procedure avoided the usual sealing of the buildings' surroundings through car parks, and sustained the idea of a continuous garden.

The architect initially envisaged planted balconies to create a genuinely green facade, but the plan was abandoned for maintenance reasons.

The depth of the facade provides a high sculptural quality which changes aspect depending on the point of view.

ARCHITECTURE

From an architectural point of view, the concrete balconies are the most striking design elements of the whole scheme. Prefabricated by the building contractor Bouygues, they form the distinctive skin around otherwise fairly standard and mass-produced rounded facades. Their relatively generous size and height corresponds to two explicit intentions of the architect: firstly, to provide privacy from neighbouring properties, and secondly, to serve as extensions of the fairly small and standardised interior surfaces. Inspired by Henri Sauvage's studies on hanging gardens and the tiered terraces of the Rue Vavin building in Paris (1912), they were meant to be planted. This, however, did not happen, and Grandval's idea of an eventually green facade did not see the light.

The floor plans are in essence fairly simple, and allow a relatively large freedom of interior organisation despite the obvious complications of a radial geometry. A drawback of the building's round form is the mono-orientation of the apartments and a fairly large amount of dark spaces in the inner parts of the 15-storey towers whose centre is a staircase with an adjacent communal corridor. An advantage of this round form is that it offers numerous angles of view, covering over 90 degrees in the case of a standard three-bedroom unit. The typical floor plan comprises two two-bed (61 square metres) and two three-bed (75 square metres) apartments. This also means that one of the nine balconies has to be shared by two families (see plan layout).

A typical characteristic of modern housing is the fact that the towers are purely residential. Even the non-elevated ground floors contain apartments and are protected from passengers' views through the raised relief of the green surfaces and small protecting fences along the narrow entrance walkways.

SUMMARY

The importance of including a *grand ensemble* – essentially referring to a post-war housing development with over 500 dwellings – in this book cannot be overemphasised. The high-rise residential building, etched into the French and European collective memory, is still closely connected to this 'quantitative urbanism' (elaborated by technocrats) to provide a quick and simple solution to the urgent housing needs of the post-war era. Over the years – from its origins in 1953 to its abolition in 1973 – the *grand ensemble's* usual mixture of slabs and towers had become increasingly bland from a spatial and architectural perspective, and it was eventually branded as a failure. Grandval's project stands in stark contrast to these depreciating tendencies, and he shows that alternative

1:1250 typical floor plan.

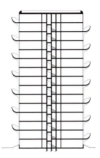

1:1250 tower section.

View of the car parks that have been included in the landscape concept.

solutions of large-scale social housing projects, even without separate involvement of an urban designer or landscape architect, were possible. It is interesting to note that his project predominantly makes use of the point-tower typology, while most social housing developments of that time relied on a mixture of slabs and, to a much lesser extent, towers. In this context it is also worthwhile noting that the controversial debate sparked by the construction of the unpopular Tour Montparnasse – which in 1974 led to the ban of tall buildings in the city centre – was in form disconnected from the housing issue and the outskirts, but eventually contributed, in conjunction with the 1973 ban on constructing any further *grands ensembles*, to establishing a link in the minds of the wider public between high-rise buildings and failed urbanism.

In the case of Créteil, the tower typology proves its plus points in terms of creating only a small footprint compared with an elongated slab and, despite several drawbacks with regard to the rigid planning system, the Quartier du Palais manages to create a strong identity as a residential garden with an elaborate artificial relief.

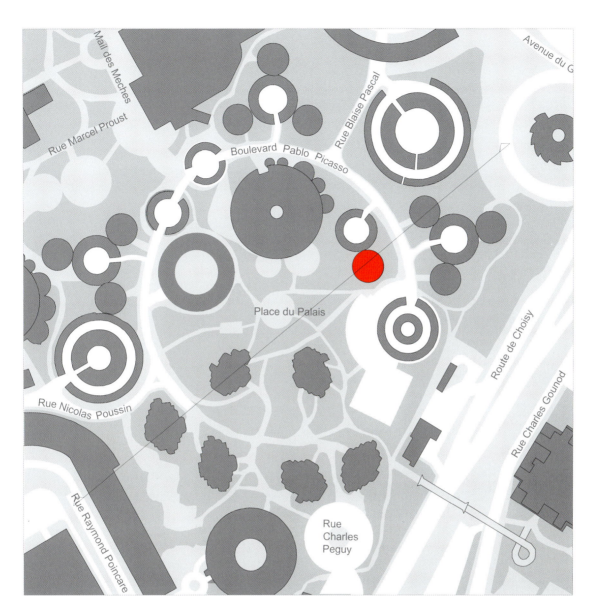

Urban plan 1:2500

Urban section 1:2500

JIANWAI SOHO

LOCATION: BEIJING, CHINA
DATE: 2004–7
ARCHITECT: RIKEN YAMAMOTO, WITH MIKAN AND C+A

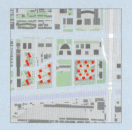

Situated between the second and third Beijing ring roads, and approximately 5 kilometres east of Tiananmen Square, this mixed-use development by SOHO China consists of 20 residential towers and four so-called 'villas'. The ensemble of several super-blocks is a remarkable and rare example of a high-rise compound that successfully combines a predominantly non-street-oriented masterplan with the creation of bustling life at the towers' base. The even massing of the strictly repetitive white towers with their abstract facades can hardly be missed as a reference to modern architecture and urbanism, reminiscent of Le Corbusier's plan for the Ville Radieuse (1935). The secret of the scheme's success lies therefore primarily with the three-storey base buildings – designed by Mikan – which enable the rich mix of uses and organise the complex spatial sequence in and around the pedestrianised super-blocks.

STUYVESANT TOWN

LOCATION: NEW YORK CITY, USA
DATE: 1946–9
ARCHITECT: METROPOLITAN LIFE INSURANCE COMPANY

On a plot of over 32 hectares, these 35 residential blocks at 13 storeys were built just after the Second World War in Manhattan's Lower East Side. The 8,755 apartments were privately developed, and targeted the middle classes. The construction of the gigantic development required the clearance of the notorious Gas House District, and the move of over 10,000 people. This was exactly the project's motive, and the Metropolitan Life Insurance Company was the first developer to benefit from a 1943 law which aimed at the regeneration of the city's slums. It essentially enabled the city to expropriate the owners at an affordable price and to grant the land to private house builders together with long-term tax waivers in return for rental concessions. Distributing the buildings like loose elements in a park, the scheme expresses its introverted character through the closure along the block perimeter and the creation of a central space.

Sheikh Zayed Road

CLUSTERS: LINEAR CLUSTERS
LOCATION: DUBAI, UNITED ARAB EMIRATES
DATE: 1990s ONWARDS

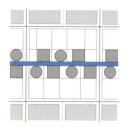

Framed by an impressive collection of similarly tall skyscrapers, Sheikh Zayed Road serves as the central spine of Dubai's extensive road network. It spatially organises the Emirate's exponential growth and provides a robust backbone to an increasingly dispersed city.

**Typological group: Clusters
– linear clusters**
Building height: 355 metres
Site coverage: 30%
Plot ratio: 6.01

HISTORY / DEVELOPMENT PROCESS

The history of Dubai as a metropolis is certainly very young. However, for a fairly long time before its urban explosion it demonstrated itself as a strategically well-located place, due to the existence of Dubai Creek as a natural port. Trade passed through the settlement and until the First World War the pearl industry represented its major source of income. The connection to the water

View from the northwest of the rear of the buildings fronting Sheikh Zayed Road. The generous spaces are predominantly used for garages and exterior car parking.

Since September 2009 a new metro line has run along Sheikh Zayed Road. At some stations, pedestrian bridges now link the formerly separated two sides of the street.

and the stability of the Al Maktoum dynasty since 1833 have remained its major trumps until today, but a new scale of development followed the discovery of oil in 1971. It was the same year in which Britain left the region as its former Protectorate, and Dubai together with Abu Dhabi and five other emirates formed the United Arab Emirates. Port Rashid opened in 1972 and initiated an urban and economic expansion of ever-increasing speed and magnitude. Jebel Ali Port was established

as the world's largest man-made port in 1979, and its surroundings were declared a free zone in 1985. It was the successful model for many subsequent free zones and offered attractive tax incentives to new businesses. Often obfuscated through the sheikhdom's overly ambitious marketing strategies in the tourist sector, these zones are Dubai's economic *raison d'être*. The Port Authority – with Jebel Ali Free Zone and Port Rashid as major stakeholders – stands also at the origin of the

Dubai World Holding Company which owns most of Dubai's assets, including Nakheel as the client for the well-known Palm Island projects. The Emirate, whose modest oil reserves are essentially exhausted, has diversified its economy in many sectors and increasingly attracts foreign investment, but the majority of the recent real-estate developments are still controlled by the Al Maktoum family who also own all land. As the Emirates' major transport connection, Sheikh Zayed Road – also known as the E11 – is linked to the foundation of the Emirates in 1971. It opened in 1980, when the Dubai part of it was still called Defence Road. It was expanded to its current size between 1993 and 1998.

URBAN CONFIGURATION

The specificity of planning in Dubai is the fact that only a small part of the city is directly controlled by the Dubai Municipality. A fairly orthodox zoning system, including predefined floor-to-area ratios and prescriptions for building uses, is therefore centrally applied only to the northern city core next to the old town and parts of Sheikh Zayed Road. Most of the newly developed areas, such as Dubai Marina, Dubai Internet City and the Downtown cluster around the Burj Khalifa (see page 31), have the aforementioned special legal status, and follow their own rules. Their masterplans – usually residential or commercial high-rise clusters – have been negotiated and elaborated together with the Municipality, but they do not depend on it legally. Seen from this point of view, Sheikh Zayed Road, theoretically just one segment of the Emirates' main motorway, has a very important role: it is the strongest link between several rather autarchic areas that, due to the distance between them, would not automatically form a city as a single legible entity. While the high-rise part is only about 3.5 kilometres long, it is still by far the most spatially impressive element of the average journey through the Emirate. In order to understand Dubai's urban momentum, comparisons could be made with the multi-nodal organisation of cities like Tokyo or São Paulo, but major differences include the breathtaking speed of the development, a far lower population figure and the fact that the former city centre on the northern shore of the Creek has so quickly lost its leading position. This situation will be further strengthened after the opening of the new Al Maktoum airport in the southern region of the state. The reasons for this intriguing development are, however, not without any

The northern section of Sheikh Zayed Road, as seen from the podium of the Emirates Tower.

historic background, as the Jebel Ali Port had been built almost 40 kilometres to the south of the historic Creek. In the last 25 years the vast urban space towards the north has been gradually filled up with tower clusters and villa compounds, unifying a metropolitan area that was previously not considered as such.

ARCHITECTURE

The strength and simplicity of Sheikh Zayed Road's urban form prevents the highly playful and at times importunate architecture of the skyscrapers themselves from becoming overly dominant. 'The higher, the better' might be a simple slogan, but somehow it seems to cope in an appropriate way with the fact that Sheikh Zayed Road is probably the only metropolitan boulevard that also works as a state motorway. On both sides and in both directions, service roads try to reconcile these two speeds, the local and the national, and several of the towers accommodate retail and shopping facilities on the ground floors. Despite Dubai's harsh climate, they help to transform the generous pavement to a more lively place than one might expect. The relationship of the towers to the front and to the back is asymmetric and reveals the Municipality's intention to stage a strong spatial experience. While the main facades are aligned along the plot perimeter in the style of a dense American grid city, the back of the plots with their loose car parking spaces and detached garages follows a much more suburban logic. The land for the construction of the parking garages was donated to the developers of the towers in order to provide the most attractive business environment. This part of Sheikh Zayed Road is strongly reminiscent of Auguste Perret's 1922 'Maisons-Tours' ('Tower-Houses') proposal for the gates of Paris; and both schemes – the French vision and Dubai's built reality – are examples of a linear monumental urbanism.

SUMMARY

It is generally assumed that the reasons which motivate building tall are linked to scarcity of land supply and the existence of an unsatisfied demand for space. In the case of Dubai, this assumption is challenged on numerous levels, and it reveals better than any other place in the world the fact that the emergence of high-rise seems to follow not one but many different rules, and that its rationality is complex to define. First of all, Dubai has no lack of space. Secondly, high-rise construction has not led to overall high densities, as the metropolitan area of approximately 1.9 million inhabitants covers already over 700 square kilometres of former desert. With 2,650 inhabitants per square kilometre, the overall density is actually not particularly

FROM TOP: Towards Sheikh Zayed Road, the towers are positioned along the plot boundary and address the pavement with a diverse mix of uses.

The gap between two towers, clearly revealing the linear character of the pedestrian environment.

Auguste Perret's vision for 'tower-houses' which were meant to delimit the boundary of Paris and also to lead along the royal axis from Paris over La Défense (see page 178) to the forest of Saint-Germain-en-Laye.

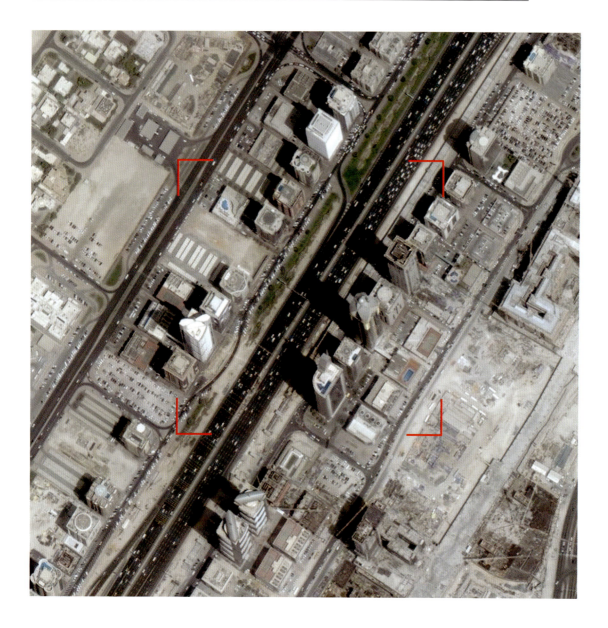

low, but this has to be seen against the fact that its swift and recent development has been masterminded and that there is no historic reason for urban sprawl. The intriguing combination of tall buildings and relatively low densities therefore provokes a reversed question: can high-rise be the result of an especially low – rather than high – price of land, in which these non-costs can be invested in expensive structural works, if possible with an international marketing effect? This at least seems to be the case for the beginnings of Dubai's building boom, when most of the development was centrally controlled. Of course, building high-rise in the desert is technically challenging, and Dubai's construction industry can pride itself on being one of the world's leaders in this field.

The combination of rapid expansion, high-rise construction and overall fairly low densities is obviously not a model in which sustainability is high on the agenda. Even if the construction and maintenance of the towers were to become ecologically friendly, the consequent creation of traffic and the necessary construction of roads is not. It will therefore be of particular interest to see the impact of Dubai's new metro network – partially opened in late 2009 as an elevated rail system along Sheikh Zayed Road – and the redevelopment phases which could gradually intensify a momentarily still under-used urban geography. The linear layout along the seashore leaves from this point of view a great development potential for the proud ambitions of one of the world's most remarkable places.

Urban plan 1:2500

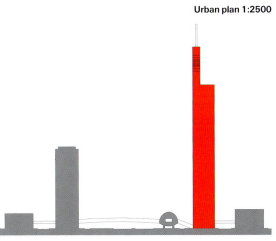

Urban section 1:5000

PLAYA DE LEVANTE EXTENSION

LOCATION: BENIDORM, SPAIN
DATE: 1963 ONWARDS

With over 370 towers of more than 12 storeys on a surface of just 18 square kilometres, the Spanish beach resort of Benidorm has one of the world's greatest high-rise densities. The majority of these developments are situated to the east of the old town along Playa de Levante in an American-style grid with urban blocks of approximately 110 metres width and length. Each of them comprises on average three apartment or hotel towers with surrounding, usually private, leisure areas. In contrast to this rather loose and typically resort-style interior organisation stands in many cases, though not consistently, the very urban delimitation of the blocks towards the street through single-storey retail and restaurant structures. This unusual mixture of scales and functions supports the extension of a *paseo*-style street life outside the historic core. Only the beach-fronting high-rises are invariably set on the southern plot boundary, forming in conjunction with their neighbours Benidorm's notorious skyline.

RUE DE LA LOI MASTERPLAN

LOCATION: BRUSSELS, BELGIUM
DATE: 2012–25
MASTERPLANNER: ATELIER CHRISTIAN DE PORTZAMPARC

In contrast to the Masséna-Nord masterplan (see page 80), predominantly new-built, this phased project for the Belgian capital applies Portzamparc's spatial ideas of the '*îlot ouvert*' (open block) to a piecemeal transformation process of a linear and already existing piece of the city. Based on an analysis of the perimeter block developments along Rue de la Loi – the centrepiece of the link between the historic core and the European district – the Parisian office defined a strategy of punctual interventions in which the buildings at the end of their life cycle will eventually be replaced by open spaces and taller buildings. The aim is to get rid of the prevalent monotony and claustrophobic character through spatial as much as programmatic interventions. The use of high-rise allows the crucial combination of public space with a sharp increase in density, needed for the construction of new European institutions, retail and apartments. A simple rule, in which the setback from the street perimeter is organised by building heights, will help to provide enough light and air, and to drain activities into the heart of the blocks and their surroundings. This 'soft masterplanning' approach, in contrast to the tabula rasa, demands for each urban situation a high level of coordination and negotiation with the respective plot owners.

Moma and Pop Moma

CLUSTERS: HIGH-RISE COMPOUND
LOCATION: BEIJING, CHINA
DATE: 2000–7
ARCHITECT: BAUMSCHLAGER EBERLE
CLIENT: THE MODERN GROUP

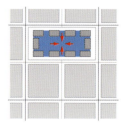

Typological group: Clusters
– high-rise compound
Building height: 105 metres
Site coverage: 24%
Plot ratio: 4.48

A typical example of China's housing developments of the last 10 years, the Moma compound represents one of the success stories. Built in three different phases, it avoids the endless repetition that is the unfortunate driver of many similar developments.

HISTORY / DEVELOPMENT PROCESS

China's spectacular economic success of the last 30 years has led to an even more spectacular urban growth. In the case of Beijing, this expansion translates in the recent completion of the sixth ring road around the old town, with the Forbidden City as its nucleus. The second ring road was only built in the 1980s and delimits more or less exactly the area of the formerly walled town with its traditional *hutong* structure and courtyard houses. These traditional elements are fast disappearing, subsumed by the encroaching redevelopment of the last few years which has not been limited to the area outside the old town's perimeter. In this urban landscape which has lost the dimensions and structure of a pedestrian environment, the Moma compound is strategically well situated. Just outside the northeastern corner of the second ring road, and right next to a connecting radial road leading to the new capital airport, it is therefore very popular with local businessmen as well as an important expat community.

Initially a state-owned paper mill covered the site. But after the mill was closed, the developer Zhang Lei and his Modern Group signed a long-term lease with the state, which by definition remains freeholder of all land. The freehold system is not a requisite imposed by the Communist government, but emanates from tradition which designated the emperor as owner of the Chinese land. The Modern Group successfully specialises in green architecture and is also the client of Steven Holl's Linked Hybrid (informally known as Grand Moma), located north of Pop Moma just opposite the motorway.

URBAN CONFIGURATION

The compound's masterplan was designed by a Hong Kong architect who also realised the five towers of the project's first phase, the so-called 'Megahall'. The building is subject to height restrictions due to its position along the second ring road and relative proximity to the historic old town. The urban layout is simple and clear, a clustering of 10 towers and two low-rise amenities in a green environment around a central lake of generous proportions. The site's clear delimitation to the north is fairly recent and stems from the massive reorganisation of the area's infrastructure through the construction of a new motorway and canal. Now it covers the northeastern half of the quasi triangular-shaped block. The oval hotel which can be seen on the urban plan is still in construction. The plan appears essentially as a compromise between a rather loose tower-in-park configuration and a perimeter block development which strengthens the northern and eastern street boundaries through the hard edges of the building masses and their podiums. Most ground floors and partly the basements of the new developments (Baumschlager Eberle's Moma and Pop Moma) accommodate publicly accessible retail uses, but are set back from the pavements. They are not permeable, in order to control access to the privatised interior of the otherwise fenced compound. The three towers of Pop Moma and their four-storey commercial podium are separated from the noisy motorway through a double range of car parks.

The development has several entrances to the underground car park, but only one main entrance on the southeastern side. The skilful and dexterous landscaping of the park and lake was created by the Japanese company Tamagushi Saishu.

ARCHITECTURE

The Modern Group's decision to work with the Austrian architects Baumschlager Eberle was based primarily on the company's experience in energy-saving construction rather than on the architectural language

of their frequently published work. In the first project phase of the Moma compound, the Austrian architects were actually subcontractors of Keller Technologies, headed by Professor Eberle's colleague at the ETH Zurich, Professor Bruno Keller. It is interesting to note that the sustainable qualities of the new construction have also been marketed as being healthy, a potentially more tangible quality than the energy-saving attribute which might not be of central importance for all future potential buyers in the fast and speculative Chinese market. Through the use of the most advanced building technologies, the interior temperature and humidity remain constant despite a continuous supply of fresh air. The temperature and humidity regulation in addition to other features have been made possible through a centralised ceiling and facade technology based on geothermal heat. Such a system is normally only used for large office spaces, and is far more energy-efficient than the usual installation of numerous independent air conditioning units.

For a Western observer it is surprising to find that these luxurious and exceptionally spacious apartments have no private external spaces in the form of balconies or terraces. This is partly due to the specificity of the energy-saving concept, but more importantly stems from Beijing's weather conditions, the wind issues as a result of the height of the buildings, and also local traditions. In mainland China, where sunbathing is a rather recent and still peculiar phenomenon, the balcony does not play the same role as in Western

View from Xiangheyuan Road into the interior of the compound. The dark towers on the sides are Moma, the reddish-brown ones Pop Moma, and the building in the background is Steven Holl's Linked Hybrid. The latter is a separate development by the same client.

LEFT: The sunken basement of the Moma towers accommodates retail, and can be publicly accessed from Xiangheyuan Road.

BELOW LEFT: The entrance area of one of the two Moma towers. They face the interior of the compound.

countries. In many cases the balcony is actually used by developers as an additional living area that is not incorporated in the maximum surface as stipulated in the building permit. After purchase, the owners often transform these spaces into enclosed winter gardens, and use them as extensions of their living rooms or bedrooms.

Another country-specific phenomenon observed by the architects is the rather more standardised appreciation of the plan layout, in which southwards orientation and the hierarchic respect of specific dimensions for each room are considered to assure a certain standard of quality and status. Interestingly, and in contrast to Western traditions, the living room together with the lobby tends to be the most public part of the apartment, the dining room being reserved for more private use.

SUMMARY

It would be negligent to describe the Moma developments without mentioning the term 'gated community', because that is what they explicitly are. In a city where the urban and architectural tradition has been conceived on the notion of enclosure, the 'gated' element as such does not arouse negative connotations. In most of the traditional *hutongs*, people walk along closed and impenetrable walls, where the courtyards are completely private and closed off to the public. The larger streets of the old town, however, are now commercial zones and have active street fronts which cater to the public in very much the same way as in any traditional city in Europe. The issue is therefore not so much that the compound is closed to the uninvited public, and that it encloses a socially homogenous 'community', but rather that there are not enough active street frontages that could sustain pedestrian movements around it, and this despite its central location. Moma is to this extent a very positive

1:1250 typical floor plan of the black-and-white Moma towers.

ABOVE LEFT: The kitchen of a Pop Moma apartment. The partition between it and the dining room is completely glazed.

ABOVE: View from the western tower of Pop Moma towards the east.

example, because its permeability – though recessed from the street – allows public access to the shops of the ground floors. Gated or not, the compound still has a suburban character, and is from that point of view comparable to the equally central but non-gated and less car-dependent Hansaviertel in Berlin (see page 128). What remains for the general discussion is the question of how to sustain public life next to tall buildings. Interestingly, it might be claimed that the relationship between high-rise architecture and gated communities works in both directions: towers seem to be a favourite choice of gated community developers – due to a mixture of market demand and land-efficiency – but without high densities and typological ingenuity, the tower and its tendency to create undefined exterior spaces somehow implies the gated solution, and this

even in a country with very low levels of street crime. In this case the enclosure and management by a single private company prevents the maintenance problem of underutilised exterior public spaces that is notorious in low-scale residential developments in other parts of the world.

Another way to understand this phenomenon stems from a simple quantitative fact: the availability of large plots of land, liberated from any cadastral constraints, and the demand for such plots through ever-growing development companies, logically supports the emergence of these privatised city pieces. Without interference from the planning authorities, the constant repetition of these proven concepts is not surprising, especially against the background of a continuous urban evolution.

Airport Expy

Airport Expy

N Erli Zhuang Road

Xiangheyuan Road

Urban plan 1:2500

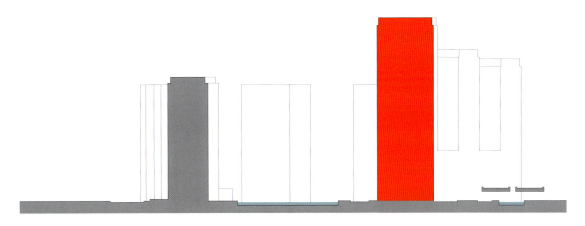

Urban section 1:2500

MARINA BAIE DES ANGES

LOCATION: VILLENEUVE-LOUBET, FRANCE
DATE: 1969–93
ARCHITECT: ANDRÉ MINANGOY

Situated on the French Riviera, between Nice and
Antibes, this impressive residential ensemble orientates
itself at the scale of the mountains and the sea, rather
than at its direct surroundings. The four undulating
pyramids with their 1,300 apartments in total – rising
up to 70 metres – encircle the pleasure port and shield
the publicly accessible interior from the nuisances of
the railway line. Attached to the base of the longest
and most northern one of these curvy slabs, a linear
single-storey construction provides restaurant and retail
facilities, and parking spaces underneath. Now a listed
structure, Marina Baie des Anges has been acclaimed
for its architecture, but mostly criticised for its rather
brutal integration in a sublime natural setting. Since
1973 the *Loi Littoral* (Coastal Law) has forbidden the
alteration of the coastline through private initiative.
The project is contemporaneous with the even larger
La Grande Motte development in the Languedoc region,
and symbolic of France's efforts to develop its tourist
industry in the 1960s and 1970s.

ICON BRICKELL

LOCATION: MIAMI, FLORIDA, USA
DATE: 2006–8
ARCHITECT: ARQUITECTONICA

This condominium and hotel development is the largest and most spectacular example of a new generation of residential towers that contribute to the revitalisation of Miami's inner-city districts. Three towers are positioned around a central podium which contains mainly car parking space, along with other uses. On top of this massive base, a communal and publicly inaccessible swimming pool and entertainment area allows spectacular views over the city, Miami Beach and the Biscayne Bay. As a mixture of a gated community and a Vancouver-style podium-tower, the development maintains a slightly paradoxical relation to its surroundings: though apparently conceived for a population that appreciates an urban setting, the building and especially its ground floor do not explicitly address and enliven the adjacent streetscape, as could have been expected in a downtown area. Icon Brickell therefore finds itself in a local tradition of large-scale resort architecture, which recently started adjusting the suburban and car-oriented lifestyle to the demands of a planned downtown revitalisation.

Roppongi Hills Mori Tower

CLUSTERS: HIGH-RISE MEGASTRUCTURE
LOCATION: ROPPONGI, TOKYO, JAPAN
DATE: 2000–3
ARCHITECT: KOHN PEDERSEN FOX ASSOCIATES (KPF)
MASTERPLANNER OF ROPPONGI HILLS COMPLEX: MORI BUILDING
CLIENT: MORI BUILDING

Like a modern version of the Tower of Babel, the bulky mass of KPF's Roppongi Hills Tower dominates its surroundings and further contributes to the high-rise reputation of a city that built its first modern office tower – the Kasumigaseki Building – only in 1968.

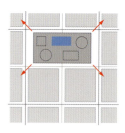

Typological group: Clusters
– high-rise megastructure
Building height: 238 metres
Site coverage: 65%
Plot ratio: 7.12

HISTORY / DEVELOPMENT PROCESS

It took over 17 years to complete. Unlike most other projects of this size, the 11 hectares of the total development area are not a result of the site's history and initial shape, but the fruit of a long process of piecemeal land acquisition and negotiation between landowners and the developer Mori. In 1986 the Tokyo Metropolitan Government had designated the area, officially Roppongi-6-Chome, a 'redevelopment inducement area', and some 500 landowners were involved in Japan's largest private-sector redevelopment project. Approximately 400 of the rights holders in the district, 80 per cent of the original number, participated in the project. Following stipulations of the Japanese City Redevelopment Law, they converted their rights into a participation in the project: that is, ownership of floor space in the newly developed residential towers. Construction as such was thus the least complicated part of the mega-project, and took only three years. Roppongi Hills is one of six conceptually similar mixed-use programmes by Mori Building, the famous Ark Hills development in Akasaka from 1986 being the forerunner and most comparable scheme in terms of size and length of implementation process.

Roppongi Hills incorporates not only the Mori Tower, but a whole cluster of high-, middle- and low-rise

structures, including a hotel, several residential towers, a park, an exterior arena and the TV Asahi broadcasting studios, designed by Fumihiko Maki.

URBAN CONFIGURATION

It is interesting to realise that the client and design team have, on the one hand, chosen to disguise the complementarity of the above-mentioned cluster of buildings through the subdivision of design tasks and the avoidance of a repetitive architectural language – a rather unusual design attitude for a holistically planned private project – and that they, on the other hand, artificially emphasised the visual presence of the main tower. The whole masterplan therefore appears as a single condensed and super-densified megastructure that sits upon a sea of far smaller structures without however completely losing touch with the surroundings' scale and character. A gargantuan space invader of indefinable elegance, the development appears at the same time as a vertical extrusion of its surroundings, and as a form that grows through a multitude of carefully designed terraces and public spaces out of Roppongi's usual small- and medium-scale fabric. The reason for this contextual design philosophy – arguably reminiscent of an old castle town – is probably

not only a question of choice, but a result of the aforementioned development history and the gradual extension of the site. It is also quite typical for the Japanese development world to separate the design of iconic structures – often commissioned from international star architects – from the more repetitive tasks like housing which tend to be designed in-house. Many of the large Hong Kong developers like Sun Hung Kai or Squire work in a similar way.

The loose geometry of the masterplan stands in any case in stark contrast to the strictly orthogonal and grid-based tower districts of Nishi-Shinjuku (see page 64), Toranomon or the recently redeveloped Marunouchi area. Even the design of the shopping and eating areas in the base of the tower – undertaken by the Jerde Partnership – seems to follow a slightly maze-like and chaotic structure, not that different from the surrounding streets and lanes of the Roppongi or Harajuku districts.

The developer Mori was ingenious in maximising the site's development potential through the exploitation of the city administration's bonus system. This was attained through the increased public permeability of the site, additional roads and the insertion of a large art gallery, the Mori Art Museum, on top of the building. These interventions have helped to raise the permissible

View of the public space in front of the tower's northern entrance. This zone is situated on top of a podium and features direct access to an underground station.

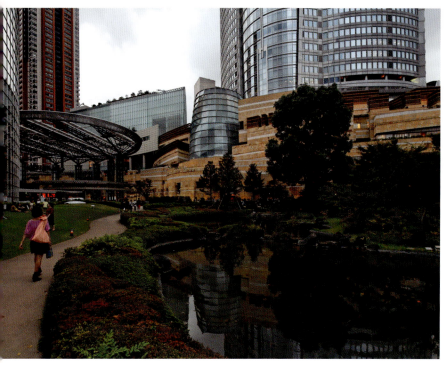

floor area ratio from approximately 320 per cent to 725 per cent.

The extensive mixture of uses – a museum, an art gallery, bars, restaurants, retail, offices, hotels, cinemas and apartments – is part of the city's policy, but constitutes also a central idea of the Mori development model. Rather than to support mixture on the scale of a district, the company's ideas of a compact city prescribe a maximum mixture within each single site – a principle that is perceived, together with extensive interior and exterior greening, as fundamentally important for a future sustainable city development. Direct access to the public transport network is part of this strategy. The company has undertaken comparisons with central areas of other world cities, especially New York, and has realised that Tokyo's generally low building heights and lack of residential spaces produced far too long travelling times and a surprisingly low level of green spaces per inhabitant.

ARCHITECTURE

The imposing size of the main tower is not only a visual impression: it is indeed a building with very deep floor plates, and finds itself in a tradition of such buildings in Japan. The central core of the tower is square-shaped with an impressive side length of 39.8 metres. It comprises technical equipment, elevators and toilets. The surrounding office floor plates have a varying depth of 14.1 to 22.1 metres, a dimension that would

barely be acceptable for European standards in terms of natural light levels in the workplace. The tendency towards such deep floor plates can be explained through the early Japanese adaptation of the 'open-plan' configuration for offices, at a time when most employees in other countries were still accommodated in rooms with single or double occupancy. This tradition, supported by rather developer-friendly building regulations, might be challenged through future restrictions of light and energy consumption. From an urban and architectural point of view, the bulky feature, however, gives the building a very individual and iconic expression, strengthened by the asymmetrical facade design which has been broadly likened to an oversized suit of samurai armour.

The office tower has 54 levels above ground, of which the first six floors are used as a shopping mall, and the top six floors for the Mori Art Museum, a viewing platform, a private club and a library. Though increasingly proposed and applied also in European developments, the success and insouciance of the vertical layering – possibly heralding a genuine vertical city – still appears to the foreign visitor as an Asian particularity. This is even more striking in the older mid-rise buildings of Tokyo's densest entertainment districts like Ginza, Shinjuku or Shibuya, where one can find restaurants, hairdressers and small-scale retail on each single floor.

ABOVE LEFT: View of the park with the TV Asahi broadcasting studios to the left and the tower's landscaped base to the right. It seems to grow out of the soil, and skilfully deals with the site's hilly geography.

ABOVE: The tower quickly became one of Tokyo's major urban icons. Its facade has been interpreted as samurai armour.

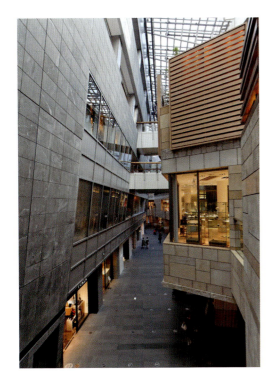

FAR LEFT: The design of the shopping mall in the tower's base echoes the formal language of the exterior landscaping.

LEFT: Despite the dense tissue of Tokyo's urban fabric, and due to its height and elevated situation, the Roppongi Hills Mori Tower can be seen from far away.

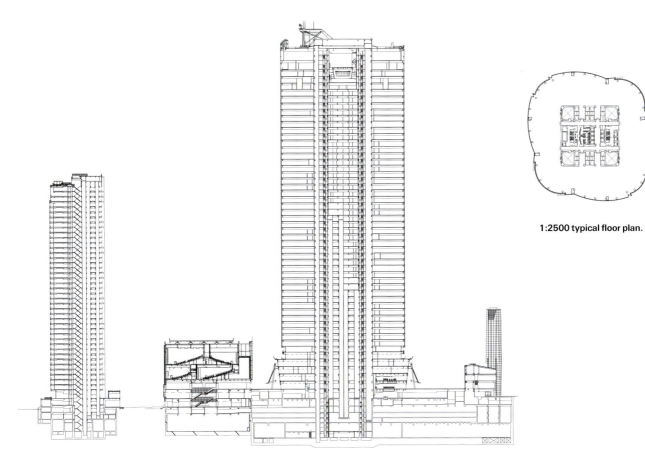

1:2500 typical floor plan.

1:2500 section through the Roppongi Hills Mori Tower, its base and one of the adjacent residential towers.

SUMMARY

Minoru Mori's strong development vision, the size and success of his company's built projects and the proud use of his ancient family name is reminiscent of the Rockefeller case (see page 88), with the difference that real estate constitutes the Mori family's central activity. This raises the question as to the impact of self-interest and personal motivation on the quality of the result; or, rather, whether a family business will create a different or even a 'better' urban environment than a listed development company. Such an idle question is difficult to answer, but it might be worthwhile to mention a rather more tangible economical dimension: the Mori Company stresses the fact that the lengthy negotiation with landowners, and a development period of over 17 years in total, can only be sustained through the long-term vision of a private company which is not obliged to satisfy the financial demands that go along with the notion of shareholder value, fundamental for a listed stock company. This notion could arguably be described as the way of least resistance and fastest profits, which indeed cannot be perceived as a warrant of sustainability and design quality. In this specific case, the question was the modification of an existing cadastral structure, the effort that it demanded, and the tools that were available for its implementation. The example of Roppongi Hills – legally very different from tabula rasa examples like La Défense or Pudong – shows that change through private initiative demands a strong vision and a long development perspective.

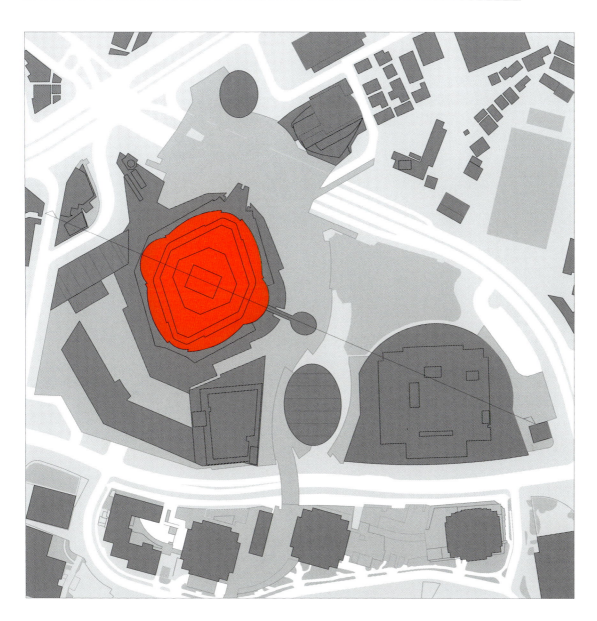

Urban plan 1:2500

Urban section 1:5000

PARQUE CENTRAL

LOCATION: CARACAS, VENEZUELA
DATE: 1970–84
ARCHITECT: SISO, SHAW & ASSOCIATES

Due to the length of the planning and construction period, this ensemble of gargantuan dimensions and apocalyptic expression features stylistic elements spanning from the early 1970s to the early 1980s. Centrally located along Avenida Bolívar as the city's major extension and traffic thoroughfare of the post-war period, the development consists of five 44-storey residential slabs and South America's tallest office towers: 56-storey twins. These volumes, with their 3,500 apartments and office space for 16,000 workers, are set on a podium that comprises among a multitude of other uses a museum complex, a swimming pool and 8,000 car parking spaces. Protrusions of the podium and several pedestrian bridges span the busy thoroughfare and connect Parque Central with neighbouring structures. The size of the intervention, the uncompromising concept and architecture as much as the mix of uses, appear as an even bolder Latin American version of London's Barbican Centre.

PINNACLE@DUXTON

LOCATION: SINGAPORE
DATE: 2005–9
ARCHITECT: ARC STUDIO ARCHITECTURE + URBANISM

As a result of Singapore's first international competition for public housing, seven towering blocks with a total of 1,848 apartments have been built by the Housing & Development Board (HDB) on a centrally located site in Tanjong Pagar. Two sky bridges with playgrounds, gardens, a gym and a jogging track on the 26th and 50th floors provide the pedestrian link between the 50-storey-tall elements. The spectacular setting and architecture – highly unusual for public housing – is also reflected at the ground level with a carefully designed park and sloping surfaces. The irregularity of the facade layout is based on the buyers' choice of bay windows, planter boxes or balconies. The exceptional development – today hardly imaginable in an American or European city – supersedes HDB's first housing slabs in this area from 1963 which were situated on the same site. It symbolises the city's very positive attitude towards high-rise living.

Hansaviertel (Interbau)

CLUSTERS: TOWERS IN NATURE
LOCATION: BERLIN, GERMANY
DATE: 1956–60
MASTERPLANNER: GERHARD JOBST, WILLY KREUER, WILHELM SCHLIESSER
(WITH OTTO BARTNING)
CLIENT: HANSA AG

The post-war housing situation was characterised by a need to build cheaply and quickly and to find solutions for the urgent housing shortage. Just 30 years after Stuttgart's avant-garde Weissenhof Exhibition, Berlin's Interbau of 1957 provided architects with the opportunity to put into practice the revised early Modernist precepts and to lead the way towards the future.

Typological group: Clusters – towers in nature
Building height: 52 metres
Site coverage: 11%
Plot ratio: 1.72

HISTORY / DEVELOPMENT PROCESS

Like many parts of Berlin, the well-to-do and much sought-after Hansaviertel had been almost completely destroyed during the Second World War. Built at the end of the 19th century on swampy ground north of Berlin's inner-city Tiergarten park, the typical perimeter block developments were generally built with three upper floors, a raised ground floor and a mansard. At the end of the war, 300 out of 343 were no longer standing, and others were heavily damaged.

In 1953 the city of Berlin organised a masterplan competition, following an earlier initiative of the Tiergarten district. The Hansaviertel eventually emerged as the only area that would at least partly incorporate elements of Hans Scharoun's green plan for the redevelopment and spatial reorganisation of Berlin after the war, commissioned in 1946 by the Allies. Due to very practical considerations of time and cost, Scharoun's radical ideas for a *Stadtlandschaft* (city-landscape) within a strongly modified infrastructural

network were quite promptly put to one side. But his ideas were not forgotten, and as a member of the jury which, out of 98 entries, chose the proposal put forward by Gerhard Jobst, Willy Kreuer and Wilhelm Schliesser, Scharoun's input had a lasting impact on the development of Berlin.

URBAN CONFIGURATION

The winning scheme's urban proposal mapped out a design of the Hansaviertel which was extraordinary in its outright refusal to create any orthogonal relationship between the distinct elements of the plan. Only at a second glance does it become clear that one of its main precepts is the rather loose delimitation of two open spaces towards the Tiergarten park. The progressive nature of this proposal, for which few precedents exist except the Aluminum City housing project in Pennsylvania by Martin Gropius and Marcel Breuer (1941–2), should be considered in direct political relation to the construction of the Stalinallee in East Berlin, finished only months before the Hansaviertel

competition was held. In the East, based on Berlin's historical spatial order, the Communist regime had orchestrated a monumental housing axis, reconstructing to the workers' glory a Classical spatial order under socially altered conditions. In the West, on the other side of what would become the Iron Curtain, Jobst and Kreuer's scheme stood in complete opposition to this, holding high in celebration the virtues of Western freedom and progress through the application of Le Corbusier's Athens Charter of 1943 and the vision of a green city that had literally nothing in common with the area's pre-existing order. It is also due to the explicit refusal of the Stalinallee scheme and its political background that the land on which the Hansaviertel was built was eventually reconverted into private small-scale ownership. Temporarily, however, all land was under the legal control and ownership of the public body Hansa AG, and the historic plot structure was erased for good. Crucially, the communist model of communally owned land as a definite solution, initially equally cherished by Western planners, was not to be repeated.

TOP LEFT: Hans Schwippert's tower seen from the city train. It marks the eastern end of a row of five point-towers along the railway tracks.

TOP: Schwippert's tower is immersed in the landscape concept.

ABOVE: The base of Gustav Hassenpflug's tower, with Eugène Beaudouin's (see also Monaco, page 162) and Raymond Lopez's (see also Front de Seine, page 136) proposal to the right.

ARCHITECTURE

One of the most striking features of the Hansaviertel is the aforementioned lack of architectural repetition. Most housing developments of that time, or at least the well-known ones like Roehampton in southwest London or France's *grands ensembles* (see page 96), are characterised by their impressive size and a holistic planning approach which often led to the collaboration of a single public client and just one architect and urban designer in the same person. Dependent on, or arguably independent of, the person's talent the result was often repetitive and lacking in complexity.

In the case of the IBA, such a holistic approach was not practical, as the fundamental concept of the Interbau was to invite many architects to be involved in the project and its construction, rather than have a competition with a single winner. The concept of the Internationale Bauausstellungen, a great success of German planning initiative that still continues today, can therefore, almost by chance, be seen as an urban planning principle in its own right – an approach which encourages and supports architectural diversity, independent of contemporaneous planning philosophies.

In this spirit, 1,160 units in 35 buildings have been built by 43 national and international architects, including well-known figures like Alvar Aalto, Oscar Niemeyer, Max Taut and Egon Eiermann as part of a who's who in Modernist architecture.

The six point-towers – five along the northern boundary of the site, and one on the southwestern one – share little resemblance, except for a similar height between 15 and 17 storeys, and an almost square-shaped footprint. Highly inventive in terms of plan layout as much as elevation and sculptural appearance, they equally all share an exposed and abrupt relationship to their surroundings, in which the geometrically simple building masses hit the ground with a modest expression of a base, if any. In terms of uses, the westernmost tower of the row, by the Italian Luciano Baldessari, is the only one to include a bank as public amenity. As objects in a green park, the buildings tend to gain attractiveness through distance, from where the careful green landscaping appears in perfect harmony with the building masses.

SUMMARY

The Interbau in the Hansaviertel was and still is considered to be a great success. It not only represents a random assembly of 'star architecture', but manages to put all these precious elements in an urban logic based on the adjusted masterplan of Jobst and Kreuer. The balance between nature and built elements has been masterfully implemented, and is also a

LEFT: The two towers by Hermann Henselmann at the Frankfurter Tor in East Berlin are part of the grandiose Stalinallee development, the ideological and urban counterpart of the IBA 1957.

Symbolic polarisation was further emphasised by the last-minute decision to elevate the status of redevelopment in the Hansaviertel from a local initiative to an Internationale Bauausstellung (International Building Exhibition – IBA), scheduled to be a major event in Germany's post-war cultural agenda for 1957. From a practical and urban point of view, the main consequence of this was the fact that the winning scheme's repetitive use of the slab type was deemed to be utterly inappropriate, and under the supervision of Otto Bartning the scheme was amended in order to accommodate a great variety of types, including single-family houses and point-towers. The point-towers were actually inspired by the competition entry from the architect Kurt Kurfiss, and have a dual function: positioned along the train tracks, they on the one hand divert the attention from the infrastructure as an inappropriate constituent of a residential area, but on the other hand – visible from afar – clearly demarcate the tracks in the collective memory as the spatial boundary of the whole site.

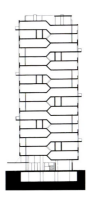

**1:1250 section of the Bakema
and van den Broek tower.**

**1:1250 floor plans of the residential tower
by Bakema and van den Broek. It comprises
skilfully designed split-level apartments.**

consequence of the inclusion of landscape architects right from the beginning of the project. Many of the flaws of comparable undertakings, such as endless architectural repetition and the neglect of open spaces, have been avoided.

The architectural excellence of the Hansaviertel is undeniable, yet there remains a certain perplexity. On reflection, this perplexity appears to be inextricably linked to the very concept of the antagonistic *Stadtlandschaft*. Integrating 'metropolitan living in the park' into the proposal was a crucial element of the design brief, and rather than opt for a more bucolic or suburban concept, an alternative vision of urban life was sought. From this point of view, the relatively low density of the new district appears to be questionable, as much as the whole concept of spatial 'freedom' as counter-model to Berlin's past as a crammed *Mietskasernenstadt* (city of rental barracks). This concept urged the express avoidance of direct geometric relations between the buildings, and appears

**Bakema and van den
Broek's colourful tower
contains with its
multitude of split-level
apartments a particularly
inventive and complex
interior organisation.**

today as an overly symbolic relic of architectural theory and social history. Both of these elements combined – low densities and the deliberate avoidance of a streetscape – may now be considered as handicaps for the creation of a successful urban environment, and it is essentially the quality of the green spaces which holds the project together. The use of high-rise further underlines this relationship, as the considerable effort and cost associated with building tall are generally counterbalanced by the high density it affords, a logic which does not seem to be dictated here. From today's pragmatic perspective, the spatial strength of the green 'city-landscape' concept seems diluted by the even greener neighbourhood of the adjacent Tiergarten park, and it is surprising that the immediate vicinity of such

an extraordinary green feature has not been used for a denser development along the border, with the example of Central Park, New York. Ironically, though in a low-rise *fin-de-siècle* version, this was also the project's historic starting point before war destruction, when the site was still covered by *Gründerzeit* apartment buildings. An economic and less subjective analysis might also question whether the present density would justify the existence of the current excellent transport connections, were it not situated in the centre of an otherwise more densely populated metropolis.

Urban plan 1:2500

Urban section 1:2500

UNITÉ D'HABITATION (CITÉ RADIEUSE)

LOCATION: MARSEILLES, FRANCE
DATE: 1947–52
ARCHITECT: LE CORBUSIER

Le Corbusier's 18-storey slab was conceived as, and eventually also became, one of the most influential high-rise models for the residential architecture of the post-war era. Based on theories that he had developed since the 1920s – including references to French philosopher Charles Fourier's early-19th-century utopian vision of the Phalanstère, as well as medieval cloisters and modern passenger ships – his scheme was meant to solve housing needs and to offer a vertical alternative to the horizontal vision of the garden city. Implemented with the use of modular construction techniques, it was a city in a house, and offered – with a gym, kindergarten, swimming pool and internal shopping streets – everything that an autarchic community needed. The great architectural quality and complexity, including cross-ventilated duplex apartments and a roof garden, resulted in higher costs than expected, and in the following years Le Corbusier received only four opportunities to replicate the Unité in other cities, including the 1957 Hansaviertel project in Berlin (see page 128). The relation of the strictly east–west-oriented slab to its urban surroundings is rather apathetic, and betrays the project's spiritual relationship with Le Corbusier's earlier proposals for a radically new city structure of a similar name, the Ville Radieuse (1935).

NEWTON SUITES

LOCATION: SINGAPORE
DATE: 2004–7
ARCHITECT: WOHA

Roughly 20 per cent smaller in surface than Berlin, the prosperous island country of Singapore has, with over 7,000 inhabitants per square kilometre, almost twice the (low) residential density of that German city, but the world's third highest as a country. Due to its modest size and the flatness of the island – especially seen in comparison with the dramatic geography of Hong Kong – the population is scattered over its entire surface, creating a very specific urban setting with only the historic core as a genuine high-density environment. In this context, high-rise helps to protect the rather green character of the city-state with its constantly growing population. The 36-storey Newton Suites does so in an especially literal way, and as such optimises the advantages of its tropical climate. The building provides planted walls, sky gardens and generous balconies as if landscape were a construction material. It forms, together with neighbouring structures, a high-rise cluster with a rather exceptional character as a mixture of suburbia, park and city centre.

Front de Seine (Beaugrenelle)

CLUSTERS: TOWERS ON PODIUM
LOCATION: PARIS, FRANCE
DATE: 1967–90
MASTERPLANNER: RAYMOND LOPEZ, HENRI POTTIER, MICHEL HOLLEY
CLIENT: SEMPARISEINE

Typological group: Clusters
– towers on podium
Building height: 98 metres
Site coverage: 48%
Plot ratio: 4.17

Just five minutes' walk south of the Eiffel Tower, a very different – though no less radical – vision of French high-rise construction can be found. From the first sketch in 1959 until completion of the last building in 1990, the project spans more than 30 years, and survived this long period with gradual adjustments, but without fundamental loss of the initial concept.

HISTORY / DEVELOPMENT PROCESS

In a plan commissioned in 1959 by the city of Paris, the quarter of Beaugrenelle in the 15th arrondissement had been identified as one of the priority zones for urban renovation. The author of this study, the architect Raymond Lopez, was eventually chosen to join forces with Henri Pottier and to elaborate a vision for the 29-hectare site whose largest existing user was a Citroën factory. Together with Michel Holley as leading designer, they developed for the newly created semi-public development company SEMEA 15, now SemPariSeine (with public majority and headed by the local mayor) a masterplan that strictly adhered to the ideas of CIAM and Le Corbusier's 1943 Athens Charter. In building high- and mid-rise structures above a podium of considerable dimensions, the project indeed represents one of the most impressive and radical inner-city schemes of late Modernism. The separation of circulations and functions, the autonomy of the built elements, the liberation from the ground and the use of high-rise buildings of homogenous height (98 metres) are almost literal translations of the urban principles of that time. The vertical layering as solution for the separation of movements actually surpassed the zoning

prescriptions of the Athens Charter, and was inspired by utopian visionaries reaching back to the late 19th and earlier 20th century such as Eugène Hénard and Ludwig Hilberseimer. Beaugrenelle, or 'Front de Seine', was, however, not the only French podium development of that type, and the simultaneous projects of La Défense, Maine-Montparnasse and the Italie-Sector in the 13th arrondissement followed similar approaches. Compared with these developments, however, the site's susceptibility to floods – one reason for its historically sparse construction density – complemented the rationale for the creation of an artificial ground and an elevated circulation level. As a matter of fact, and despite the radicalism of its formal approach, the authors did not consider the project to be disconnected from its local context. It was actually praised for being very Parisian due to the constant height of the towers, recalling the fixed datum of the traditional perimeter blocks.

URBAN CONFIGURATION

Above the service streets and the parking decks of the podium, with their universal 9.45 by 9.45-metre structural grid, Lopez and his team 'sculptured' an urban landscape for mixed use of residential, office and commercial activities. They also precisely prescribed the location and building envelope of all built structures. The dispersed spatial arrangement of the towers and lower buildings towards each other purposely avoids defining any clear hierarchies, central axes or preferred perspectives, and the scheme appears conceptually as an overlay of three-dimensional networks and patterns rather than a designed composition of spaces.

A particularly interesting aspect of the project is its complex legal structure. Initially, SemPariSeine planned to sell the development sites of the towers as leaseholds, eventually returning to local authority ownership after 70 years. In reality, however, this did not work out, as most of the towers were private residential developments, whose initiators did not believe in finding buyers based on such an, at least in France, unusual model. The leasehold solution was therefore only practised for the lower, non-residential buildings which were constructed on the podium, rather than the towers whose foundations obviously went down to the ground. In the final scheme, SemPariSeine remained owner of the slab itself, signing maintenance contracts with the private users of the spaces on its top. The developers of the residential towers acquired only the area of the building footprint, and not the land around it. The city

ABOVE LEFT: View from the southwest to the northeast of the podium's upper deck.

ABOVE: View from the corner of Rue Linois and Rue Emeriau.

became the owner of the public circulation spaces underneath the slab, but this only after an unusual legal manipulation, because the traditional definition of a public street would have included all the air space above ground – something that was not possible wherever the street was covered by the podium.

ARCHITECTURE

The towers themselves are mostly residential and were developed by private companies and their respective architects. For practical reasons and reasons of experience, many developers decided, however, to continue the architectural design work with the authors of the masterplan, and many towers were indeed built

CLOCKWISE FROM TOP LEFT: View from the upper deck over the lower level of the service streets.

The dimensions of the towers' (here Tour Rive Gauche, developed by Batima) 'wasp-waists' were based on the structural grid of 9.45 by 9.45 metres. This was introduced to liberate the maximal amount of podium space to the public, but can also be considered to be an aesthetic choice of the masterplanners.

The Hachette building, one of the mid-rise constructions in the northern part of the podium.

The podium's edge along Rue Emeriau. The spatial and functional hierarchy between the top and the fringes is not clearly defined.

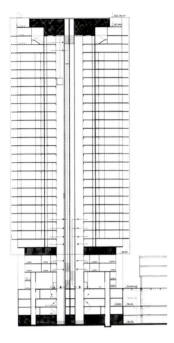

1:1250 section through Tour Rive Gauche, developed by Batima, showing the wasp-waist concept on top of the podium.

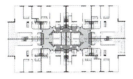

1:1250 typical floor plan of the Tour Rive Gauche with eight apartments per floor, designed by Isaac Mory and Michel Proux. The layout offers flexibility through the possibility of attaching one room of the four corner units to the apartments in the central part of the building.

by the office of Lopez and Pottier's partners and successors (Lopez died in 1966). Over time, this procedure was identified as problematic, and SemPariSeine started to appoint other architects and to organise competitions, sometimes reselling a finished project together with a valid building permit. The architectural freedom in the frame of the masterplan was admittedly very limited, and in several cases the invited architects declined participation in such competitions. Next to height and footprint, the design brief even prescribed a 'wasp-waist' base for each tower over a height of five storeys.

This procedure left the architect with even less influence than in the often-criticised development structure of the 19th century – most notoriously under Baron Haussmann – when the architect of a specific plot had to respect and follow not only fixed street lines, predefined heights and setbacks, but often even constraints regarding the aesthetic appearance of the buildings. Due to the spatial logic of the tower, which prescribes an extroversion of the apartments around a central spine, the architects of Beaugrenelle's towers did not even have the possibility to shape the relation between courtyard and building masses, as was necessary in the traditional example, and had to content themselves with alterations of the plan and facade layout as purely artistic modes of expression. This alteration and quasi-abolition of the artistic borderline between architecture and urbanism marks certainly one of the most complex changes in the history of the built environment, and cannot be that quickly analysed and explained in the context of this book. The extraordinary interest of the Front de Seine development lies, however, in its ability to show this phenomenon especially clearly, and to relate the large-scale approach almost symbolically to the above-mentioned legal questions and the balancing act between public and private initiative and interests. One might attempt the thesis that the podium is not only a practical problem and a reason for legal complications, but that these problems and complications are also revealing symptoms for crucial changes in the development logic of our cities. These changes also occurred in schemes

A service street that runs underneath the podium. The towers have secondary entrances at this level. For reasons of comfort, they are often used as main entrances.

without podium and without any private investment, but in these cases they can more easily be dismissed as purely formal considerations.

SUMMARY

The Front de Seine is hardly the French capital's most adored district, even though the tower apartments have kept high values due to their central location and spectacular views. One – and probably the main – reason for this is the nature of the podium architecture and the difficulty of creating a sense of place on an elevated level. Several changes to the initial proposal did not help, and it might be regretted that the podium has not been extended further west as a belvedere over the Seine river. It is also perhaps regrettable that

the rough character of the covered access and service streets has been gradually and purposely lost, abolishing the necessity to use the podium and to allow the establishment of a critical mass of movements and social interaction. This is especially true for the commercial uses which tend to be positioned along rather than, as initially planned, on the elevated level.

The whole development is currently undergoing major works in order to resolve these problems. The landscape design of the podium will be completely redefined and a major shopping centre will be built in order to lead the post-war dinosaur into the 21st century.

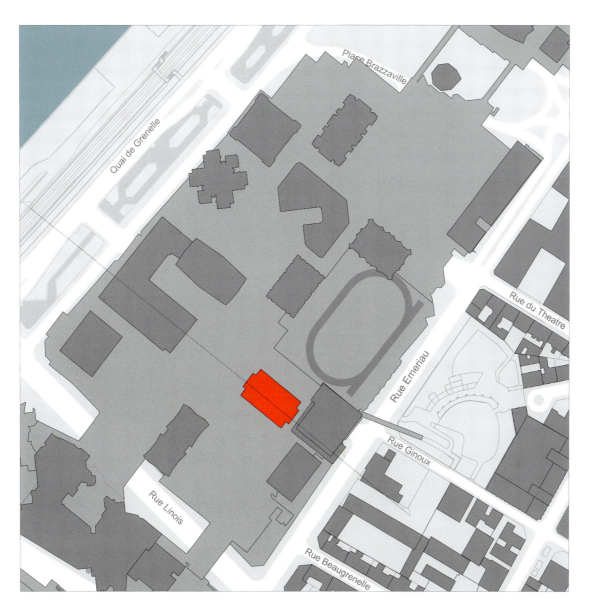

Urban plan 1:2500

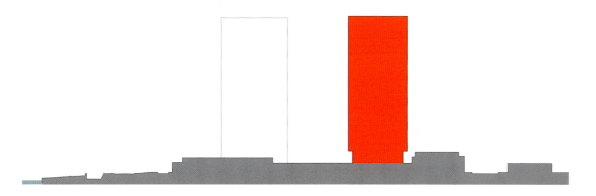

Urban section 1:2500

JUMEIRAH BEACH RESIDENCES

LOCATION: DUBAI, UNITED ARAB EMIRATES
DATE: 2007
ARCHITECT: WATG

Built by the developer Dubai Properties, this two-million-square-metre development comprises 36 residential and four hotel towers. The podium level contains car parks and extensive commercial uses, but – despite the existence of an internal mall – it still manages to address the surrounding streets through active shop fronts. The development covers several blocks and spans over the open perpendicular streets with pedestrian footbridges. The block interior and its elevated level is publicly accessible, but has been designed as a community garden for the residents of the towers.

As a matter of fact the development appears rather as a tower-on-base type with a roof garden than as a podium scheme, which usually suggests that the elevated level is the project's main focus. Unusual for European inner-city standards, the modest height of the base is not surprising in the context of low-rise Arabic architecture. Through their high density, the existence of an elevated community garden and the occasional post-modern design feature, the Jumeirah Beach Residences clearly evoke Hong Kong's residential megastructures (see page 188).

TOUR 9

LOCATION: MONTREUIL, PARIS OUTSKIRTS, FRANCE
DATE: 2007–9
ARCHITECT: HUBERT & ROY ARCHITECTES
MASTERPLANNER: ÁLVARO SIZA

Tour 9, developed by The Carlyle Group, is part of an ongoing regeneration masterplan in Montreuil, the fourth most populous community of the Parisian agglomeration. Through a metro line, the site is directly linked to the boundary of central Paris only two kilometres away. Until 2006, Tour 9 and two neighbouring buildings were connected by a two-storey podium that covered almost the totality of the large urban block. In 1992 Álvaro Siza was commissioned to develop a vision for the heart of Montreuil that included the retrofit of this ambitious Modernist development which was eventually regarded as an urban failure. As a result, the three tall structures are preserved, but their surroundings and the spatial logic of the block will be completely altered through the insertion of public spaces and a multitude of cultural, commercial and residential uses. The podium has disappeared and the freestanding Tour 9 appears now, with its playful colour scheme and a height of 26 storeys, as the symbol of Montreuil's ambitious urban renewal. The tower is not only the first high-rise renovation to reach the French HPE level (high energetic performance), but it also constitutes a good example of how the character and efficiency of a sinister building can be substantially improved without the costly destruction of its intact structure. The concrete slabs have been extended by 120 centimetres along the building perimeter, allowing the continuous glazing of the formerly opaque envelope.

Downtown Houston

VERTICAL CITIES: US-AMERICAN DOWNTOWN
LOCATION: HOUSTON, TEXAS, USA

Downtown Houston appears as a pure example, if not abstraction of a North American city centre. Its perfectly flat geography strengthens the urban grid structure of the city, and the lack of zoning restrictions suits the picture of a spatial system that is based on capitalistic development laws.

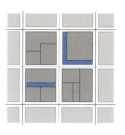

Typological group: Vertical
Cities – US-American
downtown
**Estimated site coverage
(as seen on urban plan):**
90%
**Estimated plot ratio
(as seen on urban plan):**
13.99

HISTORY / DEVELOPMENT PROCESS

Real estate speculation is a crucial part of, if not at the origin of Houston's history. In 1836, two brothers from New York, Augustus Chapman and John Kirby Allen, bought the land next to Buffalo Bayou and started an aggressive marketing campaign in which they strategically presented this new place as a future booming port town with an agreeable climate. Named after Sam Houston, a war hero and president of the Republic of Texas since September 1836, the city was incorporated in 1837. Due to land donations and skilful negotiation, the Allen brothers convinced the Congress to choose Houston as the state's capital, a status that the city was stripped of in 1839 for it to be given to Austin. The economy depended on cotton and commerce, but due to the shallowness of the Bayou's river bed the access to the sea revealed itself to be more problematic than initially expected. After experiencing rapid growth from a low level, the momentum slowed, and it was not until the dawn of the 20th century – with the construction of a canal, a deep-water port and Texas's most extensive railway network – that Houston marked its place as a major economic capital. Key to firmly putting Houston on the map was the discovery of oil, which fuelled the development of an energy sector that still accounts for about half of the local economy. Today, however, the actual production of oil no longer plays a major role, and since the 1970s the city has developed into a strategic node in the global energy and energy finance sector.

The real estate sector has followed these steps, and local developers like Gerald H Hines have had a major impact on the globalisation of modern office spaces, which were deeply influenced by the city's rapid need

for fully air-conditioned offices for very large companies. A know-how evolved that was exported all over the world. The relative freedom and availability of space compared with much older cities like New York helped to establish these new benchmarks. So did the nation's second-highest density of Fortune 500 companies.

URBAN CONFIGURATION

Apart from the city's lack of zoning laws, and taken from a strictly urban and formal point of view, the reason to choose Houston as a typical though extreme example of a US downtown is linked to the quasi-perfection of its square-shaped grid and to the comparatively small dimensions of this grid. At approximately 85 metres in width and length, it is about 20 metres shorter than, for example, the Chicago or Los Angeles grid, and features at least in its central part a very small amount of geometrical exceptions. In combination with the city's strong economy and the subsequent need for large floor plates, this means that many of the plots are covered by a single building. To this extent Houston is rather an abstraction than a model, because such a situation is actually very rare, and even the tallest buildings in Chicago or New York tend to share the

View from the corner of Dallas and Fannin Street to the northwest.

surface of a block with neighbouring structures. The consequence is a peculiar urban landscape which pushes the towers to prominence as autonomous and freestanding elements and provides a particularly high sculptural quality.

The flatness of the ground strengthens this effect, as does the relative lack of physical barriers. Compared with Manhattan's island position, San Francisco's hills and Chicago's winding Chicago River, the importance of Houston's Buffalo Bayou as a natural element appears to be, at least from today's point of view, fairly marginal. More substantial interference arrived with the construction of the motorways which border Downtown along the river bed to the north and

LEFT: The base of Johnson/Burgee's Bank of America Tower. Together with a mid-rise appendix it covers a whole block.

BELOW LEFT: Johnson/Burgee's Pennzoil Place and Bank of America (right), seen from IM Pei & Partners' JPMorgan Chase Tower.

northwest. It is hence intriguing to observe that even in the opposite direction, to the south and to the west, the high-rise section finds an abrupt end, and low buildings like the George R Brown Convention Center and the Minute Maid Park baseball stadium are – at less than a kilometre away from IM Pei's JPMorgan Chase Tower – surrounded by hectares of flat car parks.

Another particularity of Houston is its extensive system of underground pedestrian tunnels which connect the towers under the street surface. Much more than just circulation areas, this network also includes a wide offer of retail and restaurant facilities. Air-conditioned throughout the year, these privatised spaces allow the city workers to avoid stepping into the hot and humid air, but obviously have the side effect of draining activity from the public street space.

ARCHITECTURE

Houston's high-rise architecture is marked through an impressive concentration of extraordinary buildings in a range of just a couple of hundred metres: Johnson/ Burgee's Bank of America and Pennzoil Place are both milestones of American corporate architecture, and are flanked by IM Pei's slender JPMorgan Chase Tower, as Texas's tallest tower, and the Wells Fargo Center by Skidmore, Owings & Merrill. The last two towers in particular have one thing in common: in terms of ownership they cover a whole block, but through a narrow footprint they leave a fairly large percentage of the plot unbuilt. This is remarkable, because Houston's planning regulations do not operate with a bonus system for public space provision like Tokyo or New York. The developer's decision not to cover the entire

plot is therefore not motivated by the increase in permissible floor-area-ratio, but by the deliberate application of the commercially most attractive floor plan. An aesthetic consequence of this is a further accentuation of the above-mentioned sculptural quality in the almost literal form of an urban chequerboard. Architecturally, the flat facades of the towers and their expression as monoliths comply with these urban aesthetics. Due to the almost consistent lack of retail uses in the ground floors, this is much easier to accomplish than in a mixed-use environment where the programmatic change between the lower and the upper floors is usually reflected in a corresponding design response in the form of a base.

Through its peculiar architectural aesthetics and the formidable flatness of the land and grid, Houston's Downtown streetscape emanates a strong and sometimes ghostly atmosphere which is reminiscent of classical representations of empty Italian cityscapes, and especially the Surrealist work of Giorgio de Chirico. This impression is amplified through low levels of pedestrian activity and the specificity of the hot and humid climate. As subjective as this reading might be, it is worthwhile noting, because it suggests that high-rise is able to generate urban beauty in the classical sense, and to ground itself in architectural history, rather than to symbolise its sudden break. The appropriateness of the solution as such is a different question.

SUMMARY

The coexistence of an impressive high-rise core in combination with an equally impressive city extension clearly demonstrates that the use of the tower in the typical American downtown has nothing to do with a quest for overall high densities. The lack of public transport as much as the comparably very low level of mix of uses therefore only underlines the unsurprising fact that sustainability has historically not been the city's main driver. This apparent simplicity, however, has the advantage of highlighting some other interesting features more clearly than in older and more complexly layered cities like New York or Chicago. It makes clear, for example, that – at least in terms of office uses – Downtown is 'the place to be', rather than 'the dense nucleus of a historically grown structure where it seems worthwhile and obvious to build tall and to continue to do so'. In a city where everybody drives and almost nobody lives downtown, it is far from obvious that developers would pay the highest land prices just to

build in the city centre. This raises a lot of questions about the logics and dynamics of land value, and the importance of being at the right address and in the neighbourhood of the right people, but it also illustrates the vulnerability of the system if it is not balanced by a sustainable and comprehensive mix of uses. If housing and retail leave the city centre, and the existing, fairly inflexible transport network is not of major importance, the 'address' can quickly lose its attraction and will eventually be superseded by a more modern offer in a different place. The Galleria district in Uptown Houston is a good local example of this. Developed since 1970 by Gerald Hines, it was kick-started with America's most spectacular shopping mall, a commercial replica of Milan's Galleria Vittorio Emanuele II, but evolved later also into a major business quarter and competitor

Johnson/Burgee's Williams Tower (formerly the Transco Tower) in the Galleria district of Uptown Houston. At the time of construction, in 1983, it was at 277 metres the tallest skyscraper outside a central business district.

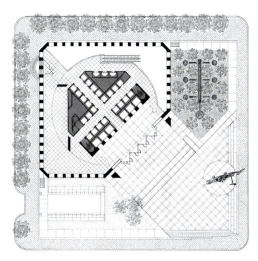

1:1250 ground-floor plan of the JPMorgan Chase Tower, by IM Pei & Partners.

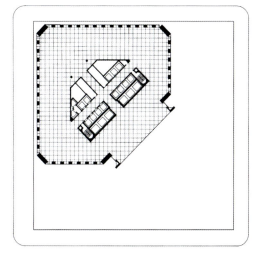

1:1250 typical floor plan of the JPMorgan Chase Tower.

of the Downtown area. In contrast to La Défense on the outskirts of Paris, Canary Wharf in London, or other European examples, its major selling point was not the provision of floor plates that could not be accommodated in the inner-city areas. Similar planned or unplanned, successful or unsuccessful multi-nodal urban developments have occurred in many other cities around the world, highlighting the constant pressure and dynamics of the real estate market.

Another economic rather than architectural observation concerns the size of the market for super-tall buildings. In 2010 the entire city of Houston counted 31 towers with a height over 150 metres, only 14 over 200 metres, and just three over 250 metres. For one of the best-known and wealthiest high-rise capitals

in the world, whose development into the sky is unencumbered by any planning restrictions, this is arguably less than expected. But even the city of Chicago counts only 11 towers over 250 metres, New York nine and San Francisco just one. These figures suggest three things: that the market for these prominent buildings is in reality fairly small; that the actual stake still remains with smaller constructions; but also that the fragile emergence of super-tall buildings, apparently the result of a rare superposition of several factors, cannot easily be masterplanned or controlled without stifling the initiative behind it.

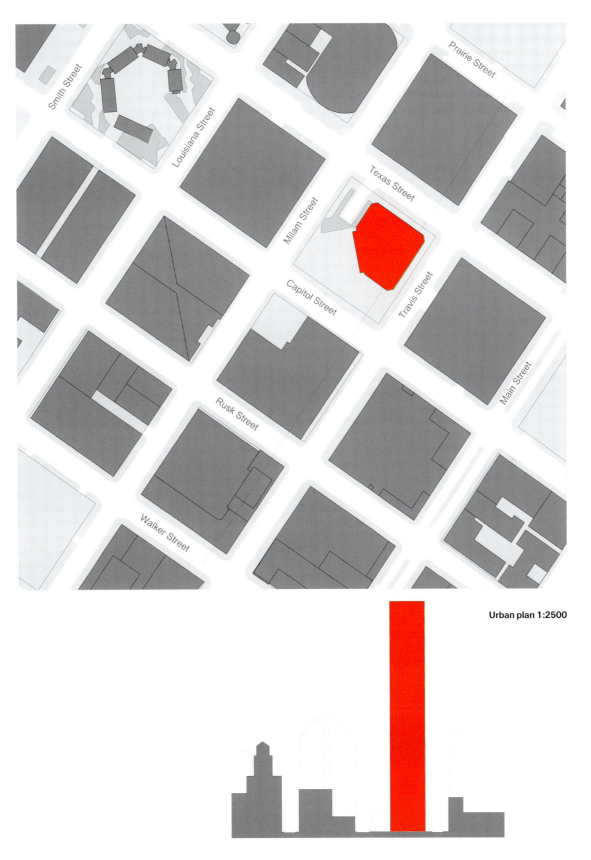

Urban plan 1:2500

Urban section 1:5000

Higienópolis

VERTICAL CITIES: HIGH-RISE AS NORM
LOCATION: CONSOLAÇÃO DISTRICT, SÃO PAULO, BRAZIL

Higienópolis in some ways would have been like Manhattan if it had grown out of row houses and not out of a garden city. Representative of a whole typological group, it exemplifies in an especially coherent way the relationship between the limitations of a traditional plot structure and the emergence of high-rise buildings.

Typological group: Vertical Cities – high-rise as norm

Estimated site coverage (as seen on urban plan): 41%

Estimated plot ratio (as seen on urban plan): 4.76

HISTORY / DEVELOPMENT PROCESS

São Paulo was founded in 1554 by Jesuits as a village on top of a hill on the Piratininga plateau. For the first two centuries of its existence, arduous access due to its geographical situation and the lack of natural resources prevented the town from achieving the same pace of development that some more privileged Portuguese foundations had managed. It was only after the discovery of gold in the city's surroundings and, subsequently, the highly profitable trade in coffee and sugar, which enabled the transformation of São Paulo in conjunction with the port town Santos into a major trading point of first national and later international importance. The first railway line opened in 1869, and significant immigration from Europe further accelerated the city's growth which in terms of population would

eventually, during the 1950s, surpass its eternal rival
Rio de Janeiro, the Brazilian capital until the construction
of Brasilia. Compared with Rio (or 'the Marvellous City',
as it was also known), where development as a
politically important place underpinned state aspirations,
the industrial capital São Paulo – not without a certain
pride – followed a 'Wild West' approach to urban
development, in which the administration's role was
notoriously limited to prevent as much as possible the
worst outcome of ongoing ferocious and partly chaotic
real estate speculation.

Interestingly, the foundation of the city on a relatively
steep hill led initially to a slow and continuous
redevelopment process of the city-centre structures,
rather than a major expansion of the city's total surface.
The considerable effort required to gain access to the
elevated centre, which was lacking in efficient transport
means, led to a development logic whereby the core
of the city was constantly being demolished and
rebuilt. Since the turn of the 20th century, the
spectacular population growth and the emergence
of efficient public transport turned this logic inside out,
and development quickly spread from the historic
nucleus to the surrounding hills which offered the
highest quality of living. The most famous example
demonstrating this is Avenida Paulista, situated on
a ridge to the southwest of the historic centre.
Eventually, this led to the creation of one of the world's
largest cities in terms of surface, and one of the rare
genuinely multi-nodal metropolises in which the
notion of 'centre' is not easy to define.

URBAN CONFIGURATION

Higienópolis was one of the first upper-class housing
developments outside São Paulo's historic centre.
Initially called Boulevard Burchard after one of its
founders, Martin Burchard, who was of French descent
– the other founder, Victor Nothmann, being of German
origin – the new quarter and its main artery soon
marketed itself under a name that expressed one of
its most important advantages: the elevated and airy
position on a slope that rises up towards Avenida
Paulista, at that time still an undeveloped area. In 1893
the two entrepreneurs had bought the land from Baron
de Ramalho and Joaquim Floriano Wanderley, and
started to lay out a street grid and to subdivide the
resulting blocks into parcels that met the demands
of the rapidly growing bourgeoisie. The surrounding
land, which had previously been used for farming,
would subsequently be developed in a similar way.

Not dissimilar to an early European garden city, the
forward-thinking founders of Higienópolis ensured
the long-term viability of the upper-class claim

ABOVE: A typical street
view in Higienópolis.

LEFT: View through two
residential towers into
the centre of the block.
It is indeed difficult to
imagine further
densification.

through careful design of the exterior spaces, including the opening of Parque Buenos Aires in 1913, and the establishment of a previously unknown set of building statutes for the sold plots. Among other restrictions, a minimum retreat from the street boundary had to be respected, a special licence had to be granted for all non-residential uses, and the construction of hygienically doubtful alcoves was forbidden. Some of these rules proved so successful that they were copied by other private developments or – like the retreat from the street line – adopted for the whole city, when in 1934 the city administration enforced the building recess. The new owners and inhabitants, many of whom were coffee barons, built their ostentatious villas in an eclectic European style on plots of a size of usually 700 to 1,000 square metres. Along the cemetery, a location that was deemed inappropriate for the highest standards, the parcels were limited to a surface of approximately 300 square metres and filled with terraced houses. A tram line connected the sought-after district with the city centre only 2.5 kilometres away.

BELOW LEFT: This particularly long building fills the totality of the plot's depth.

OPPOSITE ABOVE: Looking from the corner of Rua Itacolomi and Rua Piaui to the northeast.

OPPOSITE BELOW: Most buildings are set back from the street and fenced. Underground parking was one of the main reasons for the sealing of the formerly green surfaces.

ARCHITECTURE

The transformation of vast and ample farmland into a fairly orthogonal allotment with mid-sized plots was already an impressive urban accomplishment. From the 1930s, the aforementioned demographic explosion and the popularity of the area led, however, to a very different and rather architectural change, in which the plot sizes did not vary considerably. The first apartment building had been erected in Rua Alagoas in 1933, and in several incremental steps, but with ever increasing speed that was also influenced by changing zoning and building regulations, the formerly horizontal district grew upwards into the sky. The number of structures with more than two storeys grew from 12 in 1930 to 652 in 1979. The pinnacle of high-rise construction was reached during the real estate boom of the 1970s, and the height of the tallest structures often surpassed 30 storeys. As the recess from the street boundary still had to be respected, the increase of plot coverage – wherever the purchase of the neighbouring parcel was not possible – occurred at the back and to the side of the former single-family plots. A major impact on the geography and ecology of Higienópolis was the construction of underground parking that had become increasingly popular since the 1950s. In conjunction with the extension of plot coverage, these heavy construction works led to the complete sealing of the surface in a blanket of concrete, concealed in part by the decorative use of plants positioned on concrete foundations devoid of natural soil. Seen in section along the rising Avenida Angélica, this also meant a complete transformation of the slope: the previously undulating ground appeared now as a concrete landscape of steps, a phenomenon that is best observed along the interior boundaries of two plots where the levels of two streets often collide into a separation wall. Despite the soil's sealing, which has usurped real nature, the recess of the constructions from the street boundary and the quality of the well-designed landscaping of the entrance sequences create the effect of a much greener environment than could be expected from a perimeter-block environment. Another consequence of these fenced recesses is the relative difficulty of accommodating retail and restaurant uses in the ground floors of the buildings, for which reason the district's fairly complete mix of uses happens rather horizontally, with the Patio Higienópolis shopping mall as the most important example.

It would be overly simplistic to describe the spectacular vertical development solely on the basis of demographic pressure and the consequent need to provide alternative living options in the form of apartments rather than villas. The initial process was

ABOVE: One of the earlier mid-rise apartment buildings that has kept the notion of the front garden, reminiscent of the quarter's history as a garden city.

OPPOSITE: View of Avenida Paulista and its predominantly office towers. This area developed later than Higienópolis, and is now the heart of one of São Paulo's major business districts.

piecemeal and linked to the maintenance problem of the first-generation mansions. Due to changes in the social structure, a decline of the coffee market, and the multiple-inheritance problem, several of these large houses fell into decline, and were good targets for increasingly professionalised real estate investors. As this process started slowly in the 1930s and 1940s, the application of the apartment typology was fairly obvious, especially in a district that since its foundation was oriented towards European-style architecture.

SUMMARY

As modern, programmatic and ideological as its name may appear, Higienópolis – in its contemporary form – will stir mixed feelings and disillusionment in anyone who believes in the principles of modern urbanism and the functional city (as defined by the Congrès International d'Architecture Moderne (CIAM)). The direct reasoning behind this has to do with an obvious over-density which, at least in some areas, suggests a lack of light and air for the lower levels of the apartment

1:1250 typical floor plan with two apartments of a residential high-rise slab from 1970. The separation of service and master areas highlights the status of the owners.

buildings. From a more theoretical point of view, it is the almost ironic mixture of a modern architectural style of freestanding structures within a repetitive and traditional plot structure dating from the late 19th century, which has a certain provocative quality. In some cases designed by prominent Modernist architects, these buildings are directly juxtaposed and form – despite their usual recess from the plot boundary – a streetscape that Le Corbusier would have critically labelled a *'rue-corridor'*. To make things worse, the Modernist rule of applying high-rise in exchange for generous green spaces is completely flouted. Higienópolis therefore appears as the radical countermodel of Le Corbusier's radical *'Plan Voisin'* for the partial redevelopment of Paris, and it represents one of the most extreme cases of how to use the freestanding tower. Next to it as high-density alternatives stand the Manhattan type with its party-wall logic and Hong Kong's podium approach. Arguably thus ridiculing the modern concept of the residential point-tower, Higienópolis shows how modern design principles can be put *ad absurdum* when private initiative acts under population pressure in the context of an existing and naturally grown plot structure. However, this is not to imply that the result is a failure; indeed, Higienópolis is one of São Paulo's few central districts that has avoided the flight of its residential population in the last 30 years, and remains today a prestigious address.

Urban plan 1:2500

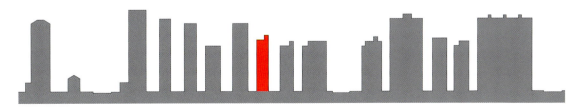

Urban section 1:2500

Monaco

VERTICAL CITIES: HIGH-RISE AS GEOGRAPHICAL OBLIGATION
LOCATION: PRINCIPALITY OF MONACO

With barely more than 32,000 inhabitants on two square kilometres, the Mediterranean city (and country) is certainly the smallest of the featured urban entities in this book. Densely built-up and bursting at the seams, it is, however, also the only one for which vertical construction is not just a concept and efficient tool, but a simple necessity to accommodate growth.

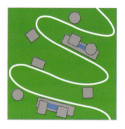

Typological group: Vertical Cities – high-rise as geographical obligation

Estimated site coverage (as seen on urban plan): 25%

Estimated plot ratio (as seen on urban plan): 2.22

HISTORY / DEVELOPMENT PROCESS

As a principality, the history of Monaco is strongly linked to its founding family, the Grimaldis, and dates back to the mid-12th century, when a statesman by the name of Grimaldo became Consul of the wealthy Republic of Genoa. The following 150 years were marked by turmoil and civil war, and parts of the family left Genoa in order to take control of the castle on Monaco's well-protected *Rocher* (Rock), where they have now been based as sovereigns for over 700 years. The Principality included until 1861 also the seigneuries of Roquebrune and Menton, the stretch of land which lies between Monaco and the Italian border. Its history as the second-smallest country in the world – barely two square kilometres in area – is therefore relatively short, and has experienced a strategic shift. Lacking in natural resources and the potential for agriculture or any conventional industry, the Principality had to find alternative ways to exploit the remaining piece of land in order to preserve its status and wealth, and did so through gradual development into a luxury resort as much as an economic and financial stronghold. Conducive to and symbolic of Monaco's financial status was the construction of the famous Casino in 1856 and the decision not to levy

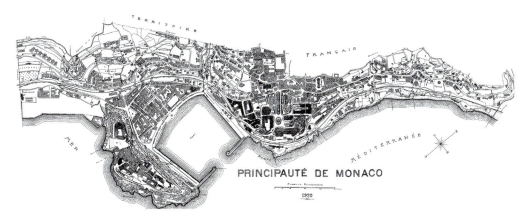

LEFT: Map of Monaco in 1920, when there was still plenty of land to be developed.

BELOW: View from the port of the reclaimed Fontvieille district towards the northwestern heights of Monaco. The Patio Palace (see drawings) can be perceived in the middle back.

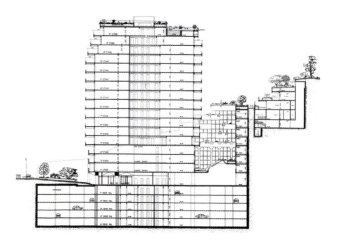

1:1250 10th-floor plan with eight apartments of Le Patio Palace by Joseph Iori from 1993.

1:1250 section of Le Patio Palace along the slope.

income taxes, a policy which does not, however, apply to the 47 per cent of the Principality's residents who are French nationals. Glamorous Monaco, essentially a peaceful village until the Second World War, is today also one of the region's largest employers.

Its small size, the spectacular geographic situation and an elongated position along the shore mean that Monaco exploits very rich and complex natural features. Over the years, the impressive land reclamation efforts have recuperated over 40 hectares from the sea and

have added some flat areas to the otherwise hilly spot with its three juxtaposed natural 'amphitheatres'. The challenges to construction thus represented by the geography of the area make the Principality's population density of 16,400 inhabitants per square kilometre all the more impressive. While the title of the world's densest country might not seem very meaningful, comparisons as an urban entity are all too revealing. The country-wide population is respectively three times and eight times denser than its neighbouring French

In the daytime, the elevator of the Patio Palace can be used by the public in order to reach the city's heights. The development can be exited on the upper level and is connected to the street.

cities Nice and Menton, and stands at a similar level to the predominantly flat French capital Paris (20,800 inhabitants per square kilometre).

URBAN CONFIGURATION

Exploiting the benefits of high-rise to accommodate the predominantly non-Monegasque population has been modestly but increasingly applied since the 1950s. Previously, the architectural image of the city had principally been determined by the Belle-Epoque style and a height of usually not more than three storeys. From the 1940s the influential French architect and urbanist Eugène Beaudouin had formalised the aforementioned naturally occurring amphitheatre as a conceptual basis and guiding line for the future development of the city and its tall buildings. Beaudouin was a pioneer of French high-rise construction, and had planned together with Marcel Lods the Cité de la Muette in Drancy (1931–4). Among many other milestones, at the end of the 1950s he was also appointed masterplanner of the Maine-Montparnasse area in Paris, best known for the tower that is still France's tallest. The amphitheatre concept manipulated the impact of high-rise to encircle and frame the small country through positioning towers along its boundaries. This vision, however, underestimated the dynamics and pressure of the real estate market, and over the years a growing number of derogations have been implemented. The scheme also oversimplified the Principality's relief, and its surprisingly rich urban diversity which has filled up the total land area as a densely urbanised zone since the late 1980s, including land reclamations and several publicly-owned amenities in the neighbouring French districts.

The effect of the hilly slopes is to massively accentuate the visual expression of high-rise in Monaco. Seen from the port, the multitude of facades merge together, and distinguishing between towers and low-rise structures is not easy. The slope influences this perception, however, not only directly through its own verticality, but also indirectly through the winding shape of the streets and the consequently 'arbitrary' position of the constructions. Such an urban setting bears parallels with the Mid-levels on Hong Kong Island and can be seen as the counterpoint of a completely orthogonal setting like Manhattan or the linear Sheikh Zayed Road in Dubai (see page 104). In the other direction, from the Moyenne or Haute Corniche, the Riviera's most famous mountain road, the view is less obstructed and reveals more easily the silhouette of the city's relatively few skyscrapers.

Another particularity of Monaco is its vast network of public elevators and external stairs and escalators.

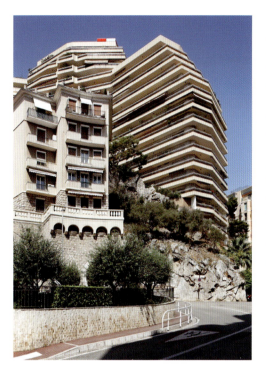

LEFT: The eclectic architectural mix is also a consequence of the Principality's complex geography.

BELOW: A photomontage of the Odeon Tower by Alexandre Giraldi in the Annonciade district. It is currently under construction and is, like the neighbouring round-shaped Château Périgord from 1972, a tower-on-podium development.

The density of construction, the city's wealth and its high safety levels, have expedited these combined public and private initiatives to minimise pedestrian efforts for the ascent of the city's heights. The upshot, spatially speaking, of this multiplication of contorted walkways, passages and bridges is an intriguing relativisation of the ground level and the emergence of a parallel urban world, emphasised through the extensive existence of multi-level and multi-connected

underground car parks. Symbolic of and embracing the Principality's 'urban madness', this phenomenon is part of the flagrant collage of architectural styles, set in naturally impressive and charismatic surroundings. Monaco is also the only example in this book in which the verticality of the tower seems directly related to, if not mirrored by, the verticality of the underground developments and their multiple connectivity. The sheer existence of a parallel pedestrian network, underneath

or above street level, is however not unique: in some respects it is reminiscent of Hong Kong and its famous Central-Mid-levels escalator, in a similar urban context, but also – and in a far more figurative way – of Houston, Texas and its underground tunnel system (see page 146).

ARCHITECTURE

Despite the city's high density and due to the arbitrary structure of winding mountain streets, at least in its upper parts, high-rise architecture in Monaco still expresses a comparatively non-urban character. This has to do with the ubiquity of the sea and the surrounding mountains, but is also linked to the fact that the landscapes of coastal cliffs inhibit the emergence of continuous perimeter developments in which the building visually and functionally merges with the urban block. Each tower design implements a specific solution for its specific natural situation, but the repetitive topic of the steep slope still suggests the emergence of something that could be perceived as a type, at least in section. In reaction to obvious light and view issues to the back and towards the rock wall, the building mass cannot simply cover the whole site surface as a monolithic structure. One solution is the construction of a level-compensative podium underneath the actual tower, exemplified by the 1960s Château Périgord and the future Odeon Tower. This low-rise and mono-oriented element will hardly be attractive for residential uses, and does usually contain car parks, restaurants and shops, with the lobby on its top as unifying element between the vertical and horizontal geometries. Another solution consists of excavating the site to its lower level, and positioning the building on the street-fronting edge. The section of the Patio Palace highlights this formally more modest strategy, with a courtyard-like space to the back. Seen from the top, the 16-storey entrenched development appears only four full storeys above street level.

As has already been mentioned, the general variety of architectural styles in the Principality is abundant, with a still-prevailing predominance of Belle-Epoque elements. Compared with an inland city of similar size, Monaco adds the notion of resort architecture as an important component, often copying in a more or less fortunate way the colour scheme and some architectural details of the earlier and more vernacular buildings.

SUMMARY

This book features many examples in which high-rise appears not as a necessity, but rather as a branding tool that is meant to express the overflowing ambitions of a developer, a multi-national company or a city: high-rise is the aim, and it is as crucial for the programme as it is

LEFT: Public stairs and escalators in the centre of Monaco.

BELOW LEFT: Over time, the combination of density, wealth and extraordinary natural setting have produced a highly unusual cityscape.

OPPOSITE: View of Monaco and its towers from the neighbouring French municipality of Roquebrune-Cap-Martin. The *Rocher* as the origin of the city can be seen in the background.

for the cost-effective structural solution to make it economically viable. The irony of Monaco is that despite building a reputation for ambition and grandeur, the reverse holds true. 'Naturally glamorous', spoilt by its geographic setting, and arguably over- or mis-branded through its status as tax haven, the city is not in need of high-rise as an expression of its aspirations. To a certain extent, it could even be claimed that high-rise, and its symbolism as component of a generic city, is quite opposed to the picturesque cliché of a resort on the prestigious Côte d'Azur. As a peculiar and fascinating mixture of Hong Kong, Benidorm and Saint Tropez, the Principality adopts the tall building quite successfully as a means to an end: the increase of density, caused by the impossibility of horizontal expansion. Another intriguing consequence of these constraints is the

emergence of genuinely hybrid buildings, in some cases including light industrial uses. Mid- rather than high-rise, they mark the counterpoint of the Modernist vision of a city with functional separation.

Relativised by its exceptional geography and wealth, the Principality appears therefore as a testing ground and model for a similar development that will arguably be followed by many other agglomerations around the world, currently still increasing their footprint on greenfield land.

Urban plan 1:2500

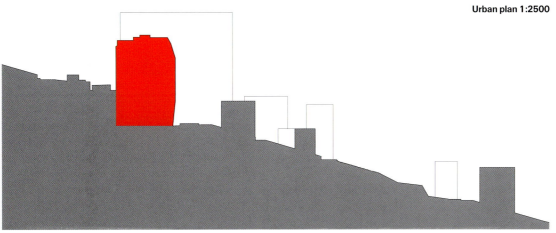

Urban section 1:2500

Lujiazui

VERTICAL CITIES: CITY OF MONUMENTS
LOCATION: PUDONG, SHANGHAI, CHINA
DATE: 1990 ONWARDS

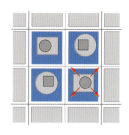

Probably the most ostentatious urban expression of China's rise to megapower, the business district of Lujiazui brings together in a comparatively small area some of Asia's most impressive high-rise architecture.

Typological group: Vertical Cities – city of monuments
Estimated site coverage (as seen on urban plan):
28%
Estimated plot ratio (as seen on urban plan):
13.97

HISTORY / DEVELOPMENT PROCESS

The background of this ambitious project is linked to the creation in 1990 of Pudong New Area as a national-level special economic zone. The Lujiazui Central Finance District is its most prominent and spectacular part, mainland China's new financial hub and the seat of already over 80 financial institutions. Over half of those are of foreign origin, reviving Shanghai's glorious past as an open place and Eastern melting pot, though under politically very different circumstances compared with the foreign occupation and colonial situation after defeat in the First Opium War in 1842. Physical incarnations of China's past and present stand directly opposite each other: the Bund area's majestic facades on the western bank of the Huangpu river, and the new towers on the eastern shore, the Pudong Peninsula. Initial urban proposals were developed in 1991 by the Shanghai Urban Planning and Design Institute, but the Mayor of Shanghai – aware of the scheme's symbolic importance – instituted in the same year after a trip to La Défense near Paris an international ideas consultation, supported by the Institut d'Aménagement et d'Urbanisme de la Région d'Île de France (IAURIF). Teams from Britain (Richard Rogers), France (Dominique Perrault), Italy (Massimiliano Fuksas), Japan (Toyo Ito) and China itself (a collaboration between the Shanghai

A photomontage of the future triumvirate, with Gensler's Shanghai Tower (right) currently under construction. The three super-tall buildings are the central component of Lujiazui's masterplan. The World Financial Center by KPF (left) and the Jin Mao Tower by SOM (centre) are already built.

Urban Planning & Design Institute and Tongji University) were invited and submitted proposals which would through their extensive publication be revealed as very efficient marketing tools. Richard Rogers Partnership's scheme won, but the following revision through a Chinese team, and the development of three further proposals based on combined elements of all entries, finally led to the official appointment of a masterplan which was actually fairly close to the initial Chinese scheme. Major modifications included the inclusion of a park and the abandonment of several podium elements.

Lujiazui's international claim does not only relate to the economic activities of the new towers' occupants, but also to their construction and ownership. In 2000, 23 out of 31 buildings were at least co-financed by foreign investors, 10 were completely foreign-funded, and 26 were designed by foreign architects. The commitment is worthwhile and the city has attracted foreign real estate investment through heavy tax incentives and occasionally through the exemption of import taxes for construction materials. In this context it might be said that since the late 1980s China's economic reform has led to a decisive change in the financing of the city budget. Previously, the budget was mainly subsidised by extractions from state firms; now it

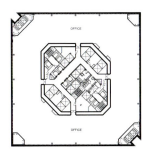

1:1250 typical floor plan of Kohn Pedersen Fox's World Financial Center.

The Lujiazui Financial District at the tip of the Pudong Peninsula.

is based on the sale of leaseholds to private companies which were formerly free of charge.

URBAN CONFIGURATION

It takes some time to realise why La Défense is, at least from this book's selection, indeed the most comparable example to Lujiazui. This has to do with the fact that there is a notion of a grand urban form which is neither directly related to the geography of the place nor to any specific infrastructural element. If American downtowns are systems in which the final shape depends on decisions taken by the developers of each plot, Lujiazui and La Défense are classic tabula-rasa masterplans and very controlled designs: the French example is based on an axis and a central space on a pedestrian podium, the Chinese one defines a green space and three super-tall towers as urban nucleus. A triangular belt of tall buildings circumscribes this space, but does not shield or ignore the relationship with Pudong's geography. In the form of a double row, it manages to relate to the new centre of Pudong as much as to the history-charged Bund on Shanghai's western side. In doing so the planners creatively solved one of the potential problems of Richard Rogers Partnership's winning scheme that seemed to turn its back on the historic centre. The connection in the other direction, with Pudong's hinterland and Century Park, is assured through Century Avenue, a five-kilometre-long mixture between a boulevard and a motorway, designed by French architects Arte Charpentier. The newly created street network is a non-orthogonal and very wide-meshed grid whose shape is strongly influenced by the peninsula's curve. Interestingly, this masterplanned though fairly pragmatic street network is in terms of shape and size not that different from the one of the territory of the former foreign concessions – outside

the historic old town – where large urban blocks had been designated as the simplest way to subdivide land. The obvious difference between the colonial and the new Shanghai is therefore not the shape of the urban grid or the large-scale development approach, but the fact that the historical blocks have been built over with low-rise residential *lilongs* as perimeter block developments, and the new ones primarily with single office towers. The equation of a block with a plot of single (leasehold) ownership as such is hence not new, and was in the historic case linked to the specific legal and social conditions of the explosively growing foreign concessions. In their home countries, the occupying powers would usually have been obliged to respect a smaller-scale development logic, based on the historically grown plot structure and ownership pattern.

ARCHITECTURE

The monumental impression created by Pudong's towers is reflected through their central position on the building plots, and the consequent possibility of admiring them in their entirety from all directions.

CLOCKWISE FROM TOP LEFT: The base of KPF's World Financial Center, developed by the Mori Group (see also Roppongi Hills, page 120).

View from the river promenade to the southeast of Pudong.

The river promenade with the towers of the Puxi district in the left-hand background.

As mentioned above, these plots often cover the whole block and have street access on all sides. This is consistently the case for the largest towers, and contributes to the simplicity of the urban grain and a certain lack of spatial complexity. Depending on the dimensions of the plot and the development programme, the relation of the towers to the block perimeter varies, but in general it steps back from the street and gathers lower building appendixes, green areas and car parks around it. This not unusual relationship to the surroundings, together with the sheer amount of super-tall structures, is in the context of this book reminiscent of the Nishi-Shinjuku masterplan in Tokyo (see Tokyo Metropolitan Government Building, page 64). A major difference is, however, the fact that Shinjuku has been conceived on the basis of an abstract and strictly orthogonal grid and not a designed urban form with a clear formal designation of different zones.

This mixture of a picturesque, if not Beaux-Arts-inspired grand urban form, typical for many ongoing projects all over the world, with the recess from the street and the provision of plot sizes that correspond to contemporary corporate needs, therefore supersedes the traditional subdivision logic of blocks into numerous single plots. The result is something like a super-sized modern garden city, in which the monumental visual impact of the built masses scribed on the city's skyline as an element of great symbolic importance is at least as important as the quality of the street space as such. Consequently, a certain tension between global aspirations and urban ambitions is all too tangible. The pragmatic construct does, however, provide a lot of advantages, and eliminates some of the problems that the few comparable 'vertical cities' in this book feature: the legal and formal problems of the podium are avoided, there are no party walls and therefore no issues of light and air, the relation to the soil is simple and clear, and the urban configuration allows a certain flexibility and robustness.

SUMMARY
Despite the lack of a strong – let alone avant-garde – concept, Lujiazui has something fascinatingly simple about it. An obvious advantage, unrelated to the urban and architectural details discussed above, is its situation opposite the Bund, and the fact that it has considerably changed the geography and image of a city that historically evolved essentially on the western shore of the river. While many Asian cities have experienced a similar growth and urban development over the last two decades, very few have had the opportunity to use their natural features to reinvent their skyline and create a completely new urban dynamic.

In relationship to its actual shape and fabric, the collage technique of several urban principles turns out to be rather successful, if one acknowledges the fact that the deliberate monumentalisation of freestanding high-rise objects cannot remain without occasionally intimidating consequences on the surrounding environment and pedestrian realm. Hand in hand with this goes a certain amorphous character which relies on the undefined position of the towers on their plots and towards the street, and the exaggerated width of these streets. In terms of activities the concept is fairly 'conservative' in the sense that the mix of uses is limited. It exists mainly through hotels, some luxury apartments and shopping malls, but essentially copies

OPPOSITE: View from the World Financial Center towards the river.

BELOW: View from the river promenade of the Mirae Asset Tower by Kohn Pedersen Fox (left) and the Aurora Plaza (right) by Nikken Sekkei.

a model that can be found in several central business districts around the world. The explicitly corporate character stands in contrast to the proposals by some of the participants in the 1992 consultation – especially those by Dominique Perrault and Toyo Ito – who tried to put forward alternative concepts in which corporate high-rise would be juxtaposed with a much smaller architectural scale that suggested different uses and development structures. In the event, this issue too is moderated through Pudong's advantageous geography as a peninsula, the large amount of green space and the generosity of the riverfront promenade. The whole western tip of the peninsula is therefore perceived and extensively used as an outdoor leisure zone, brilliantly symbolised by the playful architecture of the Oriental Pearl Tower.

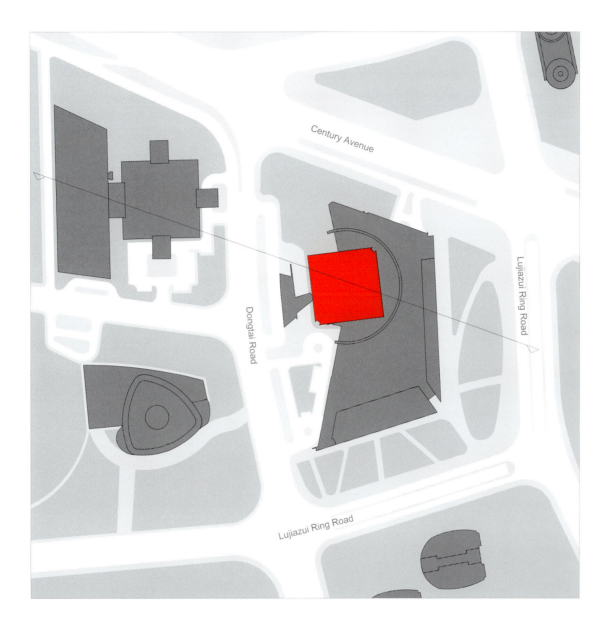

Century Avenue

Dongtai Road

Lujiazui Ring Road

Lujiazui Ring Road

Urban plan 1:2500

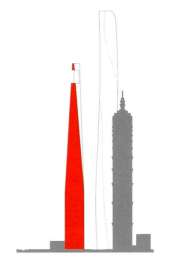

Urban section 1:10000

La Défense

VERTICAL CITIES: EUROPEAN CBD
LOCATION: COURBEVOIE / PUTEAUX / NANTERRE, PARIS OUTSKIRTS, FRANCE
DATE: 1958 ONWARDS
MASTERPLANNER: ROBERT CAMELOT, JEAN DE MAILLY, BERNARD ZEHRFUSS
CLIENT: EPADESA (FORMERLY EPAD)

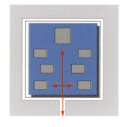

Typological group: Vertical
Cities – European CBD
Estimated site coverage
(as seen on urban plan):
24%
Estimated plot ratio
(as seen on urban plan):
2.39

At first glance, La Défense – Europe's largest business district – appears, through its axiality and the symmetry of its ring roads, to be a city that originates right from the drawing board. In reality, its history is far more complex and it has followed over the last 50 years a gradual development process that is still ongoing.

HISTORY / DEVELOPMENT PROCESS

Key to the understanding of the site's importance is its position on an important axis, the 'royal' connection of the Louvre as historic centre of power with the chateau and forest of Saint-Germain-en-Laye to the west of Paris. The central parts of this axis were prominently formalised through André Le Nôtre's 16th-century Tuileries Gardens and later the Champs-Elysées, but also the area outside the city core, situated in Nanterre, was gradually developed and a roundabout of generous size mirrored the Etoile – the site of the Arc de Triomphe – from the late 18th century. At the end of the 19th century, the neighbourhood was known for its aviation and automobile industry, and already accommodated

a fairly dense tissue of housing and industrial uses in the direct vicinity of the roundabout. The name 'La Défense' refers to the defence of Paris in the war of 1870 against Prussia, and in 1878 an eponymous monument substituted an earlier statue of Napoleon Bonaparte in the middle of the roundabout. The elevated position of this section of the axis, gradually rising from the river's shore, made it a scenic spot and predestined its future development. Additional advantages were the relative proximity to the centre as much as to the noble western suburbs of Neuilly, Versailles and Saint-Germain-en-Laye.

For a long time the public authorities had sensed the potential for a grander development, but were not clear about its nature, partly due to the financial instability as a consequence of the two world wars. Several initiatives and competitions were organised for parts or all of the axis, but a built result followed only after the Second World War, in 1958, with the construction of the CNIT (Centre des Nouvelles Industries et Technologies), an exhibition space and a technical tour de force with the largest concrete span of its time. Privately initiated, the project had been implemented in conjunction with the authorities, and eventually led to the development of an ambitious urban proposal by the same architects as those of the CNIT: Zehrfuss, Camelot and de Mailly. Even though this project already included some elements that would be realised only much later, it would be an exaggeration to see it as a blueprint of the later development: it did not feature, for example, a continuous podium, and – with the exception of a super-high-rise opposite the CNIT – was not based on a tower typology. However, the starting point had been made, and in 1958 a public development company was founded, with the initial remit to develop the area over the next 30 years. The national rather than communal or mixed status of this company (see for comparison Front de Seine (page 136) and Masséna (page 80)) is not unique but is rather unusual, and the main reason for its foundation has to do with issues of expropriation and political accountability. Approximately 20,000 people had to be moved, an undertaking that was impossible without the legal tools of public intervention, but neither of the local electors was inclined to take the political responsibility for this. The national and superordinated status of EPAD (Etablissement Public pour l'Aménagement de la Région de La Défense) solved this issue. Another detail of paramount importance for the constant renewal of La Défense is its financial and organisational logic: despite its public status, its only income consists of the sale of development rights, and it therefore auto-generates its continuing redevelopment. This includes the gradual

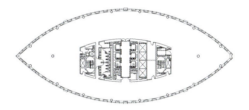

1:1250 typical floor plan of the EDF Tower by Pei Cobb Freed & Partners.

La Défense seen from Neuilly, with Johan Otto von Spreckelsen's Grande Arche as the main focus and determining architectural feature.

increase of maximum building heights, and has recently caused the emergence of several redevelopment projects in which former high-rise structures are torn down in favour of taller and technically and ecologically more advanced towers. Arquitectonica's Tour AIR2 (see page 184) is one of these examples which document the growing attractiveness of the district. The gradual rise of total development rights also explains the increasing specialisation as a business district. Initially, the mix of uses was quite balanced, but financial needs and the market's demands eventually suggested the construction of more office rather than residential space.

URBAN CONFIGURATION

The construction of a podium of formerly unknown dimensions, approved in 1964, has two major reasons. One of them is a practical consequence of the vertical layering of functions and traffic flows, and inspired by the Modernists' ideals as propagated by CIAM and the Athens Charter. Potentially more specific in the case of La Défense is the role that the podium plays in respect of the monumental east–west axis. Interestingly, the

LEFT: The central pedestrian space seen from the steps of the Grande Arche de La Défense. The CNIT on the left, built in 1958 by Bernard Zehrfuss, Robert Camelot and Jean de Mailly, was the starting point of the district.

podium in conjunction with the circular ring roads enables the retention of the axis as a pedestrian central element. It has therefore been stated that the urban configuration applied for the La Défense extremity of the axis actually resembles its very beginning, where the Tuileries Gardens as green and pedestrian heart are evenly doubled by the Rue de Rivoli and the Quais as parallel circulation spaces. This feature, in conjunction with the symmetrical composition of the podium's central space, explains why La Défense has been interpreted as a combination of the French Beaux-Arts tradition and Modernism, rather than a radical break with urban history. The Front de Seine example (see page 136) is to this extent, and despite its smaller size, a more intransigent scheme.

Equally intriguing, but socially and politically problematic at times, is the analysis of the district's relation to its surroundings and its often-stated perception as an alien implant. Historically, La Défense was seen as the very beginning of an integrated planning strategy for the Parisian agglomeration, and can therefore hardly be dismissed as an ill-considered outcome of purely economic considerations and the need for larger floor plates. During the following planning process and the gradual application of a specific set of urban paradigms – most prominently

including the podium and the circular boulevards – the physical result of the new district has, however, revealed several weaknesses, predominantly in terms of radial connections. The Tour Dexia (see page 79) and the Tour AIR2 project highlight these issues and present the efforts at finding a solution which are supported by ongoing heavy works for the 'domestication' and down-scaling of the circular boulevard.

Of crucial importance for the historical development of La Défense, and the major ecological argument for its future extension, is its excellent connection to the regional network of public transport. The extension of the number one metro line had already been envisaged in 1956, and incrementally it has been backed up by trains, buses, trams and, most efficiently, the RER network of regional trains. As a result of this, and even more so since the connection of an additional RER line, the car parks in the podium are frequently underutilised.

ARCHITECTURE

There are two major ways in which high-rise in La Défense relates to its surroundings. Those which are positioned above the podium mostly hit the ground as point-towers in the simplest way and without any attachments or expansions on the base. Tour Areva and Tour EDF are good examples of this, and contribute

OPPOSITE FROM TOP: The combination of the podium urbanism with a dense network of traffic arteries leads to unusual spatial situations along the podium's edges.

An apartment building from 1969 by Robert Camelot and Jean-Claude Finelli. Between then and now, the percentage of residential uses has gradually decreased through the intensification of office developments.

Typical for La Défense's expansion, the 'Les Miroirs' building by Henri La Fonta, built in 1981, functions as an extension of the initial podium and connects to it via a pedestrian bridge.

through their simple and almost abstract aesthetics
to the monumental character of the podium's central
part. The relation of the towers which are positioned
somewhere along the edge of the podium is slightly
more complex, and they often have to cope with three
or more levels: podium, circular ring road, parking level
and to-grade surroundings (see Tour Dexia, page 79).
Even the developments which have been built outside
La Défense's actual territory mostly relate to the podium
and its various amenities through a pedestrian bridge
over the ring road, and are revealing features of its
centralised character.

From a purely architectural and stylistic point of view
the towers are, due to the long development history of
La Défense, quite varied and cannot be attributed to a
single group. However, the monumental character of
the above-podium space certainly had an impact on
the architects, and modern monolithic simplicity seems
to be a common denominator. The actual plan layout
of the towers is strongly influenced by France's strict
fire-safety rules for IGH (*immeubles de grande hauteur*
– 'buildings of great height') which, unlike most featured
examples in this book, are not performance-based,
meaning that specific rules have to be followed rather
than an overall performance demonstrated.

In recent years, efforts have been made to adjust
these rules to the demands of more sustainable
constructions. As the French HQE label (*haute qualité
environnementale*) tends to focus on the ecology of
construction materials rather than on the minimisation
of energy consumption, all new towers in La Défense
also have to be LEED™ certified, a unique demand
among the leading business districts.

SUMMARY

This book focuses on typological solutions for high-rise
architecture, acknowledging the fact that height as such
is not a typology. In respect of urban continuity we are
especially interested in systems that allow a gradual
growth and typological readjustment on the basis of
persisting circulation networks, Manhattan remaining
probably the most impressive and extensively studied
example of that kind.

La Défense highlights a radically different strategy:
spatial separation and typological reinvention rather
than inclusion and adjustment. And it could indeed be
claimed that inner Paris's acclaimed urban landscape
of perimeter blocks with an extensive mix of uses would
not have survived the inclusion, even behind traditional
facades, of millions of square metres of additional office
space. Many European cities have followed a similar
model, with Canary Wharf in London, AZCA in Madrid
and Moscow City as prominent examples. Interestingly,

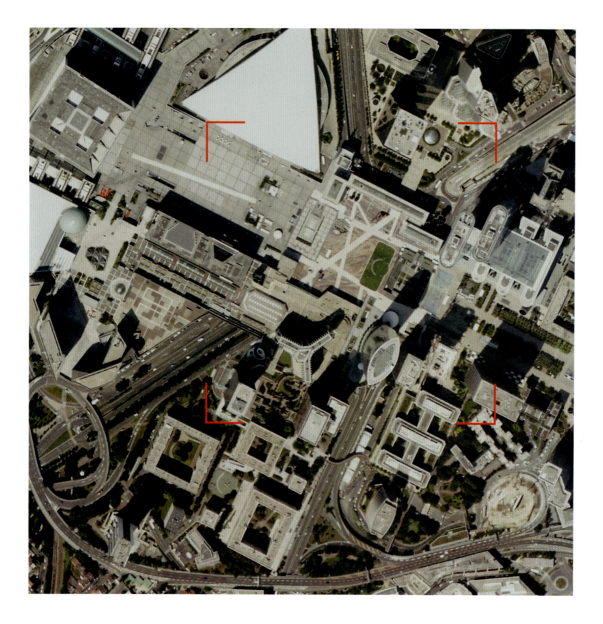

all these far more recent projects share podium features, and in doing so suggest that the French archetype was not only the result of an alleged Modernist fascination with slightly twisted urban novelties, but also and in the first place a particularly rigorous answer to apparently repetitive functional requirements. The beauty and at the same time difficulty of La Défense is its incomparable legibility as an urban entity in itself, but also – through the 'royal and triumphant axis' – as an element of an enormous metropolitan agglomeration. The political merger with its western hinterland, administered since November 2010 under the new name EPADESA (Etablissement Public d'Aménagement de La Défense Seine Arche), seems to be a symbol for the fact that this distinction cannot eternally be based on spatial separation.

La Défense, in spite or arguably because of its specific national status, can therefore be seen as an early reference for the recent and ongoing discussion about 'Le Grand Paris' which tries to better synchronise the development of the self-governed inner-city core of only 2.3 million inhabitants with its urban agglomeration of approximately 10 million inhabitants, partitioned into four separate political entities (*départements*). The obvious parallel between the Boulevard Périphérique and the Boulevard Circulaire as respective spatial and political boundaries of the city of Paris and La Défense appears as a symbol for the complexity of such an undertaking which has to happen within the constraints of political, economic, social, but also physical considerations and pressures.

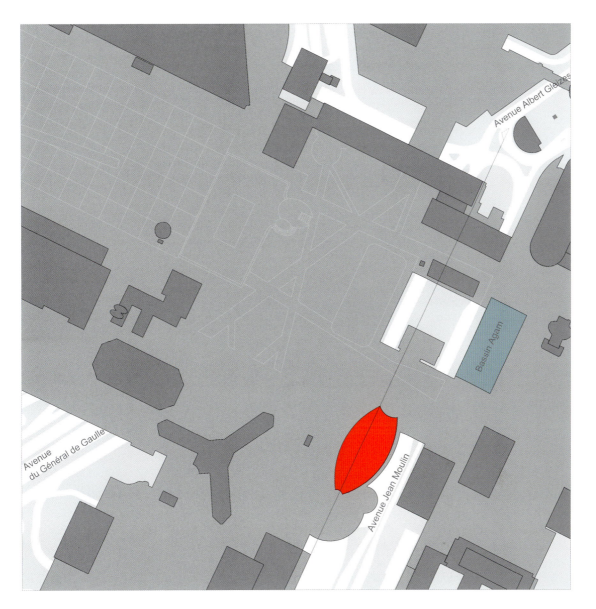

Urban plan 1:2500

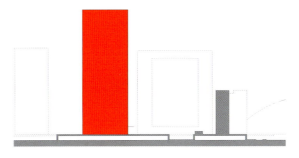

Urban section 1:5000

LA DÉFENSE RENEWAL PLAN (EXAMPLE OF TOUR AIR2)

LOCATION: LA DÉFENSE, PARIS OUTSKIRTS, FRANCE
DATE: SCHEDULED FOR COMPLETION IN 2015
ARCHITECTS: ARQUITECTONICA

Part of the La Défense business district's ambitious renewal plan and its strategy for further vertical growth, Arquitectonica's 220-metre-tall Tour AIR2 will supersede the existing 110-metre-tall Tour Aurore. Built in 1970 as one of La Défense's first-generation towers, Tour Aurore's dated interior configuration and limited ceiling heights made destruction and new-build preferable to renovation. It is an alternative development approach compared with Tour 9 in Montreuil (see page 143), developed by the same investor, The Carlyle Group. A much-needed by-product of this heavy intervention is the opportunity to redefine the tower's poor relation to the ground and the adjacent border of the podium. Trying to tackle the issue of spatial separation through the hard edge along the Boulevard

Circulaire, the new scheme's glazed lobby extends over three levels, the upper one of the podium and the lower one of the Boulevard and northern surroundings. The project also involves the construction of an exterior flight of stairs, further improving connectivity with the surrounding communities. In conjunction with similar interventions and the one undertaken for the replacement of the adjacent Veritas Building by the Tour D2, the project contributes with modest and efficient measures to the gradual opening and extension of Europe's largest business district. Historically, the built structures were solely fixed on their relationship with the central space and the strategic axis, eventually turning their back on the local surroundings.

ABOVE: Tour AIR2 as a projected component of La Défense's skyline.

RIGHT: Visualisation of the tower's three-level lobby, improving the connectivity between La Défense's central podium and its surroundings.

FAR RIGHT: View down the historic axis, with Arquitectonica's projected Tour AIR2 to the left.

Two other examples of the business district's ambitious renewal and extension programme: Foster + Partners' predominantly residential Hermitage Plaza and Manuelle Gautrand's Tour AVA.

Hong Kong Waterfront

VERTICAL CITIES: CITY OF MEGASTRUCTURES
LOCATION: HONG KONG, CHINA
DATE: 1997 ONWARDS

As one of the very few genuine high-rise cities in the world, Hong Kong combines the tower typology with an overall extremely high density. Over the last 30 years, a local development type of tower-on-podium megastructures has gradually evolved, initially applied for mainly residential purposes, but more recently also for the waterfront and Hong Kong Island's major business district.

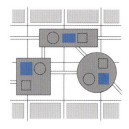

Typological group: Vertical Cities – city of megastructures
Estimated site coverage (as seen on urban plan): 52%
Estimated plot ratio (as seen on urban plan): 7.28

HISTORY / DEVELOPMENT PROCESS

Since its forced establishment as a major colonial trading point by the British in 1841, Hong Kong's spectacular and highly flexible development has attracted a level of mass immigration that it almost constantly had problems to accommodate in decent and healthy living conditions. The pressure of population influxes, the characteristic efficiency of the natives, and the low level of competition due to only a handful of large local development companies, have led to a very specific architectural culture that is often referred to as a 'quantitative approach'. This does not, however, question the rather spectacular and often breathtaking results that many people identify with urban scenes from movies like *Blade Runner* or *Ghost in the Shell*. Another idiosyncrasy of great importance for the city's unique development history is the

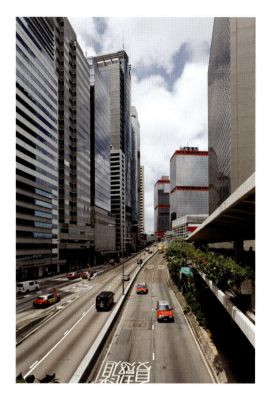

importation of the British free- and leasehold system, in which all land will eventually return to ownership of the city government. While this system is not unique to Hong Kong, due to its history and peculiarities it has had a decisive impact on the development of the city, particularly as real estate represents a major source of income for the government. This situation, that arguably creates a certain conflict of interest in terms of land regulation and policies, has not changed significantly since the return of Hong Kong to China in 1997. China also has a similar system in which the state keeps long-term ownership of all land, but the difference is that the leasehold sales did not historically have the same importance for the city finances.

URBAN CONFIGURATION

A brief look at a map or aerial photograph reveals the fact that there are at least three different development types for high-rise construction in Hong Kong.

The first and oldest type is still based on the initial land subdivision strategy in which geometric plots were designed for party-wall construction of low-rise tenement buildings along the historic waterfront of Hong Kong Island. Queen's Road is the oldest example, but roughly the same system was replicated for several stages of land reclamation to the north, gradually diminishing the size of Victoria Harbour. With time these plots have been constantly redeveloped and

the buildings gained in height, a process comparable to Manhattan, though on a narrower and less repetitive geometrical scale.

A second type can be found to the south, and is directly related to the city's spectacular topography and steep slopes. This is demonstrated by the example of freestanding towers, but which are often connected to their neighbours through the towers' bases. These predominantly residential constructions follow the winding streets reaching up to Victoria Peak, and are typologically not unlike developments in a similar extreme environment – like, for example, Monaco (see page 162) – where excessively high land prices make such costly construction worthwhile.

The third and most recent type, the tower-on-podium superstructures, are closely linked to the land reclamation strategy of the last 15 years (see below), but find their origin earlier in large-scale public and private residential developments like Tsuen Wan New Town in the New Territories or Whampoa Garden on the southeastern

CLOCKWISE FROM TOP LEFT: View down Connaught Road to the west, with the International Finance Centre to the right and the twin towers of the Shun Tak Centre in the background.

Pedestrian bridge leading over Connaught Road to the International Finance Centre (IFC).

Reclamation works to the east of the International Finance Centre for the new waterfront of Hong Kong Island.

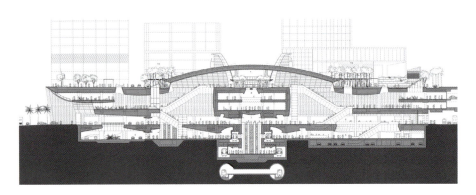

BELOW: Kowloon Station development has been built on reclaimed land and is motivated by the construction of a new metro line leading from Hong Kong station to the new Chek Lap Kok Airport.

Section through the base of the Kowloon Station development, masterplanned by Terry Farrell & Partners.

tip of the Kowloon Peninsula. Comparable to several Modernist European examples (see Paris's Front de Seine (page 136) or La Défense (page 178)), the vertical stacking of functions and movements has been adopted as an urban solution that, more appropriately than anywhere else, seemed to accommodate the complex demands of an overly dense environment. The city supported the development of the podium type in allowing 100 per cent plot coverage for the first 15 to 20 metres of new constructions, and therefore enabled the provision of generous retail and parking surfaces. New elevated pedestrian linkages were also encouraged by the city to ease traffic problems through the uninterrupted flow of cars underneath the pedestrian bridges.

ARCHITECTURE

The most interesting evolution of the tower-on-podium type has been its establishment as a megastructure for which the spheres of architecture gradually merge with the urban form, eventually losing the relation to any noticeable cadastral logic. Two specific points have had great impact on this tendency. From a financial point of view, the tower-on-podium type has become the ever-replicated typological solution for the development above the new stations of the train and metro network. In a typical case, the city government grants the above-station development rights to the formerly public, but now privatised railway company MTR in order to minimise its own financial involvement in the construction and maintenance of the network. In a following step, MTR sells subleases to one or several of the local real estate conglomerates. A second, rather more spatial and approximate influence is arguably based on Hong Kong's history of constant land reclamation which began in 1861, only 20 years after the annexation by the British. The artificial creation of large pieces of land and the application of an increasingly large-scale planning and subdivision attitude seems in the last two decades to have gone along with a separation from the formerly over-dense, but coherent urban tissue of perimeter blocks and small-scale plots.

The International Finance Centre (IFC) and the Kowloon Station scheme are good examples of the interplay between these financial and spatial constraints,

The elevated and privatised inner courtyard of a predominantly residential superstructure south of Lai Chi Kok station in Kowloon. The base of the development contains a large shopping mall.

Whampoa Garden in Kowloon, finished in 1991, was one of the earliest large-scale podium developments. It contains over 10,000 private apartments.

and establish a completely new urban paradigm in which the link with the direct neighbourhood relies on an extensive network of pedestrian bridges rather than on a more traditional network of pavements and to-grade public spaces. This paradigm is particularly apparent for the interconnected megastructures along the new waterfront, with the IFC as its most western element, which indeed sit like enormous boats on a shallow layer of reclaimed land, but it has also been replicated in places like Tseung Kwan O New Town or inland Lai Chi Kok. The generally high quality of these constructions, an outright mix of functions, Hong Kong's excessive density levels and buying power, and a clear separation of public and private spaces, have yet prevented problems arising that podium developments have previously produced in other places in the world. In the longer term, taken to the extreme, it might however be questioned if elevated connections and essentially privatised space will be able to replace streets and squares as major constituents of the urban network, especially if linear structures like the Waterfront grow into three-dimensional neighbourhoods through the addition of a similar row of megastructures.

In this respect it is intriguing to realise that this superstructure type, as one of the few genuine tower typologies of our times, represents simultaneously one of the most exceptional and extraordinary cases in this book, while the definition of a type and the idea of repetition might yet suggest the opposite. It is therefore the 'domesticated' and mainly residential version of the tower-on-podium configuration that has attracted more notice and has been widely exported, often with the support of the planning authorities in view of an inner-city revival. One of the most famous and influential examples, Li Ka-Shing's False Creek development on Vancouver's former Expo site, even originates directly from a Hong Kong investor. The highly flexible model of slender towers on low podiums – applicable in almost all types of urban fabric – has since been built in many places around the world, transposing the Asian experience and acceptance of high-rise living, but in the end also Hong Kong's building regulations which stand at the origin of this specific spatial arrangement. Variations of the same type – which seems to have ultimately superseded the slab as most replicated model of mass housing – also include the projects in Dubai (see Jumeirah Beach Residences, page 142) and Miami (see Icon Brickell, page 119).

SUMMARY

Many ingredients of the 'perfect high-rise city' can be found in Hong Kong: true density of the built mass, and this in direct relation to the protection of green areas outside the city core; a high level of mixed-use developments; and the almost perfect connection of the buildings to the highly efficient public transport network. The queen of the mighty Pearl River Delta

A tower-on-podium
example from Vancouver,
financed by Hong Kong
investors. Despite its
Chinese influences, the
base with its townhouses
is not typical of the
developments in Hong
Kong.

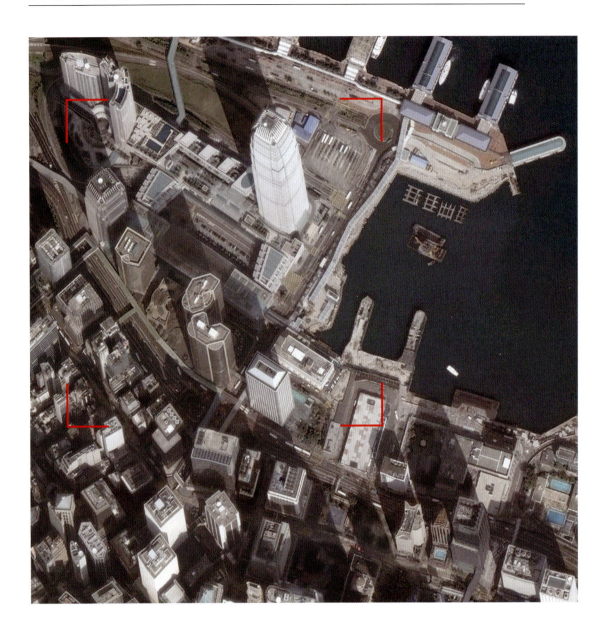

demonstrates a winning hand in the rational use of the tower typology and the – in many other places rather theoretical – deliverance of high densities.

However, in addition to some of the aforementioned reservations regarding the long-term robustness of its boldest outgrowths, Hong Kong and its extreme commercial as much as residential density levels cannot only and blindly be seen as a sustainable model to follow. In the USA and Europe, the urban sprawl and an altered demographic development over recent decades have actually led to a justifiable quest for higher densities, and the assumption that this rise of density can be accomplished through new typological inventions in high-rise architecture is one of the starting points of this book. The case of Hong Kong shows, however, that there still is a (relative) limit, and a

potential further increase will have to be sustained by new typological visions. As one recent example, the tower-wall effect of the new residential developments, created through the linear juxtaposition of towers of 40 storeys or more, has repeatedly been suspected to have a negative impact on the city's ventilation and climate, and for some is – at least symbolically – reminiscent of the sanitary problems that many industrial cities experienced at the end of the 19th century due to the constant influx of new workers.

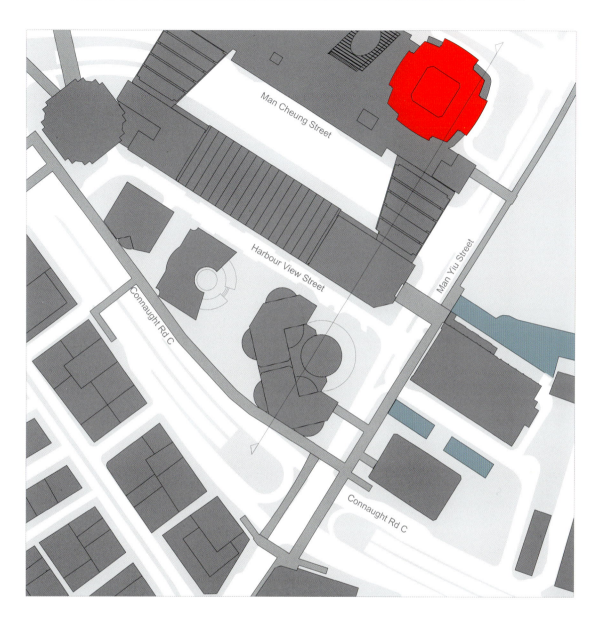

Urban plan 1:2500

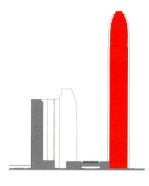

Urban section 1:10000

High-rise building regulations in seven cities worldwide

London

As a political entity, London gets actively involved in the implementation and reassessment of town planning documents that are designed to regulate and optimise the construction of tall buildings. Implementation occurs through an accumulation of bureaucratic layers, which enables private interests and pursuits to fall in line with the city's overarching urban strategy. The high-rise typology is perceived as just one of many tools in the box used for redevelopment of the city within a framework of heritage protection.

BACKGROUND / CONTEXT

At the end of the 19th century, London's urban fabric was made up of an agglomeration of boroughs, all administered by the London County Council (LCC), which was established in 1889 and which at its outset performed only a limited range of planning functions. London's urban history subsequent to this reads like a long journey with a quest to secure increased central planning powers. One of the first acts to be introduced by the LCC was the 1894 London Building Act. This incorporated the 30-metre height restriction regulation and defined a low skyline in which St Paul's Cathedral and the Houses of Parliament would remain prominent. During the Second World War, London suffered severe damage caused by the Luftwaffe's bombs, leaving gaping holes in the urban fabric. The reconstruction that was so urgently needed as a result would be enacted by the 1947 Holden–Holford Plan, which envisaged sweeping redevelopment and radical re-planning of the City. The architects in charge of the plan, Charles Holden and William Holford, proposed a plot ratio system to limit height and density of new constructions. This also ensured an adequate amount of air and light for surrounding structures. These proposals became less rigid in 1956, and exemptions were frequently granted to developers who wanted to build higher. Under pressure to increase density quickly, the City borough authorised spontaneous proposals, which were assessed on a case-by-case basis. In efforts to promote a more consistent urban pattern, the LCC – responsible for urban planning – drafted eight specific decision criteria, consolidated in 1962: visual integration, location, plot size, amount of shadow, local character, impacts on the river Thames and open space, architectural quality and night scene.

In 1969, the Greater London Council (GLC), which had replaced the LCC four years earlier, drew up a regional development plan identifying three geographical zones, which were subject to different conditions with regards to high-rise construction. Zone one prohibited high-rise construction. Zone two concerned sectors sensitive to the visual impact of a tall building and partially permitted the construction of high-rise; this included 80 protected viewpoints which were updated and subsequently reduced in the mid-1970s. Zone three finally permitted the construction of high buildings. Photomontage was retained as a project validation tool. Up until 1980, the GLC was thus in charge of all the building projects above 45 metres.

In 1986, the Greater London Council was dissolved by the government and its expertise was transferred to the 32 boroughs of the capital, under governmental authority control. In 1989, the Secretary of State for Communities and Local Government ordered a new report on protection of views and vistas, which was completed two years later in 1991 with a list of 10 strategic viewpoints voted on in that year. The subsequent *Strategic Guidance for London Planning Authorities* (Regional Planning Guidance 3, 1996), carried out by the London Planning Advisory Committee (LPAC) at the request of the government, was intended to prepare supplementary strategic planning advice on high buildings, skylines and strategic views. Work on this initiative was carried out in two parts, firstly when the LPAC drafted *Buildings and Strategic Views in London* in 1998, and one year later when its supplementary *Strategic Planning Advice on High Buildings and Strategic Views in London* was adopted by the city. LPAC was also responsible for assisting boroughs in the regulation, planning, conception and construction of tall buildings, as borough councils were required to take into account the policies and principles when revising their unitary development plans (UDP). The London Planning Advisory Committee thus defined the specifications that had to be respected by all high buildings, and supported the protection of cones and view corridors as well as that of the panoramas. Moreover, in 1999, *Towards an Urban Renaissance* – the independent and influential report of the Urban Task Force, chaired by Richard Rogers at the request of Prime Minister Tony Blair – advocated densification of the city to curb the urban sprawl phenomenon.

In 2000, the London Planning Advisory Committee became the Greater London Authority (GLA), a strategic authority with a London-wide role which was designed to support the Mayor of London and his office in the development and delivery of strategy. It also supports the London Assembly which monitors the Mayor's work on behalf of Londoners. Early 2000 provided ideal conditions for the development of towers: indeed, Mayor Ken Livingstone openly declared his support for tall buildings – both as clusters (such as in the City and Canary Wharf), and as stand-alone buildings (such as the Millbank Tower) – in circumstances where constructions of this nature contributed to the quality of London's environment. London might even have Europe's tallest buildings,

and the Shard London Bridge project (310 metres, see page 78) was a way to test the new strategic policy. Supported by the GLA, the Mayor worked on a Greater London plan based on the 2002 *London's Skyline, Views and High Buildings* study by the research department of strategic consultancy firm DEGW. The report defined necessary conditions which high buildings had to meet. Alongside this, the heritage issue took new form, defended by independent

▲ Landmark
● Built
● Projects

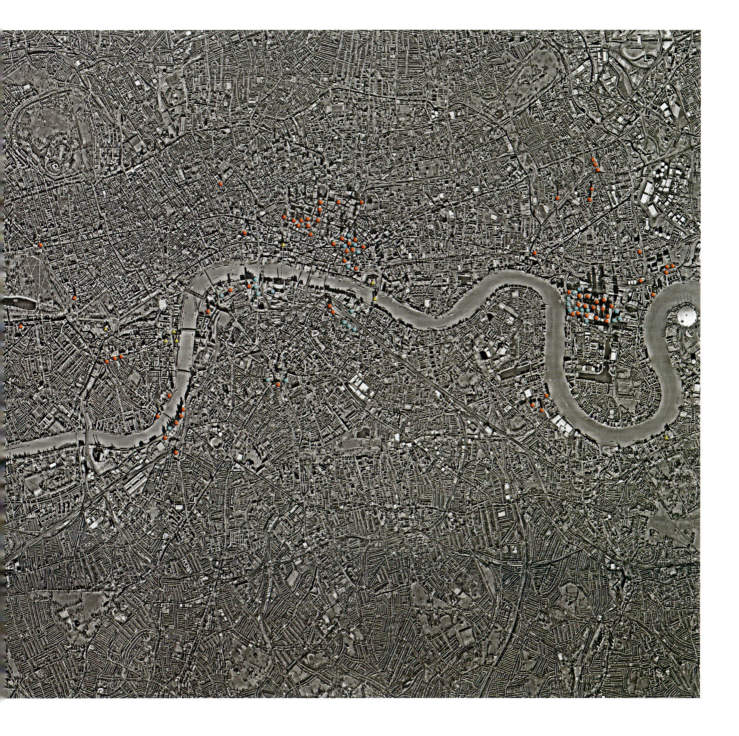

commissions: English Heritage and the Commission for Architecture and the Built Environment (CABE).

Two London sites have attached particular significance to tall building architecture, namely the borough of the City of London and Canary Wharf (Isle of Dogs). Situated north of the Thames and east of St Paul's Cathedral, the City, which had undergone intensive post-war reconstruction, had established itself as the financial hub of London. But this reputation was to be challenged in the 1980s with regeneration of London's docklands as part of the Canary Wharf project (see below). In response to this economic thread, in 1994, and again in 2002, the London Plan took up specific regulations for the City area through its unitary development plan (UDP) to revitalise it in agreement with the adjacent boroughs: the City of London Unitary Development Plan's strategy is the local interpretation of international, national and regional strategies and policies as they affect land-use planning issues in the City. A concept of town planning was pursued which responded to the evolving laws of the market but tallied with the local standards.

In 1980 the London Docklands Development Corporation (LDDC) was created. Financed by the government and based on the idea of the American businessman Michael von Clemm, it was decided to rehabilitate the old harbour quarter and to transform the docklands into a business district. The Canadian developer Olympia & York – initiator of the World Financial Center in New York – was responsible for developing the new office complex. Regeneration of the London docklands, which involved the construction and sale of buildings, began in 1981 and was coordinated by the LDDC, who were also in charge of town planning, having taken over the responsibility from the borough of Tower Hamlets. The LDDC incited companies to locate themselves on the Isle of Dogs through flexible regulations (no height limitation) and promised fiscal exemptions. Approval for projects only had to be acquired from the LDDC, thus creating favourable conditions for high-rise construction – stymied only by financial constraints and changes in ownership – and explaining the speed and ease with which the area developed into an ambitious and thriving sub-metropolis.

ORIGINATORS OF URBAN REGULATIONS AND RESPONSIBILITIES

In 2004, town planning expertise was transferred from the Secretary of State to the Mayor of London who is now designated to draft the *London Plan*, which replaced the ministerial Regional Planning Guidance (RPG3) in 2004. The *London Plan* defines the planning and development strategies of the entire Greater London area. It is the text of reference with which the London boroughs' Local Development Frameworks (LDFs) must comply (the LDF progressively replaces the UDP). LDF approval has to be obtained from the Secretary of State and by an independent inspector named by the latter, and must undergo six weeks of open consultation, during which the individual parties can voice their opinions.

London City Hall is thus responsible for outlining the core strategic direction of town planning to be implemented by London's 32 borough councils, which are not permitted to set height limitations on their own territory. On a day-to-day basis, boroughs make most decisions concerning town planning, but for skyscraper projects they must refer to the municipal authority, which can refuse the permit. Each borough is in charge of identifying sectors not suitable for tall buildings within the framework of its LDF by analysing the characteristics of the site and the potential impacts. Public consultations may be organised for major projects, but the ultimate decision rests with the Secretary of State based on the financial, housing and renovation needs as well as taking the architectural quality of the project into account.

The Mayor and the boroughs are supported in their decisions by various consultation bodies ruling on the protected views in the case of the Commission for Architecture and the Built Environment (CABE), or attending to the protection of London's historic fabric in the case of English Heritage. Their recommendations may then be included in the *London Plan*.

ZONING / URBAN PLANNING

A floor area ratios map, inspired by the American model, originally determined sites compatible with tall buildings, but this methodology was abandoned in 1986, along with dissolution of the GLC. Today, the London construction permits and town planning authorisation system is complex. No zoning system exists, and requests for building permits are simply considered on a case-by-case basis, taking into account the relative qualities of the proposal and the existence and capacity of transport services. The municipality encourages the densification of the borough of the City's and Canary Wharf's clusters through the construction of new towers. In addition to the emergence of new clusters in areas as indicated by the *London Plan*, high-rise development in zones between boroughs is endorsed and documented in the *City Fringe Opportunity Area Planning Framework* (2008), with a particular focus on borough boundaries between the Central and Eastern Sub Region. How

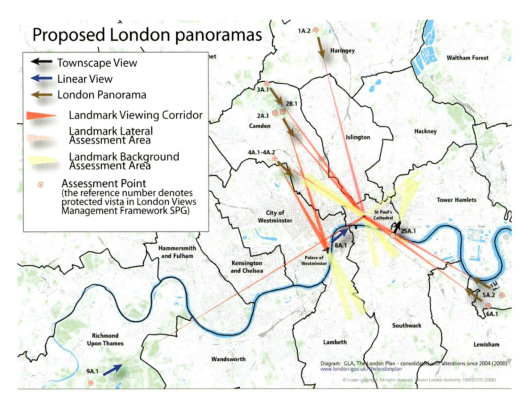

Proposed London panoramas

- **Townscape View**
- **Linear View**
- **London Panorama**
- **Landmark Viewing Corridor**
- **Landmark Lateral Assessment Area**
- **Landmark Background Assessment Area**
- **Assessment Point** (the reference number denotes protected vista in London Views Management Framework SPG)

Diagram: GLA, The London Plan - consolidated with alterations since 2004 (2008) www.london.gov.uk/thelondonplan
© Crown copyright. All rights reserved. Greater London Authority 100032379 (2008)

these proposals are integrated into the local planning framework is at the discretion of the borough and depends in part on the availability of public transport. A number of benefits can be attributed to high-rise construction in these fringe zones, with the potential for attracting economic activity, promoting mixed usage, and acting as a catalyst for local regeneration projects while sparing the historic centres.

Access to public transport is mapped out for the entire London territory and is covered by the Public Transport Accessibility Level (PTAL), which estimates the distance, per zone, from a transport (bus, Underground) hub and the connection time from one point to the other on a scale from 1 to 6. The site's accessibility is so measured using statistics, which determine the appropriate density of future urban development.

The link between tall buildings and socioeconomic activity of the city is crucial, and projects are assessed according to the *London View Management Framework Supplementary Planning Guidance* (SPG) report on the basis of the potential capacity to revitalise economic activity, not only in the vicinity but in London as a whole.

URBAN SKYLINE / CITYSCAPE

London's skyline remained low for a long time, dominated by two pinnacles: St Paul's Cathedral (the first protection decision dates back to 1934, followed by *Strategic Views of St Paul's* in 1989) and the Houses

of Parliament. There are currently 26 'designated views' defined in the *London View Management Framework SPG*, which is an integral part of the *London Plan*. These perspectives are classified in four different categories: six panoramas, three views of landmarks framed by objects in the landscape, 13 views integrating the Thames, and four landscape views (see the proposed London panoramas plan). In addition to the designated views there are the 11 corridors stretching from various viewpoints to landmarks listed in the SPG. These 'protected vistas', defined by the Secretary of State for Communities and Local Government, widen protection by integrating the background and surroundings of the landmark (see the 3D picture of the protected vista from Westminster to St Paul's). In case of interaction with a designated view, experts from English Heritage and CABE are consulted, as well as the Secretary of State. Height, scale, materials, night-impact (interferences with air routes) as well as the visual variations due to changes of weather and seasons are carefully studied. Harmony between a tower project and the landscape is gauged through Accurate Visual Representations (AVRs), which map out precise simulations of tower insertions and have to be presented by the developers, accompanied by an explanatory report.

In short, all projects must respect the SPG and *London Plan* standards and present distinct, innovative property designs appropriate to the protected zones.

3-D image of the protected vista from Westminster to St Paul's. The vista, which stretches from Westminster Pier to St Paul's Cathedral, determines the setting-up of tall buildings by protecting both the foreground and the background of the monuments.

building should favour a mix of uses, notably by reserving the ground floor for retail and cafés and creating public places around its base (ponds and green areas or squares). The Mayor can require architects and developers to provide public access to the upper floors of the tower so that all Londoners can take advantage of the panoramic views.

High-rise construction should be 'dynamic' and reflect an environmental consciousness expressed through energy-saving systems, and utilisation of responsible, renewable materials. If the building is located near the Thames, it should be in the blue chromatic range to respect a visual coherence (*Strategic Planning Guidance for the River Thames* (1997), since incorporated in the SPG). In 2000, CABE published the *By Design: Urban Design in the Planning System* guide which aimed to define conditions of architectural aesthetics in line with London tradition, in order to avoid repeating past mistakes. Guidance on the interior environment of a building in the aforementioned documents is somewhat limited, but in general recommends that 'green areas' should be integrated where possible. The *City Urban Development Plan* recommends interior spaces to be designed flexibly, permitting the building to adapt to market changes and ensuring its durability.

Safeguards exist on numerous levels in order to avoid the unwanted effect of tall buildings grouping together in the left-over spaces uncovered by the designated views and panoramas. Ultimately, the *London Plan* and SPG aim to establish a more holistic and extensive approach towards effective management of the London views than was the case under the RPG3A regulation. Urban landscape studies have become the preferred method for assessing, developing and protecting the city of London and its impressive skyline.

TOWER DESIGN

All skyscraper projects must respect *London Plan* criteria, which take into consideration the findings of the *Guidance on Tall Buildings* report piloted by English Heritage and CABE in 2003 (amended in 2007). A tower must enhance the qualities of its immediate location and setting based on its 'first-class design'. This is defined in terms of its fit with surrounding buildings, its access to the road network, public and private places and its status as a landmark in the city (see the image of the ground floor of 30 St Mary Axe). Overall it should produce more benefits than inconvenience to the lives of those affected by it. In order to exploit the full potential of the site, the

BUILDING CODES / FIRE SAFETY

The *London Plan* stipulates that all tower projects should display an intimate understanding of the microclimate in which they are to be built, and thus take into consideration issues of wind, light and shade as well as reflection impacts. They must also take the air channels and telecommunication networks into account, and fulfil the safety standards detailed in the Building Regulations. Studies on sunlight duration and shade generated are required when a new project is submitted; these influence the height and shape of buildings. More recently, in 2009, the Secretary of State commissioned – as a result of the 11 September 2001 attacks on New York – the preparation of a document entitled *Tall Buildings: Performance of Passive Fire Protection in Extreme Loading Events – An Initial Scoping Study*, which aims to assess and address issues of structure, materials, elevators and escalators of evacuation.

ECOLOGY

Environmental and ecological concerns have grown beyond the issue of non-renewable energy consumption, to a more holistic approach. This shift in attitude is complemented by requirements and guidelines which apply on not only a national but an international level, and to which construction of high-

Ground floor of 30 St Mary Axe. The Norman Foster tower embodies the London guidelines in terms of public and green spaces and commercial retail at ground level.

rise in London is subject. Environmental sustainability issues including the relative impact of a tower on its local environment, its energy consumption, and the subsequent consideration of polluting outputs formed the basis of an independent consultation in 2002, entitled 'The Tall Building and Sustainability'. The consultation, which examined the compatibility between sustainable development and vertical town planning, also assessed the building components, systems and furnishings and the potential energy loss attributed to these materials. A series of recommendations were thus made, including the use of solar heat and thermal mass of the building, higher levels of natural lighting (through shallow floor plans) and the use of wind energy.

In 2007, CABE and English Heritage made an open statement on sustainable town planning advocating that construction of tall buildings should only take place under exceptional circumstances and denouncing the case-by-case validation system. In addition, they argued, the architecture of tall buildings should respect environmental standards in absolute terms and reduce carbon emissions and energy consumption. While the *London Plan* did not corroborate this perspective on town planning, it has acknowledged the potential impact of high-rise on the environment and adopted a fairly stringent set of measures with regard to adaptation to climate change, energy renewal, natural

heating and air-conditioning systems, mixed uses and public transport exploitation.

In 2007, the Greater London Authority called for a review of the impact of the energy policies in the *London Plan* on applications referred to the Mayor. The review, carried out by South Bank University, focused particularly on the benefit of solar energy and photovoltaic panels. The city of London has also defined zones where the Environmental Impact Assessments (EIA, procedure stemming from European directives) standards are required, notably in the City borough. The architecture of a tower must thus conform to national (Planning Policy Statement 1: delivering sustainable development), regional and local ecological standards. Environmental and ecological issues have thus to be addressed in every phase of a high-rise building's life-cycle, from conception, construction and renovation to demolition.

For more information, see:

Greater London Authority
http://www.london.gov.uk/

City of London
http://www.cityoflondon.gov.uk/Corporation/

The planning portal
http://www.planningportal.gov.uk/

Frankfurt

Over the last 60 years, Frankfurt's urban fabric has been strongly marked by the superimposition of several development plans dedicated to tall buildings. The coexistence of high-rise clusters and mid-rise buildings (four to six storeys) is the result of a detailed and well-researched town planning policy. It has emerged from a combination of the control exercised over future high-rise development with the repair of some past special dispensations, linked to isolated political initiatives.

BACKGROUND / CONTEXT

Under the Weimar Republic, the Germany of the 1920s revealed an unprecedented enthusiasm for the skyscraper typology, perceived as a strong symbol for innovation and progress. This enthusiasm for building tall was underpinned by a decree issued on a national basis by the Minister for Social Affairs (*Wohlfahrtsminister*) on 3 January 1921, which permitted the inclusion of skyscrapers in local city development plans. In the midst of this climate of change and emulation, the story of skyscrapers in Frankfurt took shape with the construction of the IG Farben tower by Hans Poelzig, in the 1930s, alongside Max Taut's Trade Union House and works by the architect Martin Elsässer.

Ernst May, leading architect and city planner, headed the Frankfurt building administration between 1925 and 1930, and spearheaded a campaign of modernisation in urban planning which, notably, retained the high-rise typology for the realisation of these objectives. May's ideas steered, however, away from the trappings of a dense vertical conglomeration and were akin to Bruno Taut's Expressionist *Stadtkrone* (city crown) principle of lower structures surrounding a single focal point in the city centre. But these conceptual preoccupations were rapidly replaced in the middle of the 20th century by the practical considerations which emerged in the aftermath of the Second World War. Frankfurt had been heavily bombed and large parts of the city destroyed. This, coupled with the gradual increase of the population, inevitably precipitated a severe housing shortage. The dearth of adequate housing put pressure on city planners to build onwards and upwards and saw new builds leap from an eight- to a 14-storey standard. At the same time, Frankfurt had begun to establish itself as Germany's financial centre, and thus, in 1948, became the location for the head offices of the German Federal Bank and the Reconstruction Credit Institute. Hygienist aspirations of the post-war reconstruction marked a forward-looking approach to architecture with public welfare at its core, and incorporated many of the same Modernist ideals as projects from the 1920s. Although large sections of the city were destroyed during the war, a further proportion were deliberately demolished and the large avenues across the city core of medieval origins traced out as Frankfurt sought to reinvent its architectural identity. However, following extensive debates by elected representatives, it was eventually decided to spare the historic heart of the city, which in turn was incorporated by architect Herbert Boehm into the first 'skyscraper plan' (*Hochhausplan*). Boehm's 1953 plan therefore distributed tall buildings in a ring around the old fortifications, which were to become green areas. In the end this plan, which carried no legal obligation, was ignored; and the towers, such as the Bienenkorb Tower by Johannes Krahn in the centre of Frankfurt, that sprung up during the 1950s worked instead on the aforementioned principle of a focal point.

In 1962, the Zürich-Haus on Bockenheimer Landstrasse, designed by Udo von Schauroth and Werner Stücheli, marked the beginning of a new generation of tall buildings that were characterised by simple volumes, curtain walls or concrete aesthetics (such as the 1966 Deutsche Bank building by Sep Ruf) and embodied the will to increase the density of the western part of the city. Three years later, the Brutalist Dutch architects, Johannes Hendrik van den Broek and Jaap Bakema proposed a series of tall buildings along Reuterweg, in the northwest. In 1967 the *Fingerplan* built on and extended these principles by aligning tall buildings not only along Reuterweg, but along eight major highways radiating from the green belt towards residential districts in the city's periphery (Mainzer Strasse, Theodor-Heuss Allee – Messegelände, Kettenhofweg, Bockenheimer Landstrasse, Reuterweg, Eschersheimer Landstrasse and Eckenheimer Landstrasse). The height of the buildings, however, was limited to 95 metres, in line with the cathedral. The project, which was coupled with an extensive reworking of the traffic system, created a surge of property speculation and led to the decline and partial demolition of the area's existing 19th-century housing. Social resistance in the city rapidly built up during the 1970s and highlighted the existence of a series of conflicts between economic development and environmental protection. The end result was to halt construction of high-rise in many districts, like Holzhausen to the north, and bring it to a standstill.

In 1973, in answer to commercial pressure and to counterbalance the relative failure of the *Fingerplan*, the City West Plan defined a new high-rise development area between Rathenau-Platz, Weserstrasse, Taunusanlage and the theatre district. The raising of height restrictions and definition of a skyline complemented the city's densification strategy and consequently tall buildings sprang up and reached new heights of between 20 and 38 storeys. In 1982, Albert Speer's *City-Leitplan* gave new momentum to urban planning. His project referred to the *Fingerplan* and the Brutalist architects' work, and intended to conquer the western sector of the city through an outline plan which was inspired by a rhizome whose branches were punctuated with tall buildings. At the end of the 1980s, the increasing number of skyscrapers and their impact on the urban landscape fuelled political debates. For the first time also, the notion of architectural quality came into play for granting building permits. Meanwhile, the height of new constructions increased exponentially. In 1990, the *Bankenplan* (Novotny Mähner Assoziierte)

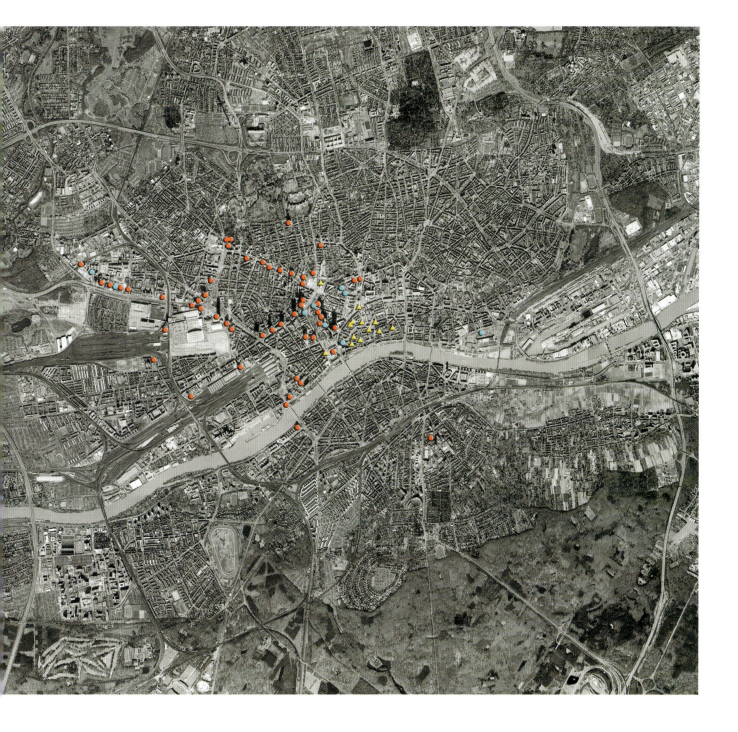

was published to further increase the density of the central business district. This led to a new development plan vote in 1994: very tall buildings were now the basis for planning and encouraged speculation. It is in this context that Norman Foster's Commerzbank was achieved in 1997.

In 1998, the *Hochhausentwicklungsplan* (tall building development plan) by Jourdan & Müller was published. This plan was drawn up in association with the City Planning Department and identified two new high-rise construction zones, the *Messeviertel* and the *Parkviertel*. The plan was ratified one year later by a wide majority at the City Council which finally decided on 16 sites in terms of being able to accommodate tall buildings. These were distributed in three cluster zones: the *Bankenviertel*, the *Messeviertel* and the *Parkviertel*. The latter was also subject to another plan known as *Frankfurt 21*, defined by the National Railway Company (Deutsche Bahn AG), to renew and develop its property in the western part of the centre. It was eventually abandoned in 2002 but without any disruption to the overall plan of the City Council. The plan, also called *Frankfurt 2000*, relied on the balance between private and public interests and made competition the basis for planning. Still in force today, the plan was revised in 2008 for two reasons: to identify new sites which should make up for the failure of the *Parkviertel*, and to make official a number of towers which – for political reasons – had received dispensatory building approvals outside the actual high-rise cluster zones, such as the Palais Quartier towers in the heart of the historic city.

ORIGINATORS OF URBAN REGULATIONS AND RESPONSIBILITIES

In 1998 and 2008, the city development service (Stadtplanungsamt) appointed Jourdan & Müller to compose and revise the tall building development plan, and both texts were subsequently approved by the City Council. An important procedural principle of the *Hochhausentwicklungsplan* is the feasibility study, which is carried out and released for each site listed, resulting in a specific development plan determined by the city to guide developers. It also serves as the basis for the contractual agreement between the developer and the town planning service, and thus for the building permission. The feasibility studies define type and level of building use, materials, colours and an approximate envelope of the construction to maximise compatibility with the immediate environment. In a next step, the competing architectural projects of interested developers are judged by a jury of independent experts. So, in spite of defined zones dedicated to very tall

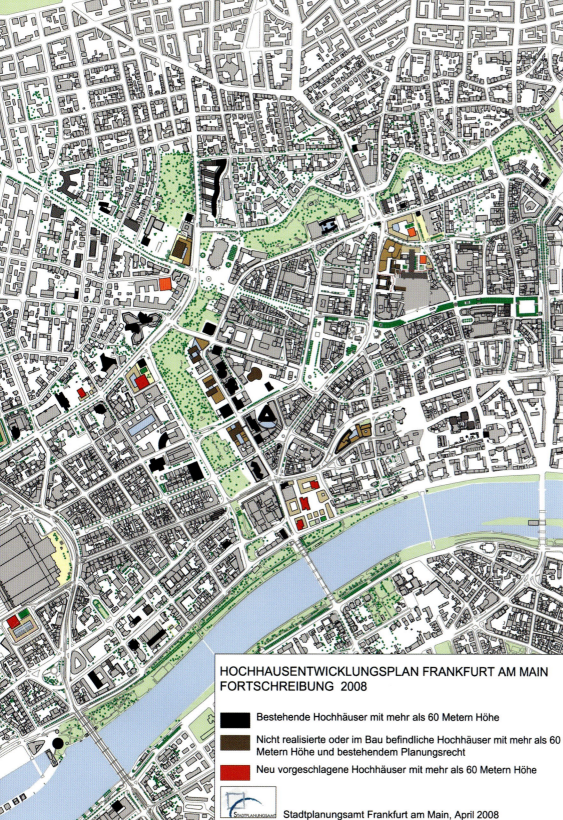

Hochhausentwicklungsplan map. The outline plan confirms high-rise developments along the major roads and the extension to the west.

HOCHHAUSENTWICKLUNGSPLAN FRANKFURT AM MAIN FORTSCHREIBUNG 2008

Bestehende Hochhäuser mit mehr als 60 Metern Höhe

Nicht realisierte oder im Bau befindliche Hochhäuser mit mehr als 60 Metern Höhe und bestehendem Planungsrecht

Neu vorgeschlagene Hochhäuser mit mehr als 60 Metern Höhe

Stadtplanungsamt Frankfurt am Main, April 2008

buildings, final approval of high-rise proposals rests on the individual and qualitative study of each project. This marks an important difference from the comprehensive approach practised in the 1970s.

ZONING / URBAN PLANNING

The creation of homogenous high-rise clusters set out by the *Hochhausentwicklungsplan* is designed to strengthen the identity and urban life of Frankfurt (see the *Hochhausentwicklungsplan* map). The *Bankenviertel* groups financial activities in the city centre and the *Messeviertel*, further west, presents a mixed cluster of tall buildings suitable to accommodate further densification (situated around the *Messeturm* (Trade Fair Tower) by Murphy/Jahn). The residential zones to the north and south are protected, and the hypothesis of small towers at the western and eastern gates of the city has been evoked. The boundaries of zones are set according to their distance from residential districts and depend on public transport networks (current and future) to limit motor traffic. The exact position of the towers is linked to the amount of daylight and cast shadow, for which specific study reports are commissioned. Frankfurt gives priority to developments in clusters as it resolves issues of incompatibility between old buildings and new constructions, and it creates a flexible demarcation line which can be shaped and that directly generates intense social economic activity, therefore contributing positively to city life. Access is thus essential and the *Bankenviertel* is considered as a vital link between the historic centre and the central station from where pedestrian traffic proliferates.

The cluster approach, however, has been amended slightly during the last revision of the plan and from now on, in specific cases, constructions of up to 60 metres are permitted outside the designated cluster areas if they create an attraction pole within the district. For example, this decision allowed the Palais Quartier towers to be included in a micro-cluster at Stiftstrasse, in the central historic district. This is the example of the will to legitimise single towers by including them in a cluster that was not originally planned (see the scale model illustration).

URBAN SKYLINE / CITYSCAPE

One of the principles of the *Frankfurt 2000* plan is to mitigate the disruption of the cityscape by preventing

***Hochhausentwicklungs-plan* scale model illustration. High-rise development projects densify the existing clusters.**

the uncoordinated construction of isolated tall buildings and, therefore, to protect the historic districts, residential zones and green areas. Potential groups of 'reasonably' distributed tall buildings are required to keep in line with the existing skyscrapers in order to create a dynamic skyline. Similarly, solitary towers must serve as a visual relay and so harmonise the townscape. As it stands, no height limit exists for high-rise in Frankfurt: rather it is studies on daylight and environmental impact that determine the construction of a tall building and the shape of its top on a case-by-case basis – for example, the 210-metre maximum in the *Bankenviertel* as opposed to 60 metres in the historic centre.

TOWER DESIGN

For the successful integration of tall buildings in the urban context, developers are asked to reserve the ground floor and the first five storeys for commercial, public or communal activities and to calibrate the office space and housing within the tower or on the overall plot (the recommended ratio is 70 per cent to 30 per cent). Interaction with the public sphere is further encouraged by recommendations which state that the top of every high-rise building should contain sky lobbies or restaurants accessible to, and for use by, the public. Recommendations also emerge from innovations represented by other contemporary projects like the vertical gardens of the Commerzbank. Projecting the structural elements of a high-rise on to the Frankfurt skyline through lighting is also subject to consideration. In general there are, however, no general specifications concerning the shape and aesthetics of a tall building except for recommendations made during the phases of individual conception.

BUILDING CODES / FIRE SAFETY

The Frankfurt building control department (Bauaufsicht Frankfurt) associates high-rise constructions with a special status (*Sonderbauten*) and they are therefore subject to meeting certain requirements. These requirements are outlined in the 'General directives on the construction and amenity of tower blocks' drafted in 1983 by the State of Hesse (*Richtlinien über Bau und Einrichtung von Hochhäusern (Hochhaus-Richtlinien-HHR) – Fassung Dezember 1983*) and are not legally binding but serve as general guidelines which the Frankfurt building department has to consider when making decisions on planning applications. The city council defines further requirements for high-rise buildings which are detailed in judicial authority reports available in the parliamentary information system PARLIS.

A building is considered a tall building if its height exceeds 22 metres. It should only be erected in a location where environmental impact is limited, be this in terms of the immediate local environment, the surrounding landscape or the sealing of ground surfaces. Developers of high-rise projects have to submit an appraisal report and then be given the go-ahead by the national institute of the environment of the State of Hesse (Hessisches Landesanstalt für Umwelt). The energy requirements for high-rise buildings are based on the German energy saving regulations (EnEV). Finally, the fire safety requirements are outlined in the Frankfurt *Hochhaus-Richtlinien*.

ECOLOGY

Environmental concerns have for many years been core to the urban evolution of Frankfurt, and are best illustrated by the comprehensive studies undertaken on mixed uses and transport connections for tall buildings. As the city strives to build up its sustainable credentials, it is simultaneously subject to economic pressures: the stakes are high. An extensive portfolio of requirements for high-rise developers consists of, in the initial stage, assessing the ecological conditions, setting out optimal systems of energy, daylight and wind management, working construction within the shortest possible time-frame in addition to using recyclable materials in anticipation of the building's destruction. In terms of operational requirements, the 'primary energy' consumption is set below 150 kilowatts per square metre, with 50 per cent of this derived from geothermal or solar-panel energy. The recent renovation of the Deutsche Bank (1985) towers into LEED™-certified 'green towers' marked a new milestone in the ecological quest for sustainable design (predominantly through the exchange of the facades with new opening windows and insulating glass). In addition, the conversion of empty office buildings into residential towers creates new challenges and approaches the topic of sustainability from a more strategic level.

For more information, see:

Frankfurt Municipality   http://www.frankfurt.de

Stadtplanungsamt Frankfurt am Main
http://www.stadtplanungsamt-frankfurt.de

PARLIS parliamentary information system
http://www.stvv.frankfurt.de/parlis

Frankfurt Bauaufsicht   www.bauaufsicht-frankfurt.de

Vienna

Vienna is the perfect example of a city with a dense historic heritage which finds itself confronted with the need to reassess its approach to tall buildings and to update its regulations accordingly. As part of this process, fundamental questions have been raised on the necessity and conditions for implementation of skyscrapers. They are symbolic of debates which have had an impact on skylines in several other European capitals, notably London and Paris. Vienna acts in a certain sense therefore as a research laboratory on regulations which constrain, but allow scope for innovation combining syncretism of legislation and innovations. In this way, the Austrian capital is able effectively to shed light on crucial differences which exist in planning methods for tall buildings: either based on regulations resulting from an empirical initiative, in reaction to the construction of the first few towers, or perceived as an inflexible prerequisite.

BACKGROUND / CONTEXT

In 1893, Vienna equipped itself with a zoning plan entitled *Bauzonenplan* following the integration of large parts of the suburbs into the city a year earlier. One of the main objectives of the plan was to classify the districts into height categories: the 1st central district was categorised as class V (with buildings ranging in height from 16 to 26 metres), the 2nd, 9th and 20th districts to the northeast as well as the 10th and 22nd districts were categorised as class IV (with buildings ranging in height from 12 to 21 metres), sectors between the ring road and the suburbs were categorised as class III (with buildings ranging in height from 9 to 12 metres), and finally residential suburbs were categorised as class I and II (buildings ranging in height from 2.5 to 9 metres and from 2.5 to 12 metres respectively). Category VI, which referred to constructions over 26 metres, was not linked to a specific zone.

In 1905 a green belt was created around the city, giving Vienna the profile of a compact urban complex. The division into height sectors, classifying streets according to their widths, as well as the calculations for fixing building cornices at a precise height, helped to shape Vienna's distinctive architectural identity. As illustrated by the gasometers, only industrial buildings were exempt from height limitations. In 1932 the first residential skyscraper, located on Herrengasse, was built by Siegfried Theiss and Hans Jaksch. The symbolic status of the skyscraper representing American permutations polarised the positions of the conservatives and social democrats and marked a turning point in the future development of the city. Height acquired a political and symbolic dimension and became a fantasised tool of Modernist planning, as it was in several other European cities like Berlin or Paris. But all things considered, until the 1950s, skyscrapers were in Vienna an epiphenomenon. The Vienna Construction Zoning Plan had created a rather theoretical class VI which it refused to actively use in the plans for the city development, thus explaining the isolated character of the few initiatives.

The *Bauzonenplan* envisioned a homogenous city with a single compact centre which would grow concentrically by incorporating satellite villages. During the Anschluss – Austria's annexation by Nazi Germany – the city was made up of 26 districts, but it lost a fraction of its territory in 1955 when Austria regained its full sovereignty. In the same year, within the scope of reconstruction, the municipal insurance company (Wiener Städtische) commissioned the construction of the Ringturm tower by architect Erich Boltenstern, located on Ringstrasse, which once again broached the issue of skyscrapers. It was considered as a special construction project and, despite breaching the historic zoning plan, was permitted and dealt with on the basis of separate legal provisions. Later on, during the 1960s and 1970s, height limits in peripheral urban expansion areas were knowingly ignored. A coherent and unambiguous concept and definition of high-rise was lacking, and regulations remained at a standstill. The residential tall building districts – Mitterhofergasse to the north and Alt-Erlaa in the south, among others – provoked in 1973 a strong break in height and scale of Vienna's urban landscape which had been disrupted and subsequently diversified. It communicated the impression of a cityscape deprived of visual or architectural rules. One year later the first historic buildings protection zones were appointed. This amendment to the construction code was the first step towards global and rational management of the city which eventually emerged in 1984 in the form of a new urban development plan (*Stadtentwicklungsplan*). New planning principles were developed and normalised. These included urban density and public transport, the development of the centre, the polycentric urban structure and the mix of uses.

In 1991, architects Coop Himmelb(l)au prepared a high-rise concept for the Urban Development Plan (UDP) of 1994. This concept took into account the aforementioned principles of urban development and improved the legal and economic framework for high-rise projects. The UDP encouraged the development of tall buildings in the Donaustadt district and in the Wagramer Strasse area, and emphasised the crucial importance of the skyscraper setting. Through the extension of the authorised high-rise construction zones, respecting the maximum distance of 400 metres from public transport, the economic environment for

towers was thus improved. The study defined 32 criteria, categorised according to eight themes: land planning, infrastructures, public space, procedures and controls, design quality, social impact (internal organisation, fire safety), ecological performance and economic impact. Nevertheless, in Vienna, tall building architecture continued to suffer from an inadequate definition and a blurred decision-making process: according to the building code, the term 'high-rise' still

▲ Landmark
● Built
● Projects

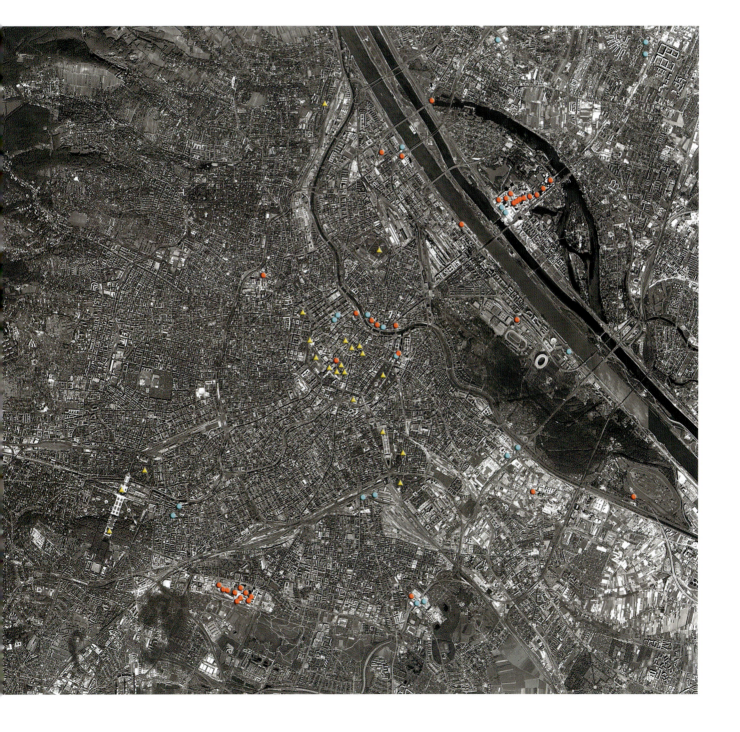

applied to any building that was taller than 26 metres and came under the legally still unclear status of building class VI. Thus, even though the Coop Himmelb(l)au conclusions may be considered an essential evolution in high-rise construction, their legal translation was not easy to establish.

In 2001, the municipality therefore decided to undertake a comparative analysis of initiatives at a global level, before setting in stone its own definition of the skyscraper concept. The *Internationale Stadtplanungs- und Hochhauskonzepte (International Planning and High-Rise Concepts)* compared the planning policies implemented in Paris, London, Los Angeles, Portland, Seattle, San Francisco, New York and Chicago. The selection criteria for choosing which cities to study were based on the existence of a historic urban heritage, experience in town planning services regarding tall buildings, appropriate location of tall buildings under effective and efficient regulations, an economy in need of offices and a positive and constructive approach to skyscrapers by the municipal actors. The study weighed up the pros and cons concerning tall building districts according to the strategic situation (whether outlying like Paris's La Défense or intramural like London's Canary Wharf), the spatial arrangement (solitaires or clusters), the control of land uses (Zoning Code in New York versus the Parisian *Plan d'Occupation des Sols*, see page 217), the floor area ratio system, the heritage protection, the implementation of qualitative criteria (such as the Design Review Guidelines in Seattle) and the presence of transport hubs. Out of this extensive research emerged a specific concept of a skyscraper set out in the *Wien Hochhauskonzept Plan* passed in 2002, later amended in 2007, and then again in 2008. But this document does not cancel out the prescriptions initially made by the Coop Himmelb(l)au plan; rather, it strengthens and completes them.

ORIGINATORS OF URBAN REGULATIONS AND RESPONSIBILITIES

Today, the municipality studies and puts into practice the tall building development plan (*Wien Hochhauskonzept Plan*) which aims in part to constrain property speculation that could potentially devour strategic sites and damage the city image. The municipality also delivers building permits and manages the land use plan (see the Vienna planning progress table). The town planning commission (*Stadtentwicklungskommission*) is responsible for outlining development directives and thus makes the decision as to which of the areas not classified as 'protected areas' (*Ausschlusszonen*) can be developed

VIENNA PLANNING PROGRESS

	Commissioned by	Participants
<u>Phase 1</u>: Urbanistic master-plan	Urban Planning Department	
<u>Phase 2</u>: Location planning	Urban Planning Department	Project developer
<u>Phase 3</u>: Project study (studies)	Project developer	
<u>Phase 4</u>: Preliminary concept / Competition	Project developer	Urban Planning Department
<u>Phase 5</u>: Public presentation	Project developer	Urban Planning Department
<u>Phase 6</u>: Project assessment / Project clearance	Urban Planning Department	
<u>Phase 7</u>: Land allocation procedure / Contract negotiations		
<u>Phase 8</u>: City Council resolution / Legally binding construction plan		
<u>Phase 9</u>: Submission of plan / Approval procedures / Building permit		

or not. Any project with a surface of at least 25,000 square metres or over 35 metres in height will be subject to a citizens' validation procedure which takes place during the last phases of the administrative procedures, before the change of land use request (land allocation procedure). The city of Vienna also imposes a time delay for developers to put forward any plans for a tall building project, beyond which the land use plan expires; such a system is designed to prevent developers from keeping key sites for speculative purposes.

ZONING / URBAN PLANNING

Since the 2001 international comparative study, the town planning in Vienna has often referred – in terms of zoning – to the San Francisco plan by Allan Jacobs (*The Urban Design Plan*, 1972), which responded to issues of city pattern, conservation, major new development and neighbourhood environment by locating tall buildings according to topography and privileged views. Inspired by this example, Vienna divided its urban territory into zones compatible in height (*Eignungszonen*) associated with sectors which would completely exclude the future construction of skyscrapers, that is any building over 35 metres. The latter, known as *Ausschlusszonen*, are decreed under Article 7 of the Vienna Building Code and concern wide green spaces, historic areas and zones insufficiently served by public transport. Unless otherwise specified in the development plan (*Bebauungsplan*), skyscrapers can be built in residential and mixed-use zones, which are now official class-VI areas. These zones are covered in part by a redevelopment and renovation plan which allows the construction of high-rise developments, in order to try to remedy the lack of an estimated 80,000 modern apartments, as long as they respect the Viennese landscape. Industrial areas remain compatible

The Vienna planning progress table. In Vienna, any high-rise project follows from a sustained dialogue between the city and the developer.

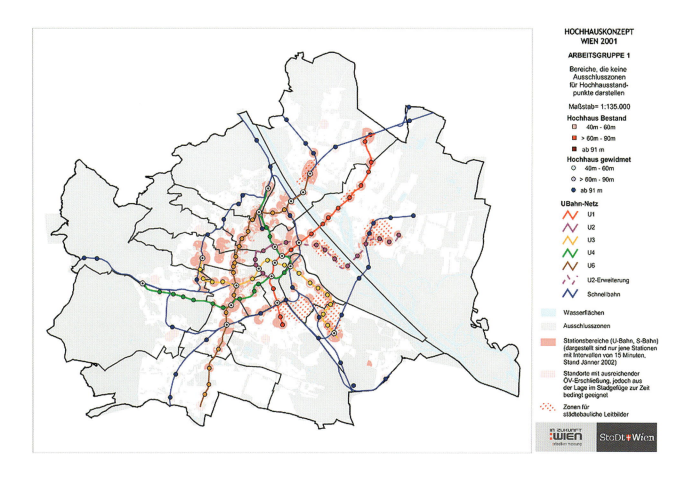

HOCHHAUSKONZEPT
WIEN 2001

ARBEITSGRUPPE 1

Bereiche, die keine
Ausschlusszonen
für Hochhausstand-
punkte darstellen

Maßstab= 1:135.000

Hochhaus Bestand
☐   40m - 60m
■   > 60m - 90m
■   ab 91 m

Hochhaus gewidmet
⊙   40m - 60m
⊙   > 60m - 90m
●   ab 91 m

UBahn-Netz
∧∨   U1
∧∨   U2
∧∨   U3
∧∨   U4
∧∨   U6
⋰⋰   U2-Erweiterung
∧∨   Schnellbahn

▨   Wasserflächen
▨   Ausschlusszonen
▨   Stationsbereiche (U-Bahn, S-Bahn)
(dargestellt sind nur jene Stationen
mit Intervallen von 15 Minuten,
Stand Jänner 2002)
▨   Standorte mit ausreichender
ÖV-Erschließung, jedoch aus
der Lage im Stadtgefüge zur Zeit
bedingt geeignet
⋰⋰   Zonen für
städtebauliche Leitbilder

IN ZUKUNFT
:WIEN   StaDt✚Wien

with high-rise developments, in addition to certain zones where the maximum height has been raised to over 35 metres. Finally, there are some specific zones for skyscrapers compatible with Vienna's traditional urban structure, in the centre or in peripheral districts.

With reference to these principles of zoning, four specific sectors have been actively identified as able to accommodate high-rise developments, within the framework of a legally binding masterplan (see the *Eignungszonen* plan). The four validated sectors are: Vienna Trade Fair/Stadium/Donaustadt Bridge (in the 2nd district); Vienna Railway Station/Arsenal/Aspang Station/Neu Erdberg/Simmering (in the 3rd, 10th and 11th districts); Floridsdorf (21st); and central Kagran-Donaufeld (22nd). A fifth private project will take place in the 15th district (Europaplatz/Western Railway Station). These compatible zones have been chosen based on several considerations outlined in the building code: minimum distance to buildings of historic interest and public gardens (100 metres in this case); respect of the perspectives and the privileged panoramas; and presence of public transport services – tram or underground railway stations have to be within a

maximum distance of 300 metres, whether they are in service or planned. The Donaustadt complex in the first sector, on the northeast banks of the river Danube, is an exemplary high-rise development with varied circulation levels (pedestrian level, underground and car parks level) and mixed activities.

Defining zones enables national and foreign investors quickly to target their location and to deal with a single party, the city. Within these zones, tall buildings must fill 10 planning criteria decreed by the city, which favour the integration of these buildings into their immediate environment and the townscape.

URBAN SKYLINE / CITYSCAPE

The overall urban profile – or townscape – of Vienna is meant to determine the location of high-rise buildings. In contrast to Paris, Vienna distinguishes its architectural identity in other dimensions than height. The legibility and understanding which we have of the city is controlled by a system of protected panoramas and perspectives: panoramic viewpoints such as the Kahlenberg or Leopoldsberg mountains, 'historic' lookouts such as belvederes or watch towers, and

Eignungszonen **(qualified zones) plan. The plan qualifies zones according to several standards, such as the distance from transport hubs and corridor views.**

finally, vantage points atop publicly accessible buildings such as the Danube Tower or the big wheel (*Riesenrad*). Visual cones and perspectives from key points such as St Stephen's Cathedral complement the city's image. These arrangements, however, do not necessarily exclude high-rise, and inside these visual axes new zones for future tower projects can still be accommodated. Alternatively, they can also be defined as zones of exclusion and be classified as protected areas (see the *Sichtachsen* map).

TOWER DESIGN

The developer in charge of a high-rise building project has to justify its feasibility as well as its environmental impact. In conjunction with the aforementioned *Hochhauskonzept Plan*, Coop Himmelb(l)au proposed a list of 10 criteria in 1991 with which each project must comply. The city of Vienna makes a final decision based on compliance with these criteria, designed to maintain architectural quality but without being an 'arbiter of good taste'.

Sichtachsen **(view axes) map. The Viennese urban landscape and heritage is protected through view corridors.**

The first of these criteria concerns the formation of a multidisciplinary team bringing together diverse experts (architecture, engineering, town planning, traffic, sustainable development, civil engineering). The second criterion demands an evaluation of the tower compatibility within the urban context, the planned purpose, planned intensity of use and effect on the urban fabric of the relevant surrounding area, even if it is assumed that the location has already been subjected to a comprehensive assessment concerning its suitability for a high-rise project and its compatibility with the urban structure and transport situation. To ensure compatibility with the transport situation, the share of private car traffic must not exceed a maximum of 25 per cent of the overall volume engendered by the high-rise project; the project must moreover be adequately connected to the high-level public transport network. The third criterion states that the high-rise building must also be aesthetically integrated into its context: the architectural conception of the single skyscraper or the cluster of skyscrapers must be submitted to a competition procedure (with the *Ringturm* and Media Tower as explicit references). The fourth criterion relates to the shadow created and the wind generated: according to the average position of the sun (for which 21 March is used as a benchmark), the tall building cannot overshadow its immediate environment for more than two hours a day or engender wind corridors.

According to the fifth criterion, the project must meet the technical and social infrastructure standards. The sixth criterion requests the provision of green spaces and indoor and outdoor public and semi-public spaces for cultural or commercial use, stemming from similar arrangements in Zurich and London. The seventh criterion relates to the sustainability of the planned project, whereby the tall building must be able to adapt to future changes, and should therefore incorporate a flexible interior organisation. The eighth criterion undertakes to use ecologically efficient and recyclable materials, keeping future renovation or demolition in mind. The ninth criterion addresses the execution of the project, assuming regular quality control, public communication of the construction phase schedule and the appointment of a person to settle complaints and disputes. Finally, the tenth criterion concerns the public presentation of the project by means of 3-D documents, real or virtual exhibits, experts' reports and conferences. This step, inspired by London's initiative, is the mandatory prerequisite for a change of land use request. Minutes must be issued recording any objections which may be made and to which the developer has to answer. The latter must

also guarantee the financing of the transport system, as well as access to the public road network.

BUILDING CODES / FIRE SAFETY

These points have not been particularly studied, but the Vienna building law (Wiener Bauordnung) sets out the common measures of safety.

ECOLOGY

The energy efficiency of a tall building is always taken into account when evaluating its overall quality. According to the building code, skyscrapers over 60 metres must undergo supplementary assessments in terms of wind, shade generated, energy efficiency and building security. The connection of the tall building to public transport further marks out environmental measures.

For more information, see:

City of Vienna   http://www.wien.gv.at

Paris

Paris's ambivalent relationship with high-rise construction combines elements of ideology, pragmatism and aestheticism. In many ways the French capital still has trouble coming to terms with its high-rise heritage from the 1960s and 1970s. A critical eye is often cast over this period of high-rise construction which is sometimes considered as going against good practice in urban design. Public opinion and the municipal authorities thus waver endlessly between accepting and rejecting a typology that essentially embodies a transgression from the long-established height restrictions of the city. Moreover, the creation in 1973 of a ring road around the historic centre added, on top of the political separation, a spatial dichotomy between historic nucleus and the suburbs – 'Paris *intra muros*' and the *banlieues* – which still holds a key position in the current planning ambitions for tall buildings.

BACKGROUND / CONTEXT

The concept of building heights in Parisian planning has its roots in the modernisation programme of Paris during the Second Empire led by the Haussmann administration in the 1850s and 1860s. With a preference for established objectives of perspective, symmetry and scale, Baron Haussmann advocated calculating maximum building heights in relation to the width of a road in order to impose visual order over the city (1859 decree). This concept of building heights was then amended on several occasions before being integrated into the 1902 decree drafted by the road architect Louis Bonnier. The decree, entitled *Décret portant règlement sur les hauteurs et les saillies des bâtiments dans la ville de Paris*, effectively regulated building heights and projections defining the envelope of a building relative to the urban context, and in doing so shaped great parts of the city. The strict alignment of buildings along the street thus defined emphasised the focus of straight lines as a key organisational component of the city.

Although the 1902 decree was revised on several occasions and waived under special exemption (such as for the Tour Croulebarbe by Édouard Albert in 1958, and for the Tour de la Maison de la Radio by Henri Bernard in 1963), it remained in force until 1967. At the time the Commission Départementale des Sites, Perspectives et Paysages de la Seine (Departmental Committee of Sites, Perspectives and Landscapes of the Seine) was given the responsibility of awarding building permits and could grant special exemptions in the 31-metre zone if the project – even if it was a skyscraper – enhanced the urban landscape. In 1967, the 1902 decree was integrated into the town planning scheme, known as the *Plan d'Urbanisme Directeur* or PUD. Drafted by architects Raymond Lopez and Michel Holley, the PUD divided the *intra-muros* area into zones of activities (residential, business, university and administrative) and fixed new floor area ratios called *coefficients d'utilisation du sol* (CUS), according to their land use (3 in residential zones and 3.5 in administrative and business zones). The PUD set the height limit in the centre at 31 metres and at 37 metres in the peripheral districts, but permitted taller buildings in designated renovation areas where a special legal status applied (in most cases being the ZAC status (*zone d'aménagement concerté*)), thereby introducing the dispensatory principle in special planning circumstances. It also permitted the construction of additional storeys when the building was set back from the street, thus disrupting the system of the Parisian alignment.

The public development operations in the urban renovation sectors were based on an understanding that the tower was a useful urban structure and thus required appropriate categorisation: *immeuble de grande hauteur* (IGH) became the national concept of tall buildings, based on security concerns. The peripheral districts such as the 15th and the 19th arrondissements little by little saw their skyline evolving, as well as two further major high-rise podium developments on the west riverbanks (Front de Seine / Beaugrenelle (see page 136)) and to the southeast, in the 13th district (Les Olympiades). Projects such as these marked a break from the past and more specifically from the Haussmann doctrine, and engaged efforts to provide contemporary housing and facilities based on elements of Modernism. For the tertiary sector, the PUD aimed to limit new *intra-muros* developments, except when they were connected to a transport hub such as the Montparnasse and Quai de Bercy areas, and advocated its 'decentralisation' into the suburbs where 'oversized' buildings became possible if 'carefully thought out'.

Following his election in 1974, the French President Valéry Giscard d'Estaing banned high-rise building from the *intra-muros* area – a reaction in part to the protests surrounding the Montparnasse tower and the many authorisations given by the Committee of Sites (in 1970, there were 42 pending building permit applications). Famously, d'Estaing stated that he did not want Paris to be another 'Manhattan on the Seine'. Efforts by the French President to mitigate the construction of high-rise extended to the *extra-muros* business district of La Défense to the west of Paris, where the first development plan had been approved by the state in 1964. In line with d'Estaing's position, the new land-use plan referred to as the *Plan d'Occupation des Sols* (POS), which replaced the PUD in 1974, introduced very strict height limitations on the Parisian *intra-muros* territory. However, the ZAC principle remained operational and exemptions thus continued to be made, with the ZAC Paris Rive Gauche as a recent example (see page 80). Since 2003, however, the ZAC status no longer provides automatic exemption from the 37-metre height restriction as set out in the current PLU (*Plan Local d'Urbanisme*), which replaced the POS in 2000.

During the 1960s and 1970s the Parisian suburbs were deeply marked by high-rise developments. The *grands ensembles* (see page 96), were high-rise housing schemes constituting point-towers and slabs which were built as part of a now-abandoned large-scale housing policy, and imposed a radical change of

Landmark
Built
Projects

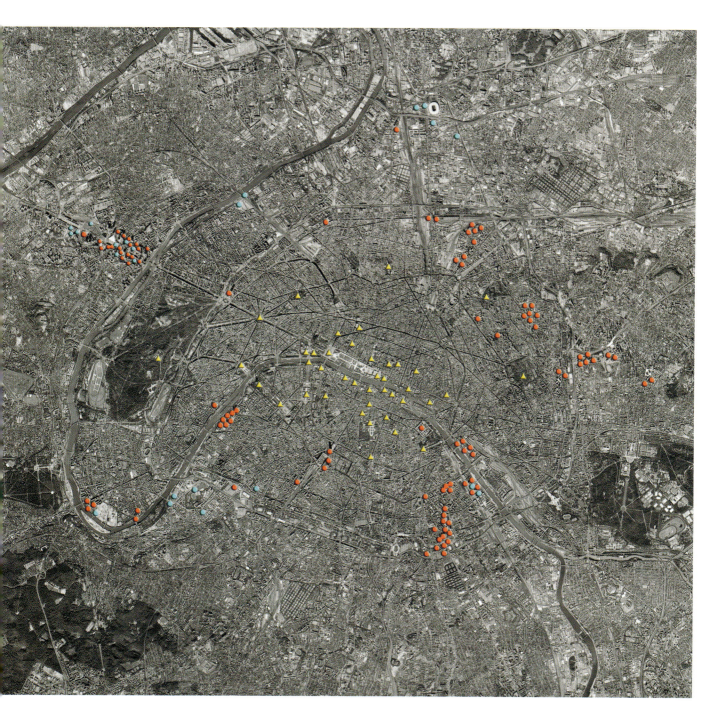

scale around Paris. Still in the suburbs, situated to the west of Paris on an important historic axis, the aforementioned financial centre of La Défense was developed (see page 178) by the national development authority EPAD (Établissement Public d'Aménagement de La Défense created in 1958).

Created in the same year as the PUD by the Paris council, the Parisian planning office (Atelier Parisien d'Urbanisme – APUR) was responsible for anticipating the needs of the city and the society, responding to these by specific studies of town planning. It was also involved in drafting future planning and development policies and legal documents. In this capacity, the APUR released a report in 2003 on tall buildings, *Les tours à Paris, bilan et prospectives*, which assessed the potential and scope for high-rise development in the city and incorporated the notions of landscape and design qualities into the functional grouping of activities by special zones (ZAC). Four zones in the suburbs were identified which could benefit from high-rise development, alleviate saturation pressure from La Défense and create new economic centres at the gates of Paris, with Batignolles, to the northwest, and Seine Rive Gauche (see above), to the east, as the most prominent examples. Secondly, the report reflected on mixed-use skyscrapers.

In 2006, the Paris council encouraged further reflection on height. In the following year, the working group, comprising elective members, delivered a summary of its findings which supported the softening of the laws on heights so as to ensure the urban development and renewal of Paris *intra-muros*. In the same way, a public audit was launched in April 2008: the Conseil d'Architecture, d'Urbanisme et de l'Environnement (CAUE – Architecture, Town Planning and Environment Council of Paris) released a report entitled *Paris demain, conférence citoyenne sur les formes urbaines et les hauteurs* (*Paris Tomorrow, Citizen Conference on Urban Forms and Heights*), which fought for mixed-use high-rise developments connected to the transport hubs. According to the report, towers could fulfil the demands of 'urban densification' by making real estate profitable and by freeing space for parks and utilities.

ORIGINATORS OF URBAN REGULATIONS AND RESPONSIBILITIES

Today, the *Plan Local d'Urbanisme* (PLU) defines the long-term direction of town planning and regulations, and is composed of the *Projet d'aménagement et de développement durable* (PADD – *Project of Planning and Sustainable Development*) and graphic documents such as the *carte des hauteurs* (height map – see

diagram) and the *Plan des Fuseaux de protection du site de Paris* (view corridor map). The PLU is drawn up by collaboration between several institutional partners, notably the state and the Ile-de-France region, as well as having input from civil society and public consultation. The PLU is then submitted for final approval by the Paris council. Building permits are handled by the town planning department (Direction de l'Urbanisme).

La Défense constitutes a special case in terms of planning and is not covered by the Paris *intra-muros* PLU. The EPAD authority coordinates and authorises planning for the site together with three municipalities on which La Défense is located (Nanterre, Courbevoie and Puteaux). The merger in 2008 of the districts of La Défense and its neighbour Seine-Arche, to the west, led to the creation in July 2010 of a new public authority, namely the Etablissement Public d'Aménagement de La Défense Seine Arche (EPADESA).

Urban development in the Parisian suburbs is subject to similar legislation as central Paris, the maximum building heights of new developments in the Parisian suburbs have to be legalised by the local PLUs of each community of the Parisian agglomeration. The application of such requests tends, however, to be simpler and less controversial than in the city centre where the architectural history is steeped in tradition.

ZONING / URBAN PLANNING

The Paris area covered by the PLU is divided into three urban zones (see the *carte de synthèse* (summary map)) – the general urban zone (*zone générale*, UG), the urban services zone (*zone des grands services urbains*, UGSU), the green urban zone (UV) – and one natural zone (*zone naturelle et forestière*, N). The majority of Paris falls under the general urban zone (UG) where construction is controlled based on floor area ratio (*coefficient d'occupation des sols*) set at 3. New constructions in UG zones must comply with the heights map (*carte des hauteurs*) which set the height limit at 37 metres. The most recent consultations on high-rise developments cited the possibility of extending this limit around the city gates as well as out in the suburbs – a tendency which has to a certain degree already become a reality with the example of the Triangle tower project (2008–15, expected completion date) by architects Herzog & De Meuron, at the southwest gate of Paris. The high-level consultation on 'Le Grand Paris' (2009) – commissioned by the Ministry of Culture and Communication – invited architects to present ideas on the future urban development of Paris, and showed that high-rise was at the forefront of many planners' minds.

The business district of La Défense is included in the local plans (PLU) of Nanterre, Puteaux and Courbevoie.

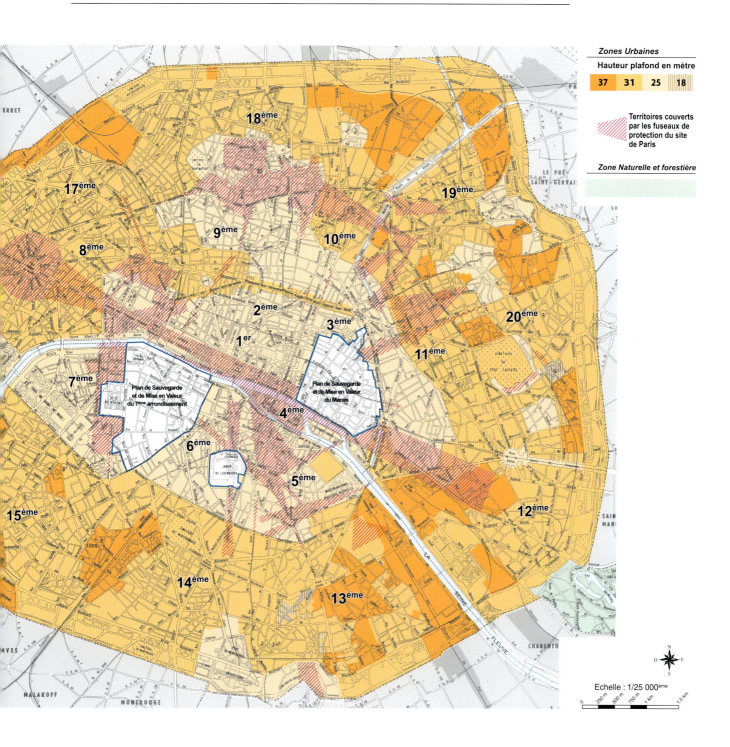

Zones Urbaines

Hauteur plafond en mètre

37   **31**   25   18

Territoires couverts
par les fuseaux de
protection du site
de Paris

Zone Naturelle et forestière

Echelle : 1/25 000ème

Carte des hauteurs
(height map). Paris
heritage is protected
thanks to height limits
and view corridors.

For example, the PLU of Courbevoie currently limits the height to 345 metres in its business zone and encourages the densification of offices, with the Hermitage Tower project of Norman Foster (323 metres) as a current example.

URBAN SKYLINE / CITYSCAPE

A 'view corridors' plan for the city of Paris indicates the location of protected panoramic views, view corridors and viewpoints which overrule the height limitations of the PLU (see the height map). These views, extraordinary sights visible from certain public places (such as the Louvre Museum and the Panthéon), are protected by legislation set out in the town planning code (*Code de l'Urbanisme*). In the business district of La Défense, the impact of a tower on the skyline is estimated using panoramic simulations made by the developers and the public authorities.

TOWER DESIGN

There is no specific mention in either the local plan of cities (PLU) or in the IGH regulation.

BUILDING CODES / FIRE SAFETY

According to fire regulations, a building is considered a high-rise (*immeuble de grande hauteur* – IGH) if it is more than 50 metres tall for residential buildings and 28 metres tall for office buildings. Constructions which exceed 200 metres are referred to in French legislation as 'super-tall' buildings (*immeuble de très grande hauteur* – ITGH). Tall buildings (IGH) are divided into sub-groups, with specific regulations applying to each: these include residential buildings, hotels, schools, control towers, health centres, offices (either between 28 and 50 metres or over and above 50 metres) and multi-use. The construction of a tall building is permitted up to 3 kilometres from a main emergency and firefighting centre. However, the prefect of the district can authorise, by decree, the construction of a tall building at a greater distance, with approval from the department advisory committee for safety and accessibility (*Commission consultative départementale de sécurité et d'accessibilité*). Tall building regulations set maximum occupation densities (one person per 10 square metres), define processes aiming to limit fire spread (fireproof devices), list prohibited materials, control the functioning of elevators and use of fire escapes in case of disaster, and control compliance with standards. The Mayor, with approval of the department advisory committee of civil protection, can require developers to have the building controlled by a laboratory registered with the Minister for Home Affairs (*Ministre de l'intérieur*).

ECOLOGY

The city of Paris seeks to promote the sustainable and economically viable development of the metropolis. This often calls for compromise between conflicting needs (such as housing shortage against the need of more green areas). As part of these efforts, the 1995 performance-based HQE certification (*Haute Qualité Environnementale*) was introduced with the aim of reaching environmental solutions without setting architectural restrictions. A number of specific criteria are highlighted such as the building duration, low energy consumption, the interior air quality and the harmonious relation between the building and its urban context. In La Défense, the Granite Tower, built by French architect Christian de Portzamparc for the Société Générale in 2008, was the first tower to be certified 'HQE' and it became the example model of application of the HQE to tall buildings (IGH HQE).

A further tool to ensure sustainable growth and development is the environmental high-performance certification (*Très Haute Performance Environnementale* – THPE) designed to reduce energy consumption in buildings by 20 to 30 per cent and to verify that a construction respects and surpasses the current legal requirements. In line with the environmental approach of the EPAD authority of La Défense, HQE criteria are actively incorporated into its tower renovation policy as illustrated by the ongoing First tower renovation (Pierre Dufau, 1974; Kohn Pedersen Fox, 2009–11).

The EPAD authority has further demonstrated its commitment to 'green issues' by ratifying a sustainable development charter (*Charte du Développement durable*) in 2007 and in 2008 by organising the first World Business Districts Summit for sustainable development, which gave rise to a 10-point charter. Current commitments aim to improve energy management in the medium and long term, harness the use of natural resources (water and air) more effectively, be more selective with construction materials, reduce and recycle waste, facilitate mixed spaces and usages, improve public transport, apply efficient governance within each business district and, finally, promote cooperation and partnership between business districts. Concerned not only with the provision of standards for future projects but also with the refurbishment or regeneration of existing projects, an urban renewal plan for La Défense has been devised (*Plan de Renouveau de La Défense*, 2010). The plan sets out strategy and support for the refurbishment of the district's first-generation towers with high energy consumption to meet the highest demands and certificates, adding to the HQE the LEED™ and BREEAM certificates (as is the case for the ongoing project of Generali Tower).

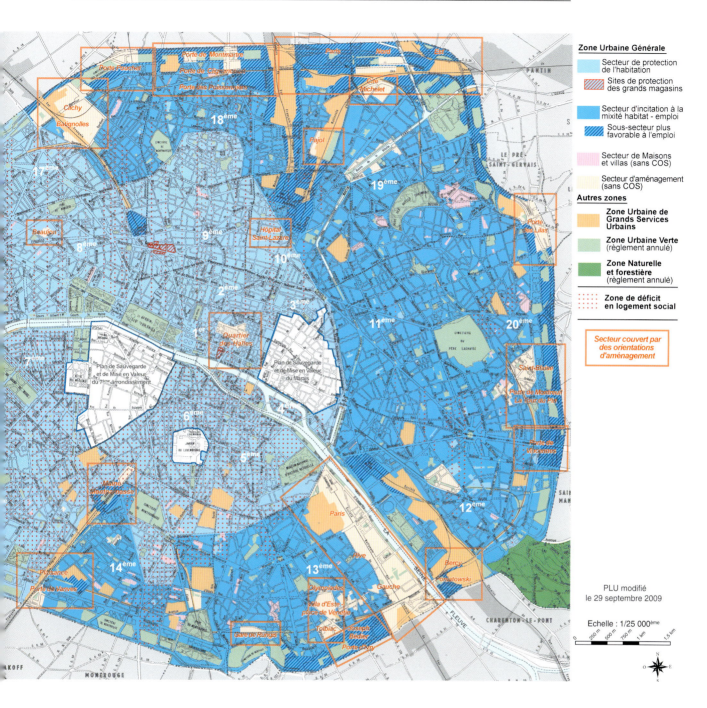

Zone Urbaine Générale

Secteur de protection de l'habitation

Sites de protection des grands magasins

Secteur d'incitation à la mixité habitat - emploi

Sous-secteur plus favorable à l'emploi

Secteur de Maisons et villas (sans COS)

Secteur d'aménagement (sans COS)

Autres zones

Zone Urbaine de Grands Services Urbains

Zone Urbaine Verte (règlement annulé)

Zone Naturelle et forestière (règlement annulé)

Zone de déficit en logement social

Secteur couvert par des orientations d'aménagement

PLU modifié le 29 septembre 2009

Echelle : 1/25 000ème

For more information, see:

City of Paris / *Plan Local d'Urbanisme*
http://www.paris.fr

La Défense business district, http://www.ladefense.fr

EPAD-EPASA: La Défense-Seine Arche
http://www.ladefense-seine-arche.fr

Planning code (*Code de l'Urbanisme*)
http://www.legifrance.gouv.fr

IGH regulation, www.sitesecurite.com

Carte de synthèse (summary map). The majority of the Paris *intra-muros* area falls under the general urban zone. Zones in red, such as the Front de Seine area, are covered by specific planning guidelines.

New York

Though the island of Manhattan with its dramatic architectural skyline is identified throughout the world with New York City, it is in fact only one of the city's five boroughs which also include the Bronx, Brooklyn, Queens and Staten Island. As the commercial, cultural and political hub of the city, confined by water, Manhattan is under considerable development pressure and maximises its density through the construction of high-rise buildings on the base of its regular urban grid. Since its early beginnings, the management of urban space in Manhattan has constantly been subject to a conflict of interest between private initiatives and public authorities which to a certain extent have been kept in check by a system of exemptions, concessions and compensations. The municipality's complex building regulations demonstrate an overarching desire to better adapt construction to the true economic, commercial and social needs of the city.

BACKGROUND / CONTEXT

New York claimed its place as the economic capital of the US in the early 19th century and was forced to undergo an urban transformation due to the spectacular demographic development. To cope with the surge in population, the municipality divided and sold off a large proportion of the land which it owned to private investors, but to maintain governance in the urban development it devised an egalitarian system of land use defined by commissioners. The Commissioners' Plan was designed in 1811 by Simeon de Witt, expert geographer for the State of New York, Governor Morris and the lawyer John Rutherford. The plan effectively rationalised the land by demarcating it rigorously into 2,028 blocks and therefore mitigated through its simplicity the predictable planning conflicts between multiple landowners. The plan provided a durable urban framework which lived up to New York's aspirations of becoming the nation's capital of economy and business. Its vast street layout was provisionally planned for a population of one million inhabitants, 10 times more than the city had at the time. The rectangular blocks were interconnected by a network of roads forming an even grid which allowed rapid traffic flow from north to south and east to west. Except for Broadway, no public building or main road strayed from this urban matrix. In this way the egalitarian governance of private and public spaces was guaranteed throughout the entire city, as was the functioning of commercial activities and traffic.

Technical advances at the end of the 19th century such as steel structures and the widespread use of elevators, in conjunction with the particularity of Manhattan's urban grid and intense property speculation, catalysed an almost logical transition to the incorporation of skyscrapers into Manhattan's urban landscape. Manhattan skyscrapers soared up and quickly surpassed the scale of skyscrapers in Chicago where regulations limited the height to 22 storeys until 1923. As Cass Gilbert, one of America's most famous high-rise architects and designer of the Woolworth Building (1913), said, the skyscraper is a 'machine that makes the land pay'. Zoning regulations in New York were adopted in 1916, following the construction of Ernest R Graham's Equitable Building (1915), whose bulky mass had led to controversy. To prevent high-rise buildings from casting Manhattan into perpetual gloom, there emerged a new era in which public authorities became involved in the governance of urban space, after several decades of non-intervention in the market. The 1916 Zoning Resolution – which may easily be mistaken for the zoning by areas – shaped the envelope of the New York skyscraper by regulating the form and the volume of the building for three quarters of the plot, according to the width of the street and the setback angles. Five types were thus defined, which gave birth to a ziggurat profile made popular by the visuals of Hugh Ferriss in his book *The Metropolis of Tomorrow* (1929). This building regulation, which only gave free rein in terms of height for a quarter of the site, put a stop to construction of buildings which were considered too bulky. Indeed, it determined a setback system: the setback was the portion of a building that was set back above the height of the building base before the total height of the building was achieved. The precise position of the first setback varied with the district. Presented as democratic progress, this Zoning Resolution was also an agreement between the regulator and the developer that guaranteed a minimum amount of daylight and air, without which constructions would have lost their value. Theoretically, the purpose was not to build as high as possible any more but to define a 'liveable height'. From now on, the number of floors was to be linked to public health requirements. Unsuccessful, however, in limiting building heights due to the developers' quest for the most efficient investment, the reformers of the 1920s demanded – primarily in vain – the reduction of plot coverage to free up public space on the ground.

This demand for public space eventually became a reality in the middle of the 20th century through a deliberate initiative led by a group of architects: Lever

House by Skidmore, Owings & Merrill (1952) and the
Seagram Building (see page 39) by Mies van der Rohe
(1958) bypassed the setback regulations through a
recess of the whole building from the street boundary,
creating a sleek and monolithic volume. The 1950s
saw such an extreme growth in densities that the 1961
Zoning Resolution attached a floor area ratio (FAR) to
all new developments. The law then granted floor area
bonuses to developers who agreed to contribute to the
improvement of the townscape by leaving a percentage
of the constructible land unbuilt, and by providing green
spaces, squares or arcades on the ground floor, with
the Seagram Building as an explicit model. Based on
a concept first proposed in 1916, the Transfer of
Development Rights (TDR) system was introduced in
1968 and applied to buildings lower than the authorised
maximum height. The owners of these properties were
allowed to sell the unused volume of land to the owner

of the neighbouring site, who could then increase the height of their building by up to 20 per cent. In the framework of this rule, 700 historic low buildings have been listed. One of the best-known examples was the sale by the Pennsylvania Central Transportation Company of the Grand Central Station rights for the construction of the Pan Am Building (completed 1963; now the MetLife Building). But Walter Gropius's skyscraper was coldly received: it highlighted how the overlay of private interests and municipal regulations was ambitious but difficult. Hence the 1961 Zoning Resolution has been continually enhanced and particularised, and the aim for mixed uses expressed through the loosening of the formerly too strict functional segregation by zone.

ORIGINATORS OF URBAN REGULATIONS AND RESPONSIBILITIES

Today, the Department of City Planning (DCP) is responsible for the Zoning Resolution. It promotes strategic development of the City by initiating changes in planning and zoning. The DCP thus reviews each year land use applications for zoning changes and the disposition of City property. The Department of Buildings enforces the Zoning Resolution as well as the directives of the City's Building Code (delivering building permits). The City Planning Commission, which is part of the Department of City Planning, is responsible, within the framework of public review (Uniform Land Use Review Procedure – ULURP, which reviews applications affecting the land use), for the election of measures linked to the use and improvement of zones under municipal regulations.

The City Planning Commission and/or the Board of Standards and Appeals (BSA – required for the small cases) consider the possibility of simple authorisations (without ULURP), exemptions or special permits when strict regulations unjustifiably limit a site's development. Any project granted exemption has to respect the State Environmental Quality Review (SEQR) and the City Environmental Quality Review (CEQR). To summarise, the DCP is responsible for amendments applied to the regulations (in the text or on the map), whether on its own initiative or that of the taxpayer, district council or the Mayor himself. Moreover, when construction rights transfer (TDR, see below) conditions are met, a report by the Landmarks Preservation Commission on the project is submitted to the Department of City Planning.

ZONING / URBAN PLANNING

The New York zoning plan divides the island of Manhattan into three zones: residential, commercial and industrial. The three basic districts are further subdivided into a variety of lower, medium and higher densities with special zoning regulations. The permitted uses of each district are listed in 18 use groups detailed in the Zoning Text (for example: groups 1 and 2 are residential; groups 3 and 4 are public buildings; groups 5 to 9 are retail trade). Any ground surface of a building is necessarily equal to or lower than the determined lot coverage – the portion of a zoning lot covered by a building – and subject to a floor area ratio. Basically, the rule sets out that the ground-floor surface and the space granted to the public sphere should determine the height of a building as well as indirectly its relation to the adjacent buildings. The setback system is codified by

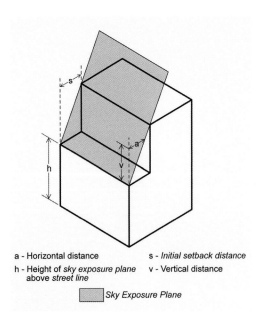

a - Horizontal distance

h - Height of *sky exposure plane* above *street line*

s - *Initial setback distance*

v - *Vertical distance*

Sky Exposure Plane

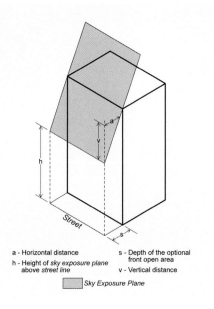

a - Horizontal distance

h - Height of *sky exposure plane* above *street line*

s - Depth of the optional front open area

v - Vertical distance

Sky Exposure Plane

Sky exposure planes. The sketches show the influence of the setbacks system on the amount of daylight in streets.

Christian de Portzamparc's LVMH Tower on 57th Street in Manhattan.

sectors according to the road width, and determines the silhouette of the building. In residential zones, regulations encourage developers to reduce congestion, by setting back from the street and by incorporating off-road parking space, thus reducing the overall mass of the building. The city bases its regulations on assessment of sky exposure planes, in order to maintain light and air at street level, primarily in medium- and higher-density districts. Structures are required by district regulations to conform to an idealised inclining plane, which begins at a specified height and ascends inwards over the zoned site; the vertical and horizontal distances are prescribed by a fixed ratio (see sky exposure planes, sketches 1 and 2). The assessments thus determine the maximum height of the tower, the depth of setbacks or even influence the shape of the building top, which may be required to slope. In this respect there is also the 'height factor building', which is a residential development whose mass is determined by a height factor (the total floor area of the building divided by its lot coverage), a floor area ratio and open space ratio, and is set within a sky exposure plane. Height factor regulations aim to develop tall buildings surrounded by open space.

In a high-density commercial area, a tower is defined as a portion of a building that penetrates the sky exposure plane and occupies up to 40 per cent of the lot or up to 50 per cent of a smaller lot (up to 1,858 square metres or 20,000 square feet): it must be set back by 3 metres (10 feet) from a wide street and 4 metres (15 feet) from a narrow street. Regulations vary depending on whether a tower is 'on-a-base' or whether its plot is lined by two streets or more. According to setback requirements, if only one point touches the prescribed (elevated) street line, the building is up to standards: contrary to what is collectively assumed, the ziggurat 'wedding cake' profile is thus not a formal obligation. The LVMH Tower by Christian de Portzamparc (1997) on 57th Street is, from this point of view, enlightening as it challenged construction customs. Situated in a high-density commercial sector, the building was allowed to be built taller thanks to the concession of a certain percentage of floor area to the city and the acquisition of the neighbouring gallery's rights (Zoning lot merger principle). The Zoning Resolution imposed recesses at the 11th and 18th storeys, the aforementioned street lines: the architect hence faceted his building so that a salient line reached these indicated storeys in just one point.

According to the Zoning law, the Zoning lot merger is 'the joining of two or more adjacent zoning lots into one new zoning lot'. It enables the shift of unused

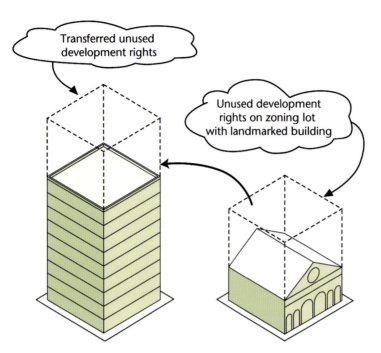

**Sketch of the Transfer
of Development Rights
system. The TDR system
allows for the transfer
of unused development
rights from one zoning
lot to another in special
circumstances.**

development rights from one lot to another, as of right.
In the same way, the TDR system applies to two
adjacent constructions or two constructions directly
across a street or diagonally across an intersection,
one of which is considered a landmark, a theatre or
any other specific structure listed by the Landmarks
Preservation Commission (excluding statues,
commemorative monuments and bridges) (see TDR
sketch). Regulations specify the floor area ratio that
the building surface cannot exceed, making a
distinction between residential and commercial zones
and taking into account the purpose of the new
building, otherwise the City Planning Commission
has to deliver a special permit.

URBAN SKYLINE / CITYSCAPE

There is no specific mention of skyline in the Zoning
Resolution.

TOWER DESIGN

In the New York Zoning Resolution, there are no
directives concerning the aesthetics of tall buildings.
The Municipality can, in certain cases, require that
a project includes public facilities such as publicly
accessible spaces, arcades or access to public
transport which in turn influence the building's
architecture.

BUILDING CODES / FIRE SAFETY

Fire safety is an important element of the New York
Building Code, especially since the terrorist attacks of
11 September 2001. The selection of materials for
internal and external design, location and functioning
of elevators as well as access follow a strict legislation.
Another section of the regulations concerns the impact
of wind on tall buildings, depending on whether they
are located in the centre or along the river, as well as
the potential hazard caused by earthquakes. Moreover,
the glass used in curtain walls is important – to limit
reverberation – as is the definition of steel structural
types. The quality of the material and the structural
design must comply with the American Institute of
Steel Construction standards.

ECOLOGY

The City Environmental Quality Review (CEQR),
introduced by the City Planning Commission according
to state law (SEQR) in 1977 (updated in 1991), aims to
identify the potential negative impacts of any urban
intervention and to find solutions which can for example
entail public review of the planning procedure. If a
zoning map or text amendment is proposed by the
Department of City Planning, its potential environmental
impact is subsequently evaluated by the City Planning
Commission. The CEQR manual published by the Office
of Environmental Coordination provides the municipal
bodies and developers with the methodology which
guides them in drafting the report to be submitted on
the impact of their project (Environmental Assessment
Statement – EAS). Based on this statement, the
Commission gives its agreement or proposes
appropriate mitigation. In 2005, Mayor Michael R

Bloomberg ratified law 86 obliging any new building to comply with the LEED™ standards developed by the United States Green Building Council. The primary objectives of law 86 are to optimise energy management, to reduce waste and to conserve water. The law is the first phase of the New York 2030 plan which intends to reduce the city's energy consumption and carbon emissions by approximately 50 per cent.

The Department of City Planning (specifically the Buildings Sustainability Board) is presently working on measures for sustainable development, notably to repaint the roofs of buildings in white or convert them into gardens, install energy recycling microturbines as well as solar panels. Any building reducing its energy consumption benefits from tax rebates according to the Energy Policy Act of 2005. In 2006, the New York Skyscraper Museum presented the 'Green Teams: How Sustainability Succeeds in Business' exhibition. This exhibition listed Manhattan's 'green' tall buildings or building projects, which include the Freedom Tower by Skidmore, Owings & Merrill (estimated completion in 2013) and the Hearst Tower by Foster + Partners

(2006). It also represented an opportunity for architects, politicians and LEED™ representatives to present a work showing future urban trends including the new technologies to be applied (transport, curtain walls, air-conditioning and structure) for sustainable development in this sector.

For more information, see:

New York City Department of City Planning
http://www.nyc.gov/html/dcp

New York Department of Buildings
http://www.nyc.gov/html/dob

New York Skyscraper Museum / 'Green Teams: How Sustainability Succeeds in Business' exhibition (conclusions on the museum's website)
http://www.skyscraper.org

The step-back logic of high-rise in Midtown Manhattan.

Hong Kong

Hong Kong, with a population of over 7 million and its mountainous topography, brings up the issue of very high densities and the importance of preparatory planning by, notably, optimising land usage, maximising public transport use and defining optimal densities. Hong Kong's current approach to town planning is unique and works on three separate yet interconnected levels: land planning, leasehold and building controls. Hong Kong thus demonstrates the crucial importance of maintaining good governance in a high-rise city which seeks to balance out the enforcement of public directives with the pursuit of private ambition.

BACKGROUND / CONTEXT

The Convention between Great Britain and China Respecting an Extension of Hong Kong Territory of 1898 was a lease which extended UK sovereignty of the Hong Kong administrative region to include, in addition to Hong Kong Island and the Kowloon Peninsula, also Lantau Island and the adjacent northern lands, the so-called 'New Territories'. This administrative subdivision was to remain in force until the restitution of Hong Kong to China in 1997.

Prior to the Second World War, construction had been governed by the Building Ordinance Regulation of 1935, limiting the height of buildings to five storeys. After the war and the Japanese occupation (1941–5), though demand for housing had skyrocketed, the Hong Kong government did not actively participate in the reconstruction of the city, faithful to its philosophy of non-intervention. In the middle of the 20th century, political unrest (characterised by the Great Leap Forward and the Cultural Revolution), refocused from the international to the internal upheavals in China, and caused many to flee the Chinese mainland in search of refuge in neighbouring Hong Kong. The pressures exerted by such a dramatic increase in Hong Kong's population resulted (almost by default) in the Building Ordinance authorising a significant amount of construction in zones where lease conditions had to be relaxed in order to physically accommodate the growth. Indeed, the territory, property of the British Crown on the basis of the aforementioned lease, was sub-leased to developers via a system of long-term leaseholds which constituted the government's main source of income. In order to keep the price of land put up for auction high, there had to be a limited supply; hence the use of land was meticulously rationed and as a result developers systematically exploited land at the maximum authorised. At the signature in 1984 of the land retrocession to the Chinese sovereignty, scheduled to take place in 1997, the agreement concerning leases between the United Kingdom and China thus took into account the pressures on real estate and stipulated that the Hong Kong government could release for construction no more than 50 hectares per year, which would increase to 159 hectares in 1992. These constraints were intended to prevent the Hong Kong government maximising cash flow through the sale of new leaseholds during the transition period before 1997.

To give a brief overview, in the post-war reconstruction context, the modification of lease conditions worked on the basis of controlling heights, densities and plot coverage. This led also to the conception and application of a floor area ratio identical to that of the United Kingdom and the United States. In 1963, three density zones were introduced, based on existing population densities (residential zones R1, R2 and R3) and control was applied by decree in zones categorised as lower-density areas. At the beginning of the 1980s, this control gave rise to further density standards introduced in Chapter 2 of the *Hong Kong Planning Standards and Guidelines*. Moreover, sites subject to height limitations due to air traffic had an even more limited density, fixed with plot ratios. The three zones were distinguished according to their geographical aspect. Zone R1 applied to the main urban areas on lower grounds and those gained from the sea: the floor area ratio was 10 (8 if the plot was lined with only one street). Zone R2 applied to higher

grounds with a maximum floor area ratio of 6.6 (also reduced to 5 if lined by only one street). Finally, zone R3 applied to steep sites like the Peak on Hong Kong Island, which constitutes an important natural heritage: the highest floor area ratio here was limited to 3.

Governance problems continued to grow until the end of the 1980s: neither the incomplete government regulations nor private initiatives succeeded in curtailing the deterioration of Hong Kong living standards (lack of financing, no central coordination, conflicts between multiple owners). Finally, in 1988, the government took action and established the Land Development Corporation to improve housing standards and the quality of the environment through the comprehensive renewal of many sites. The Land Development Corporation had the power to undertake, encourage or facilitate reconstruction within the zones defined by the Urban Renewal Plan: the Corporation

▲ Landmark
● Built
● Projects

managed the operations on its own behalf or initiated a partnership with developers or property owners. The combination of public and private initiatives within the framework of the urban renewal programme eventually led to the rapid transformation of Hong Kong's territory. Private development of targeted zones had to guarantee the fair treatment of tenants and lead to investment in and development of the city's public amenities and transport links. The overall aim was to reduce any future need for government subsidies.

In 1989, a vote was passed to decentralise the harbour and airport activities west of the bay. Two years later, the Metroplan (master development scheme), covering the entire urban area, set out objectives to enhance the visual and physical accessibility of the waterfront as part of a strategy to redistribute and lower population density in the historic core. Integral to this process were the spreading of development on to adjoining harbour reclamations; comprehensive urban renewal including the creation of high-density zones in which the floor area ratio was proportional to the distance from the nearest transport link; inclusion of green spaces; and the obligation to create public services.

However, in 1996, the *Report of Public Consultation of Urban Renewal* revealed the government's continued inability to take up the mantle of urban renovation on a sufficient scale and within a short enough period to slow down the deterioration of the townscape. It was thus decided that there was a need to create new conception mechanisms in addition to further subsidies from the government. In 2001 the Urban Renewal Authority replaced the Land Development Corporation, grouping together the Planning Department, Buildings Department, Lands Department and Territory Development Department and subsequently holding responsibility for parts of the Town Planning Board functions. Streamlining the development organisations meant town planning procedures were thus simplified. In 2003, the Design Guidelines for Hong Kong set out further objectives designed to enhance Hong Kong's profile by improving construction quality in terms of technical and aesthetic aspects and by limiting the variations from one district to the other. Based on an extensive public review, the guidelines incorporated an overarching series of measures regarding the skyline, waterfront, shape of the city, pedestrian environment and the decrease of air pollution.

ORIGINATORS OF URBAN REGULATIONS AND RESPONSIBILITIES

Today, the Planning Department is in charge of the planning policy, land use, buildings and urban renewal in Hong Kong. It takes directives from the Development Bureau and formulates, monitors and reviews land use at the territorial level. The Planning Department also prepares district and local plans and area improvement plans, and applies the *Hong Kong Planning Standards and Guidelines* (HKPSG). The HKPSG guides territorial strategies and Statutory and Departmental plans (that is, local plans) by setting out guidelines for scale, location and site requirements. Served by the Planning Department, the Town Planning Board – composed of the Metro Planning Committee and the Rural and New Town Planning Committee – is responsible for statutory planning in Hong Kong and is formed under the Town Planning Ordinance. The Town Planning Board oversees the preparation of draft statutory plans and considers applications for planning permission and amendments to plans. Two types of statutory plans exist: the Outline Zoning Plan, which determines land-use zones, development parameters and major road systems of an individual planning area; and the Development Permission Area Plan, which provides interim planning control and development guidance for rural areas in the New Territories.

In Hong Kong, town planning and the above-mentioned statutory regulations work within the complex framework of a leasehold land system. Prior to the transfer of land designated for construction, the Lands Department defines the lease conditions which the developer must respect. They relate to the floor area ratio, height, and creation of services (such as access to public transport and provision of communal areas). Finally, height restrictions relating to air corridors and special control zones are also incorporated. The process of developing a building may thus involve the seeking of not only planning permission from the Planning Department, but also a land grant or lease modification from the Lands Department and a building plan approval from the Buildings Department.

On a more general and larger scale, the Territorial Development Strategy provides a guideline to Hong Kong's future development (including provision of strategic infrastructure and housing) and forms the basis of the district plans. Thus, the Hong Kong 2030: Planning Vision and Strategy which took effect in 2007 is a territorial development strategy that encourages a further reinforcement of the governmental authority. In the same way, the Coordinated Development of the Greater Pearl River Delta Townships aims to create a regional planning framework between Hong Kong, Macau and Guangdong.

In addition, there is the Urban Renewal Authority (URA) which prepares and implements urban renewal plans within the framework of the *Hong Kong Planning Standards and Guidelines*: it speeds up the renewal of neglected urban areas and executes the Urban Renewal Strategy formulated by the government. The URA marks out restoration zones, expropriates, vacates and takes over all properties in zones to be restored, builds on or sells the recuperated sites, promulgates development recommendations, relocates the affected tenants, and manages the Rehabilitation Fund. Every developer's masterplan must be submitted to the Town Planning Board for validation.

ZONING / URBAN PLANNING

Hong Kong's geography, with the mountain range and agricultural lands in the alluvial plains, means the major urban sectors are concentrated on the northern coastline of Hong Kong Island (22 Hong Kong Planning Areas), the Kowloon peninsula (19 Kowloon Planning Areas) and in the new cities of the New Territories (nearly 60 development areas where many residential towers have been constructed). Each Planning Area respects an Outline Zoning Plan with a defined floor area ratio which can go up to 10 in residential zones and 15 in commercial zones. As one of the world's most prominent examples of a city operating within the constraints of a limited supply of land, the demographic pressure and the high floor area ratio have generated extremely high densities over the majority of the developed territory in Hong Kong. This construction density has also been limited to an extent by geotechnical conditions such as underground caves, by complexities related to conditions of land ownership or by issues of historical heritage. It is also influenced by the increase in the average size of apartments in the private sector.

The Metroplan area incorporates Hong Kong Island, Kowloon and New Kowloon and the Districts of Tsuen Wan and Kwai Tsing. The outline plan is divided in three Residential Density Zones R1, R2 and R3 – reminiscent of the zoning of 1963 – with specific categories for building heights, plot ratio, and site coverage (see the Residential Density Zones table). Zone 1 covers high-density residential development. It applies to districts served by an extensive network of public transport. Buildings in these zones can have commercial floor space spread over four levels. Developments which come under this category are then subdivided into 'existing development areas' subject to existing land leases which vary dependent on site class, and 'new development areas' resulting from new land grants. Zone 2 deals with medium-density developments, served by public transport but usually excluding floor space for commercial use. Finally, Zone 3 covers low-density residential development, and has limited public transport and special building conditions for environmental reasons.

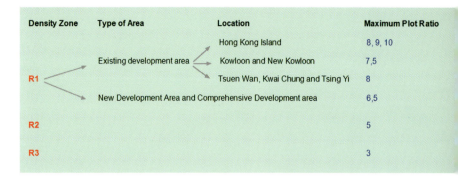

Density Zone	Type of Area	Location	Maximum Plot Ratio
R1	Existing development area	Hong Kong Island	8, 9, 10
		Kowloon and New Kowloon	7,5
		Tsuen Wan, Kwai Chung and Tsing Yi	8
	New Development Area and Comprehensive Development area		6,5
R2			5
R3			3

High-density management in the most suitable urban sectors is in fact accompanied by a process of selective de-densification in old congested districts of Hong Kong and the development of the New Territories to the north, where new cities linked to transport infrastructures are created. In reference to this it is possible to identify two urban types: the dense, old and deteriorated districts which are the priority target of the Urban Renewal Authority (eight floors on average and no green spaces); and the more recent sectors, combining tall buildings of over 30 floors with green spaces. Hong Kong's vertical town planning addresses housing as well as office or commercial use and parking use, in spite of a vast public transport network advocated and supported through Hong Kong government policy. This policy has been underpinned by a series of converging measures which include reinforcement of public transport since 1990, high taxes, prohibitive parking costs, proximity and mixed uses. As a result car circulation is relatively low. Hong Kong also boasts an extensive network of footbridges which interconnect buildings and give access between the ground floors and podiums. Incentives for developers to incorporate a footbridge section through their buildings in order to extend the existing network have been drawn up by the Hong Kong government and consist of granting a higher floor area ratio in return (refer also to first part of the book, page 188).

URBAN SKYLINE / CITYSCAPE

The Design Guidelines for Hong Kong take three principal aspects into consideration: relations between the city-dweller and the urban environment; the architectural ground disposition (volume, green spaces, bridges); and the skyline which determines the city image. Hong Kong and Kowloon define height profile by district and encourage an alternation between more or less dense zones. In contrast to the development logic of the last two decades, taller buildings are now concentrated inland, with lower developments lining

Residential Density Zones table. The Metroplan area includes three Density Zones determining planning standards.

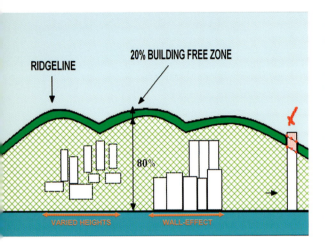

the waterfront, to avoid the disturbance of air circulation through an impermeable 'wall-effect' (see the 'wall-effect' and ridgeline sketch). The line drawn by the mountain summits as well as the views on the plain are protected by a View Corridor system. Victoria Harbour, situated between Hong Kong and Kowloon, benefits from particular measures outlined in the *Vision and Goals for Victoria Harbour* (Town Planning Board, 1999): the aim is now to vary architectural volumes and heights along the waterfront to avoid a monotonous effect, introduce landmarks, protect views of tall buildings from the harbour and thus to arrange a visual permeability between the waterfront and the internal sectors. In the same way, Urban Fringe Areas, which describe the transition between urban and rural areas, are subject to the principles of height gradation and limit the development potential towards the natural spaces.

In the New Territories, recommendations have been made to build tall and introduce the gradation of densities. Lower buildings (such as schools and the city hall) thus have to be built near the historic villages in order to avoid extraordinary differences of scale. In these areas recommendations have also been made to create strategic focal points which accommodate either commercial or civic functions.

TOWER DESIGN

According to the *Hong Kong Planning Standards and Guidelines* (HKPSG), wherever possible, the development of a site must favour the separation of pedestrian and automobile traffic (through a network of footbridges). This is sometimes prescribed in the lease conditions or can be a deliberate decision taken by the developer in order to best link the building to the surrounding urban activity. Developers also have to create an open space accessible to city-dwellers, which guarantees air and sunshine. The lease

conditions sometimes include further restrictions on the conception and position of buildings, height, types of housing and landscaping. As a consequence and defined by the situation, two principal types of tall buildings have emerged: the first is for mixed use on a podium (often with an overlay of transport station, shopping mall, car park, public spaces, housing/hotel/offices) and the second is residential only, potentially with parking spaces underneath.

BUILDING CODES / FIRE SAFETY

The fire safety standards, which are based on a combination of UK and US rules, stipulate the structure and internal organisation of tall buildings, mainly in terms of fire staircases, fire corridors and evacuation scenarios. Cool materials, which are characterised by high solar reflectivity and/or high emissivity, are required for use in the pavements, streets and building facades to minimise absorption of solar radiation. The Building Disposition chapter of the HKPSG stipulates that a suitable disposition of building blocks could help effective airflow around buildings in desirable directions (see the Building Dispositions sketch). One solution has been to create, where possible, wide gaps between building blocks to maximise airflow and minimise wind corridors. Another solution has been to allow individual high-rise blocks to capture more wind for better indoor natural ventilation – 'the angle between the axis of the building blocks and the prevailing wind direction should be within 30 degrees' (HKPSG, Building Disposition) – and heights between towers should be graduated in order to ease air circulation. In the case of podium developments, the towers must, if possible, abut the podium's edge. As compact integrated developments and podium structures often impede air movements, street-level measures for very large developments (especially in existing urban areas) have been introduced to minimise this impact. These include providing setbacks in parallel to the wind, generating voids in the facades facing the prevailing wind and reducing site coverage of the podium. In the same way, low-rise buildings and open spaces are to be located in proximity to the waterfront and in the direction of the prevailing wind.

From an architectural point of view the cruciform plan of most residential towers in Hong Kong is conspicuous. It can be explained through the legal requirement to provide natural light in each room and to maximise the unobstructed area of vision. In high-rise developments, the natural light of the lower floors comes from light reflected from the surfaces of surrounding buildings and therefore depends indirectly on the massing layout of the whole development.

'Wall-effect' and ridgeline sketch. Hong Kong fits high-rise development to its topography.

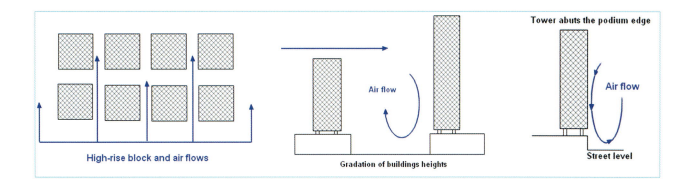

High-rise block and air flows

Air flow

Gradation of buildings heights

Tower abuts the podium edge

Air flow

Street level

ECOLOGY

The intense development of public transport is a first step towards sustainable development, but in view of the constructed density it is insufficient. Concerns regarding ecology began to be addressed in 1996 with the Hong Kong Building Environmental Assessment Method (HKBEAM), which is based on the UK Building Research Establishment Environmental Assessment Method (BREEAM) and has similar functions to the US-developed Leadership in Energy & Environmental Design (LEED™) (see page 246). HKBEAM is a very technical label adapted to the subtropical Hong Kong climate, originally conceived – and constantly updated and improved – to address the construction of new buildings as well as the upgrade of old buildings to contemporary standards. Although the label is not part of any legislation, demands in the property market have made it a valuable asset as a selling point of environmental sustainability on which Hong Kong is marketing itself (in 2009, about 200 tall buildings were, or were in the process of being, labelled). In 1997, the *Study on Sustainable Development for the 21st Century* (SUSDEV21), ordered by the Hong Kong government, introduced the sustainable development concept into the decision-making procedures and simultaneously raised public awareness by involving citizens in the process. The study subsequently led to the elaboration of guiding principles adapted to the socioeconomic structure of the city, to the development of indicators and to the shaping of the specific software, CASET (Computer Aided Sustainability Evaluation Tool). This tool helps to estimate the durability and evolution of a project based on measures taken from the analysis of statistical data. The guiding principles – which affect the economy, hygiene and health, natural resources, biodiversity, social order, environmental quality, cost of medical care and mobility – are defined by the Sustainable Development System (SDS). The establishment of a Sustainable Development Unit and the implementation of long-term strategic reflection

resulted from this guideline. As a consequence, the ever-shorter lease durations are considered to be an issue of increasing concern, as any form of construction or demolition has a direct environmental impact.

In terms of long-term strategic planning to promote sustainable development, the Council for Sustainability Development was created in 2003 and enacted the *First Sustainable Development Strategy for Hong Kong* in 2005, supporting the aforementioned measures for city ventilation. One of its priorities is to reduce growing respiratory problems among Hong Kong's population. The Hong Kong 2030 plan confirms these matters, aiming to improve the quality of life (townscape, renovation of old districts, reduction of the urban temperature, decentralisation, intensification of public transport), protecting the natural heritage and harmonising various policies supported and reinforced by the governmental authority in the construction process. The principle of density is not questioned in that it conserves land and reduces distances, but it will be combined with more lenient town planning, enhancing the microclimate and providing a more spacious living environment.

For more information, see:

Hong Kong Planning Department
http://www.pland.gov.hk

Hong Kong Lands Department
http://www.landsd.gov.hk

Hong Kong Buildings Department
http://www.bd.gov.hk

Statutory Planning Portal: OZP Hong Kong
http://www.ozp.tpb.gov.hk

Urban Renewal Authority   http://www.ura.org.hk

Hong Kong Sustainable Development
http://www.susdev.gov.hk

Building Dispositions sketch. Planning strategies provide airflow between building blocks.

Singapore

Singapore is a city-state situated on a small island south of Malaysia and is accustomed to issues of land shortage and rapid population growth, which have led to intensive land use and high-density high-rise on the majority of its territory. Singapore's planning regulations present an unusual and complex centre–suburb relation, and recent efforts have focused on the rebalancing of densities and activities on the basis of neighbourhoods, catalysed through growing environmental stakes.

BACKGROUND / CONTEXT

When the United Kingdom colonised Singapore in 1819, the planning control over new territory was loosely defined and uncoordinated. After three years during which the city grew haphazardly, it was decided that a concrete plan mapping out the city's urban development was necessary. The Jackson Plan of 1822 was the first plan that divided the land according to a regular pattern and distinguished between the various ethnic groups. Under this plan Singapore continued to prosper for the next century, until the devastating impact of the Second World War and the Japanese occupation from 1941 to 1945 brought development to an abrupt halt. At the end of the occupation a substantial housing reconstruction programme was implemented to deal with the pressing issue of housing shortage, slum clearance and resettlement faced by Singapore. The programme was coordinated and steered by the Housing Committee, established in 1947, and subsequently by the Housing Development Board (HDB) from 1960 onwards, which was set up following the election of the People's Action Party (in 1959). It signified a new direction for urban planning in Singapore. Following recommendations made by the United Nations in 1963, the city-state opted for the conurbation model structured by motorways (facilitating the transport of goods) and a system of public transport networks (provided by Mass Rapid Transport – MRT), with the long-term objective of redistributing the population over the length and breadth of the island.

High-rise housing developed rapidly, despite the scepticism of architects, town planners and economists alike who were of the opinion that other options existed to maximise land use preferable to high-rise construction. Moreover, it was considered that the spatial separation of residential and business uses would be an excessive rather than an efficient use of space. Between 1963 and 1975, the Housing Development Board commissioned the construction of more than 230,000 lodgings, distributed along a peripheral belt of new settlements determined by the Concept Plan of 1971. Home ownership was designed to increase the 'sense of nationalism'. The plan was based on demographic projections spread out over 20 years and, accordingly, rationed and exploited land resources.

Expelled from the Federation of Malaysia in 1965, Singapore was forced to turn its attention towards international trade and attracted industry and services to development on the island. The upshot was the shift in development from the centre to the sparsely built-up outskirts of the city. The priority given to a vertical growth paradigm led to the proliferation of suburban mega-complexes which continued until the end of the 1980s. These projects were initially headed by the HDB, the Jurong Town Corporation (in the Jurong and Sembawang industrial parks) and the Housing and Urban Development Company, which was dedicated to providing low-income family housing. In 1982, the latter two companies merged with the HDB which became the sole provider of public housing.

The town centre renovation was executed according to the tabula rasa principle. Its specialisation in a service industries zone with strong land pressure was realised under the aegis of the Urban Redevelopment Authority (URA). Created in 1974, the URA was independent from the Housing Development Board. Two planning paradigms appeared: small-scale neighbourhood planning on one hand and super-blocks on the other. The town centre was characterised by property speculation and the intense exploitation of the land with a plot ratio system. Some nearby residential buildings were not spared and were replaced by large-scale developments, encouraged by a new law which favoured the construction of private condominiums. In 1991, the Concept Plan was revised on the initiative of the Urban Redevelopment Authority which had become the national planning body in 1989, under the supervision of the Ministry of National Development: the new plan suggested spreading the plot ratio principle over the entire island, based on a division into five regions subdivided into 55 areas of development endowed with a detailed plan (Development Guide Plan – DGP).

Seven years later, all the DGPs were set up, marking a greater densification. Each area of approximately 150,000 inhabitants was split into sectors, each with a shopping centre. These planning principles were included in the 1998 Master Plan, which advised property owners and developers on the use of land. The 2001 Concept Plan aimed to raise Singapore to the rank of a world city over the subsequent 40 years. It was revised in 2009 and will be effective from 2011. This plan favours housing densification in already developed sectors (Bukit Merah, Bedok), construction of residential towers of 30 or more storeys, the creation of green spaces, railway transport improvement and reinforcement of a Singaporean architectural identity.

ORIGINATORS OF URBAN REGULATIONS AND RESPONSIBILITIES

Today, urban planning in Singapore continues to be strongly centralised, authority resting with the Ministry of National Development, orchestrated by the Urban Redevelopment Authority. The former ensures that the Planning Act is applied correctly. This act is the main legislative tool which dictates the terms and conditions of the planning procedures. The Urban Redevelopment Authority is the author of the Concept Plan and of the Statutory Master Plan. The former, which is not a statutory document, outlines planning and transport in the long term. The Statutory Master Plan translates the propositions of the Concept Plan into detailed

▲ Landmark
● Built
● Projects

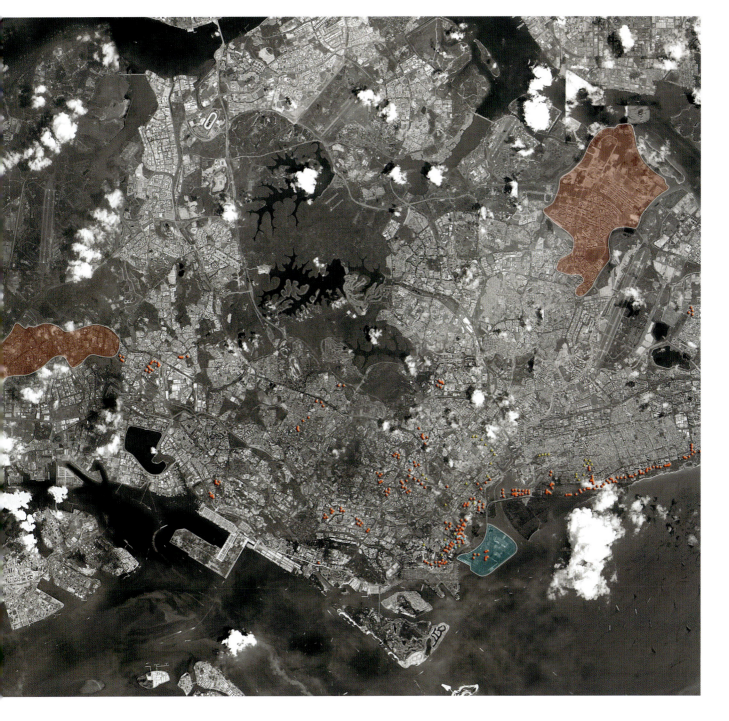

guidelines. The Concept Plan is revised every 10 years; public reviews are then organised and their results are taken into account. The Statutory Master Plan details urban planning over 10 to 15 years, adjusts zoning and the plot ratio, fixes the height limit per lot and also defines protected areas and nature reserves. It is revised every five years, its last version dating from 2008. The proper application of the Statutory Master Plan is assured through strict control of building permits by the Urban Redevelopment Authority. One of the Singaporean authority's responsibilities is the planning and sale of land to the private sector according to and in anticipation of the residential and commercial needs as well as the preservation of historic heritage (7,000 buildings are protected). Within the Urban Redevelopment Authority, the Building and Construction Authority defines the building and infrastructure construction standards (including safety standards) and is in charge of improving architectural conception.

ZONING / URBAN PLANNING

The distribution and management of land has remained unchanged since 1991. The development policy distributes plot ratios on a map and determines height limitations accordingly. This is represented in the Building Height Plan of the Masterplan 2008 which depicts the areas where specific height controls are in place. These are based on norms which are calculated in metres or number of storeys per site (for instance 50 storeys in the new Marina Bay sector) and can include planning guidelines (setback, spacing, detailed land use, building use, building form). Finally, lease conditions are applied in cases where the state is the owner of the land. Certain zones are not subject to height limits but are required to adhere to prevailing development control guidance such as the Storey Height Typology for flats and condominiums in residential developments. The zoning map defines – among other things – residential zones, residential zones with limited commercial activities, mixed zones (where commercial activities should not exceed 40 per cent of the total floor area, unless a special dispensation is granted), commercial zones, hotels (at least 60 per cent of total floor area), business parks (at least 85 per cent of total floor area), sectors dedicated to public facilities.

Since 2003, the zoning system has included a new category that groups together business and industrial activities, and which takes into account the impact on the urban environment. These New Business zones are split into two categories according to their pollutive tendencies (B1 for non-polluting uses, B2 for polluting uses) and are thus defined in terms of environmental impact. This approach encourages companies to

house several functions under the same roof and to vary activities without changing the zoning. Singapore planning regulations classify a zone as 'white' when it incorporates non-polluting activities and favours a neighbourhood-orientated lifestyle. The new plan thus aspires to increase densification of already built-up zones by advocating mixed usage. The aforementioned criticism and counterproposals made in the 1970s on density and mixed use have therefore been partially integrated, and applied with a concept of low-, medium- and high-density housing. The first is defined as a building with five storeys or less, the second as a plot with a ratio of between 1.4 and 2.1 with height up to 24 storeys, and the third as a plot ratio of above 2.1.

The urban policy is to create micro-cities and self-sufficient districts which harmonise the distribution of the population over the island's territory. According to the zoning plan, the renovation of the town centre includes the concentration of financial activities in a global business centre with a dense railway network (the MRT stations must be accessible by foot) and the construction of new adjoining housing, in particular in the new Marina district to the south. The average plot ratio in this district is planned to be between 6 and 7, in order to increase the residential population from 3 to 7 per cent through the development of a new housing category referred to as the Central Park-Style apartments.

URBAN SKYLINE / CITYSCAPE

Heritage protection is one of the main elements in Singaporean planning. View Corridors and View Cones marked out in relation to monuments or strategic points have thus protected the cityscape of the old centre since 2000 (see the Landmark and Gateway Plan). All in all there are six gateway sites (providing

The Landmark and Gateway Plan. In Singapore, protected views are associated with the definition of privileged zones for high-rise development.

comprehensive views of the city), 25 landmark sites (strategic locations, predestined for the construction of outstanding buildings), 17 focal points (popular public places), and numerous protected vistas to the harbour and the public parks. Particularly interesting, from a comparative point of view, is the description of desired future landmark sites, showing an active and aesthetic attitude rather than a solely protective one. Simulations of the projects are carried out by the municipality, which estimates their impact on the urban environment.

TOWER DESIGN

Apart from private towers, there are many types of social housing (HDB flats) whose size and composition are determined by conceptual standards with little variation (public or semi-public apartments of one to five rooms). In 2004, the Building and Construction Authority and private developers together produced *Buildable Solutions for High-Rise Residential Development*, dealing with prefabrication in reinforced concrete of floors and facade elements, as well as with the general planning and conception guidelines for such skyscrapers. Moreover, the Master Plan 2010 provides planning guidelines which have an impact on the architectural configuration (such as ground disposition and linkages through pedestrian bridges) as well as its internal organisation. If the location of the tall building can offer a panoramic view over the city, the URA may oblige the developer to accommodate a public observation deck. In addition, extensive research has been carried out by the Architecture and Urban Design Excellence programme launched by the URA on how to improve construction quality.

BUILDING CODES / FIRE SAFETY

Building Control ensures building works comply with standards of safety, amenities and matters of public policy as prescribed in the Building Control Act & Building Control Regulations. Singapore seeks to minimise energy consumption from air-conditioned buildings through the Code on Envelope Thermal Performance for Buildings. To limit the heat transfer from the outdoor environment into the residential or commercial building, the code requires architects and engineers to comply with the Envelope Thermal Performance (ETP) standards prescribed in the Building Regulations. The ETP Value inspired by the Overall Thermal Transfer Value of the American Society of Heating, Refrigerating & Air-Conditioning Engineers (ASHRAE) calculates the average rate of heat transfer of building walls.

The *Code of Practice for Fire Precautions in Buildings* sets out fire safety for high-rise buildings defined as such if in excess of 60 metres in height.

ECOLOGY

Environmental issues in Singaporean urban development emerged in the late 1960s when intense industrialisation was accompanied by a general will to create a green city. Land resource rationing and pollution control supports this aim while encouraging economic activity. In 1989, the Construction Quality Assessment System (CONQUAS) was established and approved by the Building and Construction Authority, which is responsible for estimating the ecological performance of buildings from the first phase of conception (materials of the structure, energy consumption). This label is, however, a tool, and not a legal obligation. The Singapore Green Plan of 1992, a Ministry of the Environment initiative, marked the first milestone in efforts to combine sustainable development with urban evolution management. The ministry, renamed Ministry of the Environment and Water Resources (MEWR), decided to revise the plan in 1999, creating in 2002 the current Singapore Green Plan 2012 (SGP2012), with regular updates for optimal efficiency. Its application is overseen by a coordination committee and six committees of specific experts. The objectives of the Green Plan cover air quality (pollution control via the Pollutant Standards Index (PSI), and reduction of the urban temperature), water management (supply and consumption), creation of green spaces, reduction and recycling of waste as well as hygiene and health issues (see image of green facade above). In 2005, the Building and Construction Authority created the BCA Green Mark Scheme, a certificate inspired by international standards, which developers, property owners and governmental bodies must request. One of four levels of certification is then awarded according to five specific criteria: energy consumption; water consumption; environmental protection; indoor environmental quality; and ecological innovations. In 2008, the newly created Inter-Ministerial Committee on Sustainable Development ensured that environmental objectives would be carried through to 2030 with the Sustainable Singapore Blueprint, which is currently being applied as part of the ongoing dynamic urban developments in Singapore's Marina Bay.

For more information, see:

Singapore Urban Redevelopment Authority / Master Plan 2008 http://www.ura.gov.sg

Singapore Building and Construction Authority http://www.bca.gov.sg

MEWR / Singapore Green Plan 2012 http://www.mewr.gov.sg

Green facade. Green facades of buildings highlight the environmental issues in Singapore.

High-rise and sustainability

High-rise and sustainability

A high-level assessment of the impact of the urban tower on the natural environment would conclude that low land use and possible higher density are the chief advantages, with high energy usage being the chief disadvantage. Concepts of density and of energy usage are relative, and should be examined by comparing high-rise buildings with their low-or mid-rise alternatives. Under closer scrutiny, towers do, of course, make other positive and negative environmental contributions; but the number of these, and the interaction between them, is a highly complicated subject. The purpose of this chapter is therefore to focus on the key elements, with the aim of providing a glimpse into the complex web of parameters influencing how an urban tower interacts with its environment, and how a tower can ultimately be considered sustainable.

Gordon Bunshaft (Skidmore, Owings & Merrill), Solow Building, New York, USA, 1974. A concave vertical facade – the architectural gesture reinforces the impression of the tower reaching into the skies.

URBAN INSERTION ANALYSIS: THE PRINCIPAL ISSUES

The main questions of a technical and environmental nature that must be addressed when contemplating a specific tower project and its urban implications go beyond land and energy use, to encompass subjects such as access, transportation, construction challenges and technology. Many of these issues relate both inwardly to the tower itself and outwardly to the surrounding environment and urban context. For instance, energy use can be influenced by a variety of factors, such as facade technology, local methods of energy production, international leasing market expectations, local construction and maintenance practice, and shading from surrounding buildings, to name but a few. The resulting complex interactions make each tower a one-of-a-kind project that strikes a particular balance between many factors. And even before a tower project gathers momentum, its genesis typically precedes these project-related interactions with other forces at work, of a socioeconomic, political and aesthetic nature – forces which continue to have a bearing throughout the project's life cycle. The discussion that follows outlines some of the main technical and environmental considerations associated with the development of towers.

Density issues

The concept of density is intimately related to urban integration, and more specifically to the impact the tower has on its surroundings. The reflected concept of how the surroundings may impact the tower is also of interest.

The prevalent notion explored here is how a tower fits into an existing urban context, as opposed to how a low-rise building would fit on the same piece of land. The assumption is, of course, that the piece of land is already within an existing city, and in the case of new developments, that an urban plan presides over individual tower projects. In all cases, the successful insertion of the tower will depend in part on the ability of its occupants to find fundamental amenities at the foot of the building. It may seem natural to assume that locating the tower in a dense urban fabric will automatically solve this point. However, the challenge can in fact remain even when building in an already dense urban fabric: the local neighbourhood could already be saturated and unable to cope with the sudden influx of people associated with the tower.

Conversely, the tower might be located in a developing area, where it feels somewhat isolated and disconnected from the urban context. This can happen even in the heart of an existing city, when a

Tom Wright (Atkins), Hotel Burj Al Arab, Dubai, United Arab Emirates, 1999. An isolated tower built on an island – an extreme example of urban connection.

Midtown Manhattan, New York, USA, 2010. A successful mix of towers of varying heights and different eras.

RIGHT: Philippe Chiambaretta/PCA Architects, competition design for Tour PB 22, La Défense, Paris outskirts, France, 2008. The PB 22 twin towers project was designed by Philippe Chiambaretta/PCA Architects for the 'Tour Signal' competition to improve the pedestrian connection between the business district of La Défense and adjacent neighbourhoods, providing passageways over busy highways and local roads.

BELOW RIGHT: Cesar Pelli with Adamson Associates, Winter Garden, World Financial Center, New York, USA, 1988. This enclosed atrium space serves as the nexus of the complex, with corridors leading to retail areas and escalators leading to dedicated access routes for each of the towers.

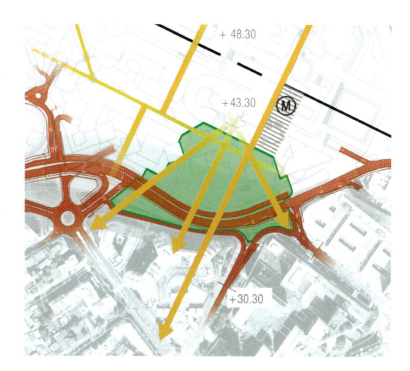

disproportionate plaza surrounding the tower tends to isolate it and make it less acceptable.

This density issue is clearly critical in the long term and therefore is central to the perceived success of the project in terms of its integration into the urban fabric.

Access issues

Resolving properly the question of access into a tower is never a simple task, when considering the various streams of people and goods entering and leaving it. A classic problem lies in the relative locations of the 'front-of-house' entrance for users and visitors and the 'backstage' entrance for all logistics associated with the building's operation. Changes of elevations can create additional challenges for a fluid circulation. Ensuring easy pedestrian access across surrounding roads is another fundamental connectivity issue.

The best way to ensure effective access into a tower is usually to provide a substantial amount of space to absorb population peaks, whether within the base of the tower itself or in its immediate vicinity. Another effective method is to establish an orderly procession of spaces that favours orientation at the base, allowing clear sight of reception desks, elevator banks and street exits. Multi-level solutions are often used, introducing monumental stairs and escalators to separate populations and provide various stages of control. With tower clusters or twins, there is often a call for generous public spaces, usually in the form of an atrium. Such spaces can serve as transition and orientation rooms, as is the case for Cœur Défense

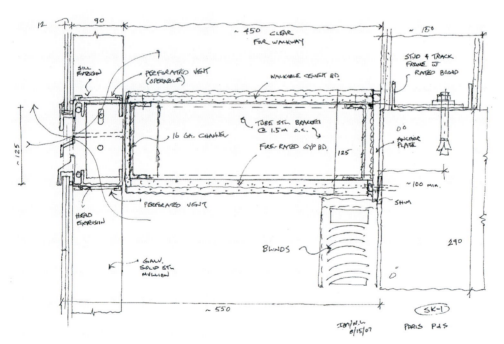

Pelli Clarke Pelli, detail of ventilated double-skin facade, competition design for Tours du Pont de Sèvres, Paris, France, 2008. The ventilated double facade is an example of 'intelligent facades' increasingly being used in energy-conscious high-rise projects.

ABOVE LEFT: Edward Larrabee Barnes, subway entrance shaped as Citigroup Center's slanted roof, New York, USA, 1988. This subway entrance was added in 1986 as part of the development of the Edward Larrabee Barnes-designed tower at 599 Lexington Avenue.

ABOVE: Hugh Stubbins Jr, sunken plaza with subway entrance, Citigroup Center, New York, USA, 1977. The Citigroup Center (originally the Citicorp Center) includes a direct connection into one of New York's busiest subway stops at 53rd Street and Lexington Avenue, via a sunken plaza at the foot of the tower.

near Paris and for the World Financial Center in New York.

Access can have a powerful impact on image, as the entrance is an important part of the standing of the tower among competing real estate. Good access can also ensure effective day-to-day operations, enabling all tower processes to function well.

Transportation issues

In order to gain acceptance both among its users and in the wider urban context, a tower's connectivity with public transport and road networks must be flawless. The classic example of high-rise structures being built on top of railway stations is a clear illustration of the relationship between towers, public transport and less car-intensive cities. In locations such as New York City, it is routine for developers to modernise and expand subway stations as part of a large tower development. The Citigroup Center tower at Lexington and 53rd Street is a case in point.

Energy issues

There is little doubt that towers consume more energy per square metre than comparatively lower buildings. This is due to increased size and usage in elevator and pump motors, and added exposure to natural elements due to lack of shielding from surrounding buildings.

Strategies are now well developed to try to reduce energy over-consumption by harnessing the specific qualities of towers, such as good access to daylight and wind. Elevators now can even regenerate some of the electrical power that they consume. However, it is likely that towers will continue to be more energy-hungry than lower-rise buildings, because of intractable requirements to lift people and water over great heights. This distinct disadvantage is obviously balanced by the need to house an ever-increasing city-dwelling and city-working population in a way that minimises land use and ground transport. So the macro picture of a city with low-rise buildings spread out over large tracts of land with many means of individual transport must be balanced against a more compact city with towers and less dependence on individual transport.

The comparison between two extreme urban examples such as the Greater Los Angeles Area and Manhattan is a good illustration of that point. According to data from the 2000 US Census, Manhattan's density is approximately 67,000 people per square mile (26,000 per square kilometre), whereas the Greater Los Angeles Area's density is approximately 7,000 people per square mile (2,700 per square kilometre) – nearly nine times less. The US Department of Energy states for 2008 that per capita energy consumption in New York State, at 205 million BTU (British thermal units), is among the lowest in the nation, due in part to its widely used mass transportation systems. It also states that California's per capita energy consumption, at 229 million BTU, is low, in part due to mild weather that reduces energy demand for heating and cooling. Although we have to compare state data rather than city data, as car transport is included in the comparison, all available data points to more energy efficiency in New York. Despite harsher weather, New York consumes less than California, due to the powerful positive impact of public transport and smaller dwellings.

TOP: Los Angeles urban sprawl, USA. A clear example of low-rise suburban sprawl, with the resulting road connectivity requirements.

ABOVE: Manhattan at night, USA. With each point of light, the vertical city of New York shows its high density at night in a lively way.

	LEED™	BREEAM	HQE
Date created	1998	1990	2000
Notation	Credits	Weighted	Multiple
Adaptable across borders	Not by design, in process though	Yes, bespoke and international schemes	Not by design
Country-centric	Yes, US	Yes, UK	Yes, France
High-rise sensitive	No	No	No
Energy calculations	In US dollars	In carbon dioxide	In weighted kilowatt-hours
Energy standard used	ASHRAE	CIBSE	Variant of ASHRAE
Mixed-use sensitive	No	Yes	No
Rating levels	Four	Five	Three
Duration of rating	Two years	No time limit	No time limit
Number of operations certified (as of 2008)	Circa 2000	Circa 100 000	Circa 500

Table comparing the LEED™ (US), BREEAM (UK) and HQE (France) sustainable accreditation systems. Sharing the same objective, these systems rely on different methods of notation and issue differing ratings that are currently not comparable.

ENVIRONMENTAL SYSTEMS AND THE TOWER

There are several systems attempting to standardise or offer a framework for sustainability in buildings. The best-known systems in the world are LEED™ (Leadership in Energy & Environmental Design), developed in the USA, and BREEAM (Building Research Establishment Environmental Assessment Method), established in the UK. Other countries have developed their own systems, such as France's HQE (Haute Qualité Environnementale), Switzerland's MINERGIE®, or Australia's Green Star. All of these systems or standards tend to classify buildings in accordance with a variety of criteria, ranging from integration in the existing urban fabric to energy consumption, from quality of indoor space to maintainability of systems, from carbon dioxide emissions to use of local resources. Most of them, being accreditation systems, require certain minimum conditions to be met, so that basic tenets of sustainable construction are adhered to. For instance, most require double glazing as a prerequisite for accreditation.

The convergence of some systems is actively pursued, for instance between the UK's BREEAM and the French HQE systems. There are of course differences between their approaches, but they lie primarily in the notation matrix and not in the underlying objectives of ensuring sensible designs for low-energy buildings that are well integrated in their surroundings. There are many ongoing discussions regarding which accreditation system is more prescriptive and which tends to state environmental objectives rather than preferred solutions. Given the very rapid evolution of these systems, it is not really possible to indicate the better system for use on a generic tower project. Using the accreditation system available in the country of the project is likely to provide good results, as most accreditation systems are intimately linked to the local way of building, of calculating energy usage, and generally of bringing environmental improvements at the local level.

However, none of these systems currently takes into account the specific nature of the tower, as compared with low-rise buildings. For instance, there are systems that ignore the energy consumption of elevators (such as the French RT thermal regulation approach, whose calculation model supports the HQE label). This is somewhat understandable, because environmental systems are meant to address the largest number of buildings, and have the objective of setting minimum construction quality standards, which are routinely exceeded by towers, due to the many technical constraints associated with high-rise construction. As standards of construction evolve rapidly as a result of ever-increasing environmental requirements, towers will soon lose their de facto advantage, and will need to have their particularity recognised in future environmental regulations.

The latest regulatory developments are now starting to address the unique nature of high-rise construction and usage, typically by creating a dedicated set of parameters that are applicable to towers. For instance, energy consumption standards will dictate a threshold of yearly energy consumption for towers that is higher than the limit for low-rise buildings. This approach is currently being discussed for French regulations, where low-rise buildings will be basically limited to 50 kilowatt-hours per square metre per year, whereas high-rise buildings may be allowed a higher number such as 100 kilowatt-hours per square metre per year. This direction brings some realism to a debate where the absence of specific regulations for towers had allowed less rational and more subjective judgements to take hold. It is encouraging to see environmental systems starting to recognise the specific nature of high-rise construction, a fact already integrated in a wide array of other disciplines, ranging from life safety to structure, from elevators to architecture.

Meanwhile, the multiplicities of labels, their rapid changes and their differing ratings are currently creating some confusion, which may at times cast a shadow of doubt over the whole environmental accreditation process. Once environmental awareness evolves from fashion to mainstream, this somewhat confused situation will mature and stabilise, bringing much-needed coherence, clarity and experience-based feedback. The LEED™ concept that a rating must be temporary is nevertheless interesting, in that it recognises the potential degradation of performance over time. Just like cars pass periodic inspections to be roadworthy, buildings would submit to periodic inspections to maintain rating levels.

COMPARISON WITH LOWER-RISE AND VERY LOW-RISE BUILDINGS

The analysis of the environmental impact of a tower should not be conducted in a vacuum. As indicated earlier, we have chosen to use the familiar form of the lower-rise building as a frame of reference. This comparative approach gives a perspective for appreciating specific aspects of high-rise design and construction, and for reviewing whether these aspects are a normal evolution of low-rise construction or represent a distinct departure from this traditional form.

So what are the key differences between a high-rise and a low-rise building?

Structure

The height is of course the main difference, but more important are the consequences of the height on the structural design. High-rise towers must be designed to take into account the lateral wind load, and the resulting wind bracing becomes a central issue in their structural design. This issue is further compounded when the tower slenderness ratio increases – that is, when the relative value of the height versus the length or width of the tower increases. Super-tall high-rise design continues to push the slenderness ratio ever higher, so that the tower attains a 'light' appearance despite its size and bulk. One approach to structural design for towers consists of using the facade to play a load-bearing role, all the while ensuring transparency and daylight access. Facade lattice grids provide an interesting and increasingly popular solution.

Towers tend to slowly 'sway' under the effect of the wind, and therefore require special measures to avoid potentially unpleasant accelerations towards the top,

such as additional stiffness in the structure or the use of tuned dampers to offset the sway. This consideration is particularly important when the top of the building is dedicated to residential use, where less acceleration is tolerated than in office areas.

In addition to the structural impact of the lateral wind, there is of course the vertical weight impact, which tends to thicken the structural elements at the bottom of the tower, and influences the foundation design. It is not uncommon in the world of high-rise for the loads in a given column to reach thousands of tons. Some ground conditions lend themselves much more easily

Tange Associates, Mode Gakuen Cocoon Tower, Tokyo, Japan, 2008. The facade lattice plays an important role in the tower's lateral stability, reducing the need for a massive core and improving the efficiency of the floor plates.

Zeidler Partnership, tuned link between trusses, Torre Mayor, Mexico City, Mexico, 2003. The patented dampers allow the building to withstand earthquakes measuring up to 8.5 on the Richter scale.

to high-rise construction, such as the granite subsoil of Manhattan, whereas some other conditions create very complex challenges, such as the muddy subsoil of Mexico, also subject to powerful earthquakes.

With the right combination of ingenuity and diligent design and execution, towers can now be built to withstand the most complex conditions of wind, soil and earthquake, which is a relatively recent development. The Torre Mayor in Mexico could not have been built twenty or thirty years ago, because special inventions to absorb energy from both vertical and horizontal forces from earthquakes had not yet been imagined.

There are clearly major differences in terms of structural complexity between high-rise and low-rise construction, which have a substantial and direct effect on place, cost and time to build. Put in simple words, the complexity of the structure grows faster than the height of the tower. The right balance between weight, stiffness, fire resistance, use of advanced materials, cost and time becomes more delicate beyond certain heights. At the R&D end of high-rise construction, there is now an increasing distinction between 'routine' 80-storey, 300-metre towers and super-tall buildings rising as high as 800 metres such as the Burj Khalifa in Dubai, which serves to demonstrate how relative the high-rise concept can be.

Beyond the purely technical considerations, there is also a direct aesthetic relationship between the structural design of a tower and its connection with the city. The technical requirements favour heavy and somewhat forbidding structures at the base of the tower, whereas the aesthetic connection requirement with the city wants transparency and column-free spaces. The challenge is therefore to create an orderly succession of spaces at the tower base, providing an inviting connection unencumbered by structural obstacles. This challenge has given rise to a variety of architectural and structural responses, from the creation of podiums and atria surrounding the base of the tower to more dramatic structural overhang situations creating a structurally free space at the bottom of the building. Examples of daring overhangs generating interesting public spaces are readily visible in the heart of cities like New York, with various iconic buildings such as the Hugh Stubbins Jr-designed Citigroup Center, the Edward Larrabee Barnes-designed IBM building on 57th Street and Madison Avenue, and the more recent Morphosis-designed Cooper Union building downtown. Examples of atria at bases of towers abound as well, from Cesar Pelli's Winter Garden at the World Financial Center in New York to Jean-Paul Viguier's Cœur Défense complex on the outskirts of Paris (see page 250).

Elevators

A key difference between high-rise and low-rise buildings lies in the provision of elevators. The invention of elevators at the beginning of the 20th century sparked the increase in building heights. Reliable elevators are the main reason why the general construction of buildings could rise above six or seven

OPPOSITE: Skidmore, Owings & Merrill, Burj Khalifa, Dubai, United Arab Emirates, 2010. At 828 metres in height, Burj Khalifa is currently – and will be for some time to come – the tallest man-made structure in the world.

storeys, the height traditionally used and commonly found in historical cities such as London, Paris or Venice.

With high-rise construction, elevators take on a new dimension, as they become an indispensable part of the building. The ever-increasing sophistication of elevators is both a cause and a consequence of rising tower heights. Vertical transportation becomes a fundamental subject in the design of super-tall buildings, with various approaches designed to minimise the number of elevator compartments at the very base, in an effort to optimise core space and costs. The traditional concept of elevators all rising from the main lobby is still used for towers up to 40 or 50 storeys, and electronic destination management techniques are now added to improve performance, over the more traditional approach of definitively allocating elevators to specific sections of the building.

Beyond this traditional pipe-organ elevator architecture, the concept of express elevators shuttling passengers directly to upper sky lobbies is now a common approach for taller high-rise design, which allows an efficient absorption of the population away from the base of the tower at the time of peak demand. The resulting multiplication of sky lobbies within a single super-tower allows easier segmentation of local elevators, which can start from various sky lobbies and use superposed shafts. With a sky lobby concept, the super-tower is considered as a superposition of regular towers, a common concept thread for various technical systems beyond elevators.

The sky lobby shuttle concept is the transposition to the vertical transport world of a well-known horizontal transport approach of express trains and local trains, commonly used with subway systems in cities like New York or Paris. It is a short step from this notion to the realisation that strongly integrated horizontal and vertical transport systems will turn sky lobbies into urban squares, with shuttle elevators becoming a natural extension of horizontal public transport systems. Transport integration is already a very important success factor for a traditional tower, when the base of the building is appropriated by the general public as a small city square complete with resting areas, coffee shops, news stands, or more extensive and diverse hospitality and retail outlets.

It is worth noting that a mixed-use tower tends to face an increased complexity for elevator design, as there is a natural desire to differentiate elevators between uses, while there is an opposite desire to contain the core size. There again, the sky lobby solution is often considered as a way of introducing gateways for each usage. These mixed-use elevator considerations are not foreign to low-rise building design; however, the size of

the population and the number of uses to be handled in a high-rise building magnify the complexity to a level where new approaches and innovative solutions have to be envisaged.

It is clear that elevators are the technical tip of a much wider issue: the fundamental connection of the tower with its urban environment. Key aspects such as orientation into the building and within the main lobby, connection with the outside at street level as well as from public transport systems, and fluidity of movement through elevator cores towards floors or sky lobbies, all form an integral part of this vertical circulation issue. Ultimately, pleasant and effective circulation through a

Jean-Paul Viguier, Cœur Défense, La Défense, Paris outskirts, France, 2001. A generous atrium linking all buildings provides the entrance into the complex.

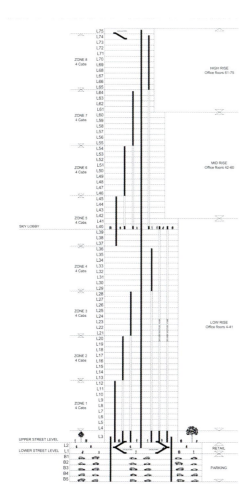

ABOVE: High-rise elevator riser diagram. For elevators, a 75-storey tower can be considered as the superposition of two towers of lesser height, with a sky lobby providing the separation.

ABOVE: Skidmore, Owings & Merrill, retail podium, Columbus Center, New York, USA, 2003. The building, with several street addresses and entrances, operates as a very successful mixed-use structure, with retail outlets, apartments, offices, a hotel and a concert hall within the premises.

tower's main public spaces significantly contributes to people's appreciation of the building's success, and therefore its overall image and acceptance. The somewhat repetitive nature of the upper floors reinforces the need for the uniqueness of the main lobby and associated sky lobbies and for a memorable experience when moving through these spaces.

Elevators are an important part of the energy consumption associated with high-rise buildings. Numbers vary widely, depending on height of tower, number of cabs, building usage, population density in the tower, traffic patterns and technology used. However we can assess the order of magnitude of elevator consumption to average from 10 to 20 kilowatt-hours per square metre per year, which brings it in line with and even above the levels of lighting consumption. To put these numbers into perspective, the latest energy targets for the overall

electrical consumption in low-rise buildings are at similar levels. The electrical consumption of a typical office high-rise with modern HVAC (heating, ventilation and air conditioning) strategies in a temperate climate is illustrated in the chart overleaf. It should be noted that the power consumed by users with their personal computers, copiers etc is not accounted for, and it could easily dwarf even the cooling consumption.

Climate

As a foreword to this sensitive aspect, we should make it clear that we are not trying to compare high-rise and low-rise construction in every climate, but rather to compare how low-rise and high-rise construction are each reacting to the influence of climate.

Architectural history shows the connection between climate and built form. This connection has been a constant in every climate for low-rise construction.

Office high-rise electrical consumption example. The chart illustrates where the energy is being used; however, it does not include computers for the office tenants, which can easily dwarf the energy consumption of any of these individual uses.

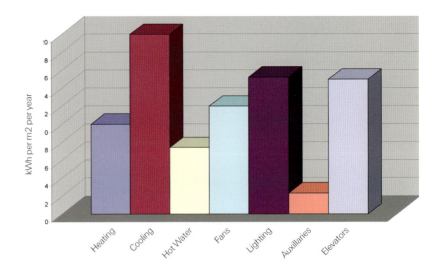

Large open windows in Paris and London betray the relatively low level of sunlight and the mild climate, whereas small Mediterranean windows cut into massive walls illustrate the need to seek shelter from the heat and sun. Bioclimatic architecture, largely inherited from vernacular forms but harnessing the latest construction technology, has been advocated in the design of some of the more recent towers.

Complex facades, integrated shading devices and energy reclaim strategies have been taking centre stage at the core of the concept. However, considerations of size, weight and lack of shading have sometimes hindered the full use of bioclimatic approaches available to low-rise buildings, such as shading from adjacent structures or from trees, or lightweight construction. To counteract this situation, rapidly advancing technology is being introduced, in particular the use of 'intelligent' facades. These facades can be as airtight as necessary in extreme weather, while they can be somewhat porous or even open in mild weather.

To prevent excessive use of technology in offsetting the effects of climate, the relationship of a tower and climate must first be reviewed. High-rise buildings are very exposed to sun and wind. On that basis, it could be argued that the more suitable climate for towers would be a mild to cold one. The tower benefits from free heating as it effectively acts as a large solar collector. It can then use a relatively simple porous or operable facade during the mild warmer months. A more 'intelligent' facade would bring variation in its openness to either sun radiation or temperature losses, to ensure optimal use of free solar energy and minimal heating needs at night.

It could further be argued that building a tower in warm or hot climates is not very energy efficient: the tower acts as a permanent solar collector and therefore requires large amounts of cooling year-round, with little

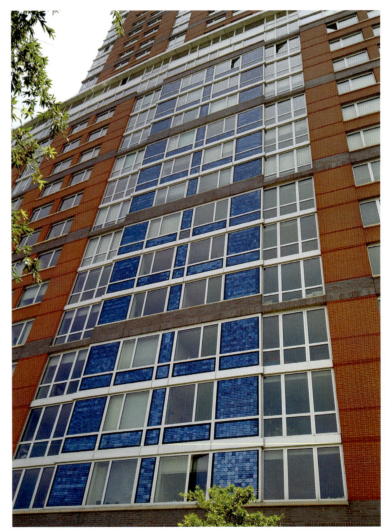

Pelli Clarke Pelli, The Solaire, Battery Park City, New York, USA, 2003. The facade integrates part of a building-wide photovoltaic array that can generate 5% of the peak electricity demand of the building.

or no relief at night. The next stage of design would logically be to cover towers partially with solar cells, to make the best use of their unusually large surfaces exposed to the sun. This is in fact currently used in some cutting-edge buildings, and may become commonplace when both the price of photovoltaic cells drops and the price of energy rises.

The climate issues facing tall buildings are not just limited to the sun, as wind can also become an important factor. There have been a number of towers in mild climates designed to take advantage of prevailing winds. The concept involves letting the energy of the wind provide natural ventilation and cooling to the tower. Again, this calls for sophisticated facade design to achieve the desired effects without suffering from high wind conditions in the occupied space.

Climate considerations have never played an important part in orienting high-rise design, at least not until recent years. While low-rise design has largely responded to climate due to its historical connection with vernacular architecture, high-rise design has started its own history as a demonstration of technical prowess. This situation is now changing under the growing influence of environmental responsibility. The subject of climate is one rare instance where low-rise and high-rise design tend to narrow down their difference over time.

Energy

The issue of energy use in the tower is at the centre of most discussions regarding their integration with the environment. Beyond energy used during day-to-day operations, one must also consider the embodied energy in the materials employed and the energy expended in the construction effort.

Energy spent in day-to-day operations

The first aspect to consider when examining energy used to operate the tower must be whether passive strategies that harness the climate in good ways and protect the interior spaces from harmful effects of the climate have been employed, be it for architectural or engineering elements.

Passive strategies typically start with the envelope. We have already mentioned the importance of facade design with high-rise buildings, particularly in connection with climate and daylight considerations. Facade design is of course very important for low-rise design as well. There are, however, some notable distinctions between the two types of buildings when it comes to the importance of the facade as an energy-saving tool. Access to wind and daylight is often more restricted in low-rise construction, particularly in a

dense urban fabric. In addition, low-rise construction must also pay particular attention to roof characteristics. There is a bigger proportion of roof area compared with facade area in a low-rise building than in a tower. Conversely, facade exposure is fundamental in high-rise buildings. This indicates that towers have a very good potential for solar collection in places where the sun stays low on the horizon. It also indicates that in tropical latitudes where the midday sun stays high, a tower elongated in the east–west direction will be naturally protected from the sun, as the long facades to the north and south do not see much direct solar radiation.

We have briefly mentioned passive strategies dependent on wind, as long as sufficient investment is made in 'intelligent' facades with operable openings that can manage the substantial wind pressure which exists at high-rise levels. So, in terms of passive measures to save energy, high-rise buildings tend to have good potential and will compare rather favourably with low-rise buildings.

Hugh Stubbins Jr, Citigroup Center in the setting sun, New York, USA, 1977. The south-facing slanted roof of this landmark high-rise was once thought of as a solar collector. The facade areas could easily play that role in the future.

Buildings do contain active systems behind their envelopes, and in this area high-rise structures are at a disadvantage when compared with low-rise ones. When looking at the energy expended on day-to-day operations, high-rise buildings tend to consume more, due to the requirement for more powerful elevators and pumps. As an additional example, besides the elevator energy issues, there are incremental energy expenditures such as permanent lighting in high-rise staircases which are rarely mitigated, if ever allowed by regulations. On the other hand, a low-rise building has the distinct opportunity of locating staircases in a way that harnesses daylight.

Day-to-day energy: the mixed-use high-rise case
There is, however, one particular type of high-rise that tends to minimise its energy consumption through extensive energy reclaim: the mixed-use high-rise.

A mixed-use high-rise is made possible when it combines different sizeable functions under one roof. Parts of the building operate mostly during the day, as office areas, convention centres and commercial spaces, while other parts are used as residential apartments or hotel rooms, with usage concentrated mostly outside normal commercial hours. This situation leads to an efficient use of shared facilities, such as car parks, elevators, lobbies and the like. It also enables heat reclaim strategies to be used in a very effective way.

Residential facilities tend to require heating year-round for hot water, while office buildings tend to require cooling almost year-round. This simultaneous requirement for heating and cooling means that the use of energy reclaim devices can be optimised. Beyond the yearly sharing effect, there is also a daily sharing that can take place: a mixed-use tower can 'recycle' the heat extracted from daytime use (solar, occupants, computers and lights) via heat pumps, in order to meet the demand for hot water and night-time heating in its residential areas. The graph shown here demonstrates how this situation tends to reduce substantially the energy footprint of a tower.

Should the mixed-use tower be associated with a waste processing plant, there are even greater opportunities to reduce the tower's energy footprint. The processed waste generates some of the energy for the tower via a cogeneration or tri-generation plant (electrical, heating and cooling). Processing waste locally also leads to less transportation of waste, which is a further positive environmental consideration.

Mixed-use considerations leading to optimal energy usage are not limited to high-rise projects: for instance, a low-rise mixed-use project comprising commercial centre, hotels and housing could benefit from similar

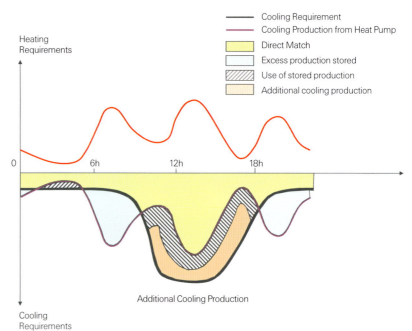

energy-reclaim strategies. So the particular case of a mixed-use project does not give an advantage to high-rise over low-rise.

In the final analysis, when looking at day-to-day energy consumption as demonstrated above, the low-rise building achieves a better result than the high-rise building.

Embodied energy
When looking at the notion of embodied energy, the actual energy mobilised to pump concrete, hoist or crane people and goods up to build a tower tends to generate energy expenditure and a mobilisation of human resources that weighs in against high-rise construction. In addition, high-rise buildings need to be constructed with high-resistance concrete and with facade panels that can withstand high winds, whereas low-rise construction can be of a more lightweight nature. So, on balance, it appears that high-rise construction is not at its best when looked at through the sole prism of energy consumption and embodied energy.

Land Use
The subject of land use is clearly in favour of high-rise construction. In fact, it is the primary reason why high-rise construction exists. With expensive investments in local transport and city infrastructures already made, it makes sense to concentrate people in buildings ever increasing in height, thus reducing the need for further commuting, and the consequent time and money spent

Cooling production breakdown via heat pump and storage. Matching heating and cooling demands – excess cooling can be stored as ice for later restitution, thus minimising wasted energy.

Skidmore, Owings & Merrill, Burj Khalifa under construction, Dubai, United Arab Emirates, 2008. There is clearly a lot of energy being spent in hoisting materials and construction workers during the course of construction.

in long-range transportation. This reduced land use is a positive environmental trait, as it reduces urban sprawl, expensive commuting and car operation, and makes the most use of long-term city infrastructures.

With a growing world population, and dwindling forest preserves, access to land already cleared for human use is fast becoming an issue, where competition occurs between tree preservation, food production and real estate development. In the longer term, it will be even more necessary to protect undeveloped land suitable for farming or reforestation, with the consequent development of denser and higher cities. In this respect, high-rise construction is more a necessity than a choice.

Building code regulations for construction

The following paragraphs specifically address technical and life safety construction code issues that regulate how buildings are constructed, as opposed to urban codes that regulate where, how large and how tall buildings can be in an urban context.

Due to the specific nature of high-rise buildings in technical and life safety terms, high-rise regulations are quite different and somewhat disconnected from low-rise regulations. There are still several countries with a mature set of low-rise regulations that do not have high-rise regulations, chiefly for lack of need. These countries often develop their regulations by adopting mature codes from another country such as the United States, the United Kingdom or another country respected for its high-rise construction. Construction codes for high-rise are often more complex and demanding than those for low-rise buildings. This stems from both a historical perspective and the impact of fire regulations. Fire authorities tend to view high-rise buildings as very specific because of issues such as fire escape, fire resistance, and the ability of firefighters to intervene.

Regarding fire escape, a low-rise building evacuates entirely in the event of a fire, whereas a high-rise building goes through a staged evacuation procedure, which means that only floors local to the fire are evacuated first. This is understandable to ensure that the staircases are not suddenly overcrowded. However, this approach of a staged evacuation requires enhanced fire resistance of structures, as well as the ability to continue occupation on floors that are not yet evacuated.

In terms of fire resistance, low-rise buildings tend to be designed on the basis of one-hour resistance to fire

Tokyo low-rise and high-rise, Japan. When traditional low-rise neighbourhoods cannot cope with population increases, high-rise neighbourhoods tend to develop, such as in Tokyo.

unsafe compromises can be made, even under pressure from economic or environmental considerations.

ARE TOWERS SUSTAINABLE?

In the preceding paragraphs, we have provided an overview of the environmental considerations surrounding the integration of towers in an urban environment, from the practical construction issues to the more theoretical environmental assessment tools available.

The myriad of factors affecting the question of sustainability of towers should not cloud the main reasons why towers are being built in the first place: increased urbanisation worldwide coupled with demographic growth in several continents. As population increases, and technology allows food production to be less and less dependent on pure manual labour, migrations occur from countryside to cities. Pressure on land use increases in several ways, and high-rise buildings are rapidly adopted as a way to contain suburban sprawl. If the notion of sustainability includes the fact that there is population growth, then towers are sustainable in their ability to minimise land use for buildings. In the short term, towers might be seen as consuming more energy, but the urban integration of towers gives rise to lesser energy spent in transport. So the overall environmental impact of towers should take into account a redeeming transport aspect.

Excessive land use due to urban development is currently without any another solution than building more towers concentrated in cities. Land is limited, hard to create on a finite planet, and it must ultimately be preserved.

The final determination of whether a tower is sustainable clearly depends on the relative value given to the energy and land use factors. Current environmental systems tend to give more weight to energy expenditure in the building than to land use, due to the short-term need to modify the environmental footprint of our energy expenditure. Land use and reduced individual transport are currently perceived as minor and less pressing environmental issues by building notation systems. So towers do not currently enjoy positive environmental ratings, but their long-term environmental benefits should not be dismissed altogether.

between floors, whereas high-rise buildings have to be designed to more stringent fire periods, and with more sophisticated requirements to prevent chain structural failure. There are also many other requirements for high-rise buildings such as sprinklers, smoke exhaust and stair pressurisation, which are not usually found in low-rise buildings.

Firefighter intervention for low-rise buildings is normally through the facade, an approach which is limited by the height of the firemen's ladders. For high-rise buildings, firefighters will have to choose between stairs or elevators, and even use dedicated firefighting elevators if included in the construction.

All these fundamental differences, as well as some other regulation items not listed here, tend to make high-rise buildings more complex and more expensive to build. Obviously, life safety is an area where no

Comparative Table

No.	Group	Case Study / Type	Location	Date	Height (in m)	Development area (in m²)	Site area (in m²)	Site coverage	Plot ratio
1	Solitaires	Kingdom Centre Monument	Riyadh	2002	302	300 846	94 230	48%	3.19
2		30 St Mary Axe Monument in block	London	2004	180	47 400	5 666	37%	8.37
3		Commerzbank Tower Tower as block	Frankfurt	1997	259	85 503	7 781	87%	10.99
4		Torre Velasca Tower in block	Milan	1958	106	42 065	7 452	45%	5.64
5		Kungstornen Twin towers	Stockholm	1925	60	16 864	2 466	91%	6.84
6		Tokyo Metropolitan Government Building Tower as team player	Tokyo	1991	243	380 504	42 941	64%	8.86
7		The Standard Hotel Tower on infrastructure	New York City	2009	71	16 457	3 106	80%	5.30
8		Tour Ar Men *1 Tower as module / Business as usual	Paris	2008	36	6 387	1 233	80%	5.18
9	Clusters	Rockefeller Center *2 Integrated in existing city fabric	New York City	1939	259	566 297	49 422	84%	11.46
10		Quartier du Palais (Immeubles 'Choux') Towers as urban pattern	Créteil	1974	38	119 743	113 270	18%	1.06
11		Sheikh Zayed Road Linear cluster	Dubai	n/a	355	470 335	78 257	30%	6.01
12		Moma and Pop Moma High-rise compound	Beijing	2007	105	274 618	61 355	24%	4.48
13		Roppongi Hills Mori Tower *3 High-rise megastructure	Tokyo	2003	238	636 354	89 385	65%	7.12
14		Hansaviertel *4 Towers in nature	Berlin	1960	52	32 560	18 971	11%	1.72
15		Front de Seine Towers on podium	Paris	1990	98	242 975	58 251	48%	4.17
16	Vertical Cities	Downtown Houston *5 US-American Downtown	Houston	n/a	305	755 437	54 000	90%	13.99
17		Higienópolis *6 High-rise as norm (grown in time)	São Paulo	n/a	115	68 024	14 284	41%	4.76
18		Monaco High-rise as geographical obligation	Monaco	n/a	170	267 212	120 625	25%	2.22
19		Lujiazui *7 City of monuments	Shanghai	n/a	632	1 095 600	78 431	28%	13.97
20		La Défense *8 European CBD	Ile de France	n/a	231	3 830 000	1 600 000	24%	2.39
21		Hong Kong *9 City of megastructures	Hong Kong	n/a	484	415 900	57 107	52%	7.28

These figures should be contemplated in conjunction with the 1:2500 urban drawings of each case study.
The site areas do not include public streets and pavements, and the development areas do not include basements and car parks.
Especially for the larger projects the indications are approximate and cannot be used as official sources.
The main aim of the table is the comparison of plot ratios and site coverage.

For Vertical Cities the height indication refers to the tallest element on the 1:2500 urban drawing.

*1   The whole Masséna Nord district has a plot ratio of 4.66 and a 77% site coverage (only for the building plots).
*2   The calculation refers only to the six oldest blocks between 5th and 6th Avenues, and 48th and 51st Streets.
*3   The figures describe the totality of the Roppongi Hills development, and not only the area as seen on the urban plan.
*4   The figures have been calculated only for the plots of the four-point towers, not for the whole Hansaviertel.
*5   The calculation is based on nine downtown blocks as seen on the urban plan.
*6   The calculation is based on the block which contains the coloured building.
*7   The figures are only based on the three super-tall buildings and their blocks.
*8   With the exception of the site coverage, the figures relate to the whole La Défense district and not only to the urban plan.
*9   These figures are based on the whole IFC project and do not include the older fabric as seen on the urban drawing.

Select Bibliography (books only)

GENERAL WORKS

Al Manakh 2: Export Gulf, Archis, Amsterdam, 2010

Aregger, Hans and Glaus, Otto, *Hochhaus und Stadtplanung*, Verlag für Architektur Artemis, Zurich, 1967

A+T Architecture+Technology, *Hybrids II*, A+T Publishers, Madrid, 2008

Binder, Georges, *Tall Buildings of Europe, Middle East and Africa*, Images Publishing Group, Mulgrave, 2006

Bossom, Alfred C, *Building to the Skies: The Romance of the Skyscraper*, The Studio Publications, London, 1934

Campi, Mario, *Skyscrapers – An Urban Type*, Birkhäuser Verlag, Basel, 2000

Cohen, Jean-Louis, *Scenes of the World to Come: European Architecture and the American Challenge 1893–1960*, Flammarion, Paris, 1995

Damisch, Hubert, *Skyline: La ville Narcisse – Essai*, Editions du Seuil, Paris, 1996

Dufaux, Frédéric and Fourcaut, Annie, *Le Monde des Grands Ensembles*, Editions Créaphis, Paris, 2004

Dupré, Judith, *Skyscrapers: A History of the World's Most Extraordinary Buildings*, Black Dog and Leventhal Publishers, New York, 2008

Firley, Eric and Stahl, Caroline, *The Urban Housing Handbook*, John Wiley & Sons, Chichester, 2009

Flierl, Bruno, *100 Jahre Hochhäuser*, Verlag Bauwesen, Berlin, 2000

Grawe, Christina and Cachola Schmal, Peter, *High Society: Contemporary Highrise Architecture and the International Highrise Award 2006*, Jovis Verlag, Berlin, 2007

Hilberseimer, Ludwig, *Grossstadtarchitektur*, Julius Hoffmann Verlag, Stuttgart, 1927

Hitchcock, Henry-Russell and Johnson, Philip, *The International Style: Architecture Since 1922*, Museum of Modern Art, New York, 1932

Höweler, Eric and Pedersen, William, *Skyscraper: Designs of the Recent Past and for the Near Future*, Thames & Hudson, London, 2003

Huxtable, Ada Louise, *The Tall Building Artistically Reconsidered*, Pantheon Books, New York, 1984

Jencks, Charles, *Skyscrapers – Skycities*, Rizzoli, New York, 1980

Lehmann, Steffen, *Der Turm zu Babel: Architektur für das Dritte Jahrtausend*, Jovis Verlag, Berlin, 1999

Lehnerer, Alex, *Grand Urban Rules*, 010 Publishers, Rotterdam, 2009

Mierop, Caroline, *Gratte-ciel*, Editions Norma, Paris, 1995

Mujica, Francisco, *History of the Skyscraper*, Da Capo Press, London, 1977

Neumann, Dietrich, *'Die Wolkenkratzer kommen!'*, Vieweg, Braunschweig, 1995

Paquot, Thierry, *La Folie des hauteurs*, Bourin Editeur, Paris, 2008

Quintana de Una, Javier, *The Skyscraper in Europe 1900–1939*, Alianza Editorial, Madrid, 2006

Riley, Terence and Nordenson, Guy, *Tall Buildings*, The Museum of Modern Art, New York, 2003

Schleier, Merrill, *Skyscraper Cinema*, University of Minnesota Press, Minneapolis, 2009

Taillandier, Ingrid, Namias, Olivier and Pousse, Jean-François, *The Invention of the European Tower*, Editions A&J Picard, Paris, 2009

Terranova, Antonino, *Skyscrapers*, Barnes & Noble, New York, 2004

Weaving, Andrew, *High-Rise Living*, Gibbs Smith, Salt Lake City, 2004

Wood, Antony, *Best Tall Buildings 2008: CTBUH International Award Winning Projects*, Architectural Press, London, 2009

WORKS ON SPECIFIC BUILDINGS OR CITIES

Balfour, Alan, *Rockefeller Center*, McGraw-Hill, New York, 1978

Bresler, Henri and Genyk, Isabelle, *Le Front de Seine: Histoire prospective*, SEMEA 15, Paris, 2003

Clémençon, Anne-Sophie, Traverso, Edith and Lagier, Alain, *Les Gratte-ciel de Villeurbanne*, Editions de l'Imprimeur, Besançon, 2004

Condit, Carl W, *The Chicago School of Architecture*, Chicago University Press, Chicago, 1973

Cybriwsky, Roman, *Tokyo: The Shogun's City at the 21st Century*, John Wiley & Sons, Chichester, 1998

Davidson, Christopher M, *Dubai: the Vulnerability of Success*, C Hurst & Co, London, 2009

Davies, Colin and Lambot, Ian, *Commerzbank Frankfurt: Prototype for an Ecological High-rise*, Birkhäuser, Basel, 1997

Dudley, George A, *A Workshop for Peace: Designing the United Nations Headquarters*, MIT Press, Cambridge, Massachusetts, 1994

EPAD, *Tête Défense – Concours International d'Architecture 1983*, Electa Moniteur, Paris, 1984

EPAD, *La Défense*, le cherche midi, Paris, 2009

Ferriss, Hugh, *The Metropolis of Tomorrow*, Princeton Architectural Press, New York, 1998

Fiori, Leonardo and Prizzon, Massimo, *BBPR – la Torre Velasca*, Abitare Segesta, Milan, 1982

Flowers, Benjamin, *Skyscraper: The Politics and Power of Building New York City in the 20th Century*, University of Pennsylvania Press, Philadelphia, 2009

Janson, Alban and Krohn, Carsten, *Le Corbusier: Unité d'Habitation*, Menges, Stuttgart, 2007

Koolhaas, Rem, *Delirious New York*, The Monacelli Press, New York, 1997

Krane, Jim, *Dubai: The Story of the World's Fastest City*, Atlantic Books, London, 2009

Lai, Lawrence and Ho, Daniel, *Planning Buildings for a High-Rise Environment in Hong Kong*, Hong Kong University Press, Hong Kong, 2000

Lampugnani, Vittorio Magnago, *Hong Kong Architecture: The Aesthetics of Density*, Prestel, Munich, 1993

Landau, Sarah Bradford and Condit, Carl W, *Rise of the New York Skyscraper 1865–1913*, Yale University Press, New Haven, Connecticut, 1999

Lee, Leo Ou-fan, *City Between Worlds: My Hong Kong*, Harvard University Press, Cambridge, Massachusetts, 2008

Logan, John, *The New Chinese City: Globalization and Market Reform*, Wiley-Blackwell, Oxford, 2002

Macedo, Silvio Soares, *Higienópolis e Arredores*, Pini: Editora da Universidade de São Paulo, São Paulo, 1987

Mayer, Harold M And Wade, Richard C, *Chicago: Growth of a Metropolis*, University of Chicago Press, Chicago, 1969

Picon-Lefebvre, Virginie, *Paris – Ville moderne: Maine-Montparnasse et La Défense, 1950–1975*, Editions Norma, Paris, 2003

Powell, Kenneth, *30 St Mary Axe: A Tower for London*, Merrell, London, 2006

Schulz, Stefanie and Schulz, Carl-Georg, *Das Hansaviertel – Ikone der Moderne*, Verlagshaus Braun, Berlin, 2007

Scobey, David M, *Empire City: The Making and Meaning of the New York City Landscape*, Temple University Press, Philadelphia, 2003

Stoller, Ezra, *The Seagram Building*, Princeton Architectural Press, New York, 1999

Tarkhanov, Alexei and Kavtaradze, Sergei, *Stalinist Architecture*, Laurence King, London, 1992

Wentz, Martin, *Die kompakte Stadt*, Campus, Frankfurt, 2000

Yabe, Toshio, Terada, Mariko, Yamagishi, Kayoko and Yokoyama, Yuko, *The Global City*, Mori Building, Tokyo, 2003

Zanella, Francesca, *La Torre Agbar*, Parma Festival dell'Architettura, Parma, 2006

Zukowsky, John and Bruegmann, Robert, *Chicago Architecture 1872–1922: Birth of a Metropolis*, Prestel, London, 2000

TECHNICAL WORKS (DESIGN, STRUCTURE, ECONOMY, ECOLOGY, SUSTAINABILITY)

British Council for Offices, *Tall Buildings: A Strategic Design Guide*, RIBA Enterprises, London, 2005

Chew Yit Lin, Michael, *Construction Technology for Tall Buildings*, Singapore University Press, Singapore, 2000

Council on Tall Buildings and Urban Habitat (CTBUH) Committee 30, *Architecture of Tall Buildings*, McGraw-Hill, New York, 1995

Craighead, Geoff, *High-Rise Security and Fire Life Safety*, Elsevier, Oxford, 2009

Eisele, Johann and Kloft, Ellen, *High-Rise Manual*, Birkhäuser, Basel, 2003

Fairweather, Virginia and Thornton, Charles and Tomasetti, Richard, *Expressing Structure: The Technology of Large-Scale Buildings*, Birkhäuser, Basel, 2004

Jenks, Mike and Dempsey, Nicola, *Future Forms and Design for Sustainable Cities*, Architectural Press, Oxford, 2005

Lloyd Jones, David, *Architecture and the Environment: Bioclimatic Building Design*, Overlook Press, Woodstock, 1998

Seal, Mark and Middleton, William and Gray, Lisa and Lewis, Hilary, *Hines: A Legacy of Quality in the Built Environment*, Fenwick Publishing Group, Bainbridge Island, 2008

Smith, Bryan Stafford and Coull, Alex, *Tall Building Structures: Analysis and Design*, Wiley Interscience, New York, 1991

Terranova, Antonino, Spirito, Gianpaola, Leone, Sabrina and Spita, Leone, *Eco Structures: Architectural Shapes for the Environment*, White Star, Vercelli, 2009

Wells, Matthew, *Skyscrapers: Structure and Design*, Laurence King, London, 2005

Willis, Carol, *Form Follows Finance*, Princeton Architectural Press, New York, 1995

Yeang, Ken, *Eco Skyscrapers*, Images Publishing Group, Mulgrave, 2007

Index

Picture Credits

The author and the publisher gratefully acknowledge the people who gave their permission to reproduce material in this book. While every effort has been made to contact copyright holders for their permission to reprint material, the publishers would be grateful to hear from any copyright holder who is not acknowledged here and will undertake to rectify any errors or omissions in future editions.

t = top, b = bottom, l = left, r= right, c = centre

Front cover image © Eric Firley
Back cover image © Eric Firley

pp 2, 6, 9, 10, 11, 14, 16, 18 (t), 21, 30 (bl & br), 31 (l, cr & br), 32 (b), 33, 34 (tl & b), 39 (l, cr & br), 40 (b), 41, 42 (t), 43 (br), 46 (c, bl & br), 47 (c & b), 48 (b), 49, 50 (tl & tr), 51, 54 (cl & cr), 56, 57, 58, 59 (r), 62 (c, bl & br), 64 (b), 65, 66 (b), 67, 70 (cl, bl & r), 71 (c, bl & br), 72 (b), 73, 74, 79 (cl, cr & b), 80 (b), 81, 82, 83 (bl), 88 (b), 89, 90, 91, 96 (b), 97, 98, 99, 102 (c, bl & br), 103 (c, bl & br), 104 (b), 105, 106, 107 (t & c), 115 (tl & r) , 118 (c & b), 119, 120 (b), 121, 122, 123 (tl & tr), 126 (cl, cr & b), 128 (b), 129, 130, 135 (bl & br), 136 (b), 137, 138, 139 (b), 142 (c & b), 145, 146 (b), 147, 148, 149, 150, 151 (l), 154 (b), 155, 156, 157, 158 (t), 159, 162 (b), 163 (b), 164 (b), 165 (t), 166, 167, 170 (b), 172, 173, 174, 175, 178, 179 (t), 180, 181, 188 (b), 189, 190 (b), 191, 192, 193, 203, 227, 237, 247, 249, 250, 256-7, 258 © Eric Firley; pp 13, 34 (tr), 42 (b) Nigel Young © Foster + Partners; p 18 (b) © Kari Searls; pp 24 (t), 29, 30 (t), 31 (t), 32 (t), 37, 38 (t), 39 (t), 40 (t), 45, 46 (t), 47 (t), 48 (t), 53, 54 (t), 55 (t), 56 (t), 61, 62 (t), 63 (t), 64 (t), 69, 70 (t), 71 (t), 72 (t), 77, 78 (t), 79 (t), 80 (t), 85, 86 (t), 87 (t), 88 (t), 93, 94 (t), 95 (t), 96 (t), 101, 102 (t), 103 (t), 104 (t), 109, 110 (t), 111 (t), 112 (t), 117, 118 (t), 119 (t), 120 (t), 125, 126 (t), 127 (t), 128 (t), 133, 134 (t), 135 (t), 136 (t), 141, 142 (t), 143 (t), 146 (t), 153, 154 (t), 161, 162 (t), 169, 170 (t), 177, 178 (t), 183, 188 (t), 195 © Eric Firley. Prepared with the assistance of Dean See Swan and David Zink; p 24 (b), 25, 26, 27 (tl & tr) © Ellerbe Becket Architects / photo Joseph Poon; p 27 (b) Courtesy of Ellerbe Becket, an AECOM Company and Omrania + Associates; pp 28, 68, 108, 116, 176, 194 courtesy Terraserver; pp 35, 43 (tl & bl), 186 © Foster + Partners; p 36 © Bluesky International Ltd/ www.blueskymapshop.com; p 38 (c) © David Guija Alcaraz; p 38 (b) Courtesy AGBAR; p 44 © Luftbild: Stadtvermessungsamt Frankfurt, Germany; p 50 (c & b) Courtesy of Alberico Barbiano di Belgiojoso; p 52 © Blom CGR; p 55 (cl, cr &b) © Behnisch Architekten / Photo Christian Kandzia; p 59 (tl & cl) © AB Centrumfastigheter; p 60 © Lantmäteriet Sweden; p 63 (cl & b) © Jesus Labrado; p 63 (cr) © photo by Klaus Fehrenbach; p 66 (t) © Mrs Kenzo

Tange,Paul Noritaka Tange Tange Associates; p 75 © Ennead Architects LLP; pp 76, 92, 152 courtesy of USGS; p 78 (c, bl & br) The London Bridge Tower © Renzo Piano Building Workshop; p 83 (t & br) © Pierre Charbonnier; pp 84, 100, 140, 182 courtesy of IGN; p 86 (l, cr & b) © Juan Pedro Sabbagh, Juan Sabbagh, Mariana Sabbagh, Felipe Sabbagh/photo Marcial Olivares; p 87 (b) © David Guija Alcaraz; p 94 (br) Courtesy of Bibliothèque municipale de Lyon; pp 94 (bl), 212, 225, 231, 232, 233, 236 © Julie Gimbal; pp 95 (c, bl & br), 111 (c & b) © Atelier Christian De Portzamparc; p 99 (t) © Gérard Grandval; p 107 (b) Fonds Perret frères. CNAM/SIAF/CAPA, Archives d'architecture du XXe siècle/Auguste Perret/UFSE/SAIF/2010; p 110 (upper c) © Balduino Martinez Muedra; p 110 (lower c) © Klaus-Henning Poot; p 110 (b) © Karl Hoskin; pp 112 (b), 113, 114 © Andrea Firley; p 115 (b) © Baumschlager Eberle; pp 123 (b), 171 (bl & br) © KPF with Mori Building; p 124 © Mori Building; p 127 (b) © Arc Studio Architecture + Urbanism and RSP Architects Planners & Engineers; p 131 Courtesy of Architectenbureau Van den Broek en Bakema; p 132 © Geobasis-DE / SenStadt III, 2010; p 134 (c & b) © FLC / ADAGP, Paris and DACS, London 2010; p 135 (c) © WOHA and Patrick Bingham-Hall Photographer; p 139 (tr & tl) © I. Mory, M. Proux/Batima S.A; pp 143 (cl & cr), 144 © CEREP Franklin Sarl/Architect: Hubert & Roy; pp 151 (tr & br), 179 (b) © Pei Cobb Freed & Partners; p 158 (b) © Luiza Cardia; p 160 Courtesy City of São Paulo; p 163 (t) Courtesy of Direction de la Prospective de l'Urbanisme et de la Mobilité; pp 164 (tl & tr), 165 (b) © Direction de la Prospective de l'Urbanisme et de la Mobilité; Cabinet d'Architecte Alexandre Giraldi - Successeur de Joseph Iori; p 168 © Direction de la Prospective de l'Urbanisme et de la Mobilité; p 171 (t) Rendering courtesy of Gensler; pp 184-85, 185 Courtesy of Arquitectonica; p 187 © Manuelle Gautrand Architecture; p 190 (t) © Farrells; pp 199, 205, 235 images created by Julie Gimbal from original satellites © DigitalGlobe (courtesy Google); pp 201, 202 © Greater London Authority; pp 206-07, 208 © Stadtplanungsamt Frankfurt am Main; pp 213, 214 © Stadtentwicklung Wien; pp 211, 217, 223, 228, 229 images created by Julie Gimbal from original satellites © TerraMetrics (courtesy Google); pp 218-19, 220-21 © Ville de Paris - direction de l'Urbanisme – 2008; pp 224 (l & r), 226 images used with permission of the New York City Department of City Planning. All rights reserved; pp 240, 241, 242, 243 (b), 244 (tl & tr), 251 (r), 252, 253, 254, 255 © Philippe Honnorat; p 243 (t) © Philippe Chiambaretta / PCA; p 244 (b) © Pelli Clarke Pelli Architects; p 245 (t) © iofoto / Shutterstock; p 245 (b) © Ilja Masík / Shutterstock; p 248 © Torre Mayor, SA de CV; p 251 (l) © WSP Flack + Kurtz, used by permission from WSP.